Resurrecting
the Person

Resurrecting
the Person

Friendship and the
Care of People
with Mental
Health Problems

John
Swinton

Abingdon Press

Nashville

RESURRECTING THE PERSON
FRIENDSHIP AND THE CARE OF PEOPLE WITH MENTAL HEALTH PROBLEMS

Library of Congress Cataloging in Publication Data

Swinton, John, 1957-
   Resurrecting the person : "friendship and the care of people with mental health problems" / John Swinton.
      p. cm.
   Includes bibliographical references and index.
   ISBN 0-687-08228-5 (alk. paper)
      1. Church work with the mentally ill. 2. Mental health—Religious aspects—Christianity. I. Title.

BV4461 .S96 2000
259'.42—dc21

                                                                00-060584

This book is dedicated to all of those people with mental health problems and their families whom I have had the pleasure of becoming friends with over the years. If this book encourages them to find strength and hope in the midst of their difficulties, then it will have been worthwhile.

Contents

Introduction

Friendship and Liberation

"The Son of Man came eating and drinking, and they say, 'Look a glutton and a drunkard, a friend of tax collectors and sinners!' Yet wisdom is vindicated by her deeds."

—Matthew 11:19

Radical Friendship

This is a book about radical friendship. It is a call to the church to rediscover its prophetic roots in the life, death, and resurrection of Jesus Christ and to reclaim its identity as the friend and protector of the poor, the outcast, and the stranger. The book is a call for the church to remember the one who offered friendship to tax collectors and sinners, and to allow that dangerous memory to reshape its attitudes, values, and practices. The God revealed within the Gospels is a God who seeks out and becomes the friend of the rejected, the despised, and the outcast (Matthew 11:19); a God who is deeply committed to justice and to the poor, whatever form poverty might take at any moment in time. This book seeks to remind the church of its responsibility accurately to image this same God in all of these dimensions.

Persons, Not Illnesses

This is not a book about mental health problems. It is first and foremost a book that is concerned with *people* whose lives have been radically altered by their encounters with mental health problems. It is a book about people who are loved by God beyond all measure and created in God's image for loving fellowship; about people whose daily struggle it is to carve out an accepted space within a society that is often fundamentally opposed to their presence. It is a book that offers a profound and prophetic challenge to the church as a community, and to each person within it who genuinely desires to become a faithful disciple.

When we reflect on the life experiences of many people with mental health problems, we find individuals who have to struggle with psychological difficulties that are frequently destructive, incapacitating, and soul-destroying. However, such difficulties are only the beginning of the story of their life struggles. Running alongside the biological and psychological history of people with mental health problems is a form of social experience that is fundamentally degrading, exclusionary, and frequently dehumanizing. When we look into the social experience of people with mental health problems, we discover a level of oppression, prejudice, exclusion, and injustice that is deeply concerning. Negative media images, powerful stigmatizing forces, and exclusion from basic sources of value are just some of the negative experiences that many people experience on a daily basis, simply because they are diagnosed as having a mental health problem. In the minds of the media and the general public, people with mental health problems frequently "cease being persons." Instead they become identified by their pathologies—"schizophrenics," or "manic depressives" (whatever these "things" might be) terms that substitute their primary identity as human beings made in God's image and passionately loved by God, for a socially constructed way of being that seriously limits their life possibilities. One of the primary tasks of this book is to explore ways of conceptually and practically separating people from their illnesses, and, in so doing, help enable the "resurrection of the person" who is often forgotten or overlooked within the process of mental health care.

Practical Theology: A Theology of Practice

This book is a study in practical theology. Traditionally, practical theology has been understood as a *prescriptive* discipline that seeks to *apply* theology to the specific needs of the church. According to this understanding, the primary focus of practical theology is on the particular training requirements of the ordained clergy. While this model has been influential in the historical development of practical theology, the second half of the twentieth century has seen a major shift away from clergy-centered models of practical theology, toward understandings that focus on the actions of the church in the world.[1] This has led to significant shifts in method and approach.

> Whereas formerly, practical theologians had first studied the Bible and the doctrine of the church in order to apply the results of their findings to the practice of the church, more recently . . . practical theologians world-wide have agreed on starting their investigations in practice itself. Practical theology has become a description of and reflection on the self-understanding of a particular religious tradition. This approach moves from practice to theory, then back to practice.[2]

Rather than simply applying theory to the training of the clergy, this understanding suggests that the task of the practical theologian is actually to *do* theology. Doing practical theology involves a process of critical reflection on the actions of the church, in the light of gospel and tradition, and in constructive dialogue with other disciplines. This paradigm sees the field of practical theology as the functioning of the church within the perspective of God's coming kingdom as it works itself out in the world. The important thing to note about this approach to practical theology is that it begins with experience/praxis and moves to theory, with a view to returning to the experience with a revised form of praxis. Thus, what emerges is a model of practical theology not simply as applied theology, but as a *theology of practice* that involves *critical reflection on the practice of the church in the world*.

Within such an understanding, practical theology assumes a natural and inseparable interconnectedness between theory and practice. As Duncan Forrester puts it,

> Practical theology is that branch of theology that is concerned with questions of truth in relation to action. This points to a deep reciprocity between theory and practice, whereby theological understanding not only leads to action, but also arises out of practice, involvement in the life of the world: "He who does what is true comes to the light." Practical theology is therefore concerned with the doing of the truth, and with the encounter with truth in action.[3]

Practical theology assumes that the actions of the Christian community are deeply meaningful and value-laden. Biblical scholars interpret texts, and systematic theologians and church historians interpret the historical documents of the Christian tradition. Similarly, the task of the practical theologian is to excavate the hidden layers of meaning that indwell the praxis of Christian communities and to test the authenticity of the praxis of the church against the vision of the coming kingdom. By critically correlating insights from other disciplines such as the social sciences with contemporary theological understandings, practical theology has as its task to interpret and explore the underlying theories and assumptions that guide practice and make apparent those areas of unfaithfulness that may go unnoticed. The model of practical theology as the theology of practice is central to the method of this book.

Practical Theology as the Praxis of Liberation

The nature of the subject matter of this book, however, requires us to approach the theology of practice from a very specific perspective: the perspective of the poor. People with mental health problems are the subject of numerous unjust practices, negative personal and social attitudes, and other forms of oppression and impoverishment. Reflection on their life experiences leaves one in no doubt that they fall firmly within the category of "the poor." The church is called to image Christ in his boundary-breaking mission of liberation and to adopt a stance of solidarity with the poor and against injustice and oppression in all of its forms. In order to enable such a critical stance, this book will focus on an important model of practical theology: *liberation theology*. The liberationist model offers a critical and prophetic approach to practical theology that gives us access to many hidden dimensions of mental health and disorder.

Liberation theology stems from a context of gross oppression within Latin America. Central to this paradigm is the quest for justice and liberation for poor and oppressed people. This perspective has been used effectively by a number of other oppressed groups such as women, people with disabilities, and people of color.[4]

Liberation theologies are theologies of *commitment, solidarity, transformation*, and *change* in the face of social and political oppression. They call for radical interpersonal, social, and political change within society, and the material, emotional, and spiritual emancipation of those who are oppressed by unjust personal and social structures. The emphasis is on *orthopraxis* (right practice) rather than simply *orthodoxy* (right doctrine), with faith and action seen as inextricably intertwined within the liberatory pastoral praxis of the church community. Whereas Western academic theology has tended to understand faith primarily as a rational construct, the liberationists refuse to separate faith from action. Faith is "the total human response to God, who saves through love; not a simple affirmation of truths, but a commitment, an overall attitude, a particular posture toward life."[5] Theology is necessarily both spiritual and rational knowledge, both elements being viewed as permanent and indispensable functions of all theological reflections.[6]

Theology is understood as *critical reflection on the church's pastoral action*, with the life and praxis of the Christian community providing a significant source for theological reflection. As such, theology is a *secondary* procedure. First comes a commitment to service; theology comes later as *critical reflection on the church's practice*.[7] Thus, unlike the applied theology model, the church's practice is not arrived at as a conclusion from theological premises. Theology does not lead to pastoral activity, but is rather a reflection on it. Gustavo Gutiérrez calls this a *new way of doing theology* that does not stop with reflecting on the world, but rather tries to be part of the process through which the world is transformed.[8]

The Centrality of the Poor

The poor hold a central role in the process of liberation theology. However, unlike applied models of theology and ethics, in liberation theology, the poor do not enter the church's thinking at the end of a process of theological or ethical reflection on the nature of Christian charity. Liberation theology begins its theologizing with the experience of the poor. One of its central themes is the idea that God has a preferential option for the poor. This is not to suggest that the poor merit preferential treatment because of a superior ontological or moral status; rather, God has a bias toward the poor because scripture reveals God to be loving, just, and a champion of the oppressed. As such, it is in the nature of God to stand with those who are oppressed or unjustly treated. God's cause is understood as the cause of the exploited, the oppressed, and the downtrodden.[9] The situation of the poor is seen as analogous to the plight of the Jewish slaves in Egypt, with the Exodus viewed as paradigmatic of God's liberating actions within history. The church, if it is to remain true to this liberating God, can be on one side only: the side of the poor.

God's work of liberation is continued and fulfilled in the life and work of Christ, that is viewed as forming part of the "Exodus movement" of God in history. As Richard Bauckham notes: "Jesus' ministry freed no slaves of men, but liberated slaves of guilt and sin, those held captive by demons, oppressed by disease and handicaps, imprisoned and subject to death. The Exodus liberation thus becomes in the New Testament a type of Christ's liberation of those enslaved to sin and death."[10] Jesus came to preach the kingdom of God, a rule that chastises the rich and the mighty and raises up the poor. In the teaching of Jesus, central concern was shown for loving the neighbor and for the poor. Jesus' mission had to do with the bringing in of the eschatological kingdom of God, and the consequent eradication of sin, that is, in the liberationist perspective, both individual and collective and, as such, evident within oppressive social structures that exploit humanity. Liberation theologians seek the manifestation of this liberation inherent within the eschatological kingdom of God, the firstfruits of which are to be seen in the liberating ministry of Jesus.[11]

Liberating the Church

The book uses a modification of the liberationist method. Liberationists draw on various aspects of the social sciences (primarily Marxism) and use them as critical tools to explore the cultural milieu of particular contexts in an attempt to unearth forms of injustice and oppression that are embedded within the social and political order. In like manner, this book uses insights from the medical and social sciences—psychiatry, nursing, sociology, psychology, philosophy, and so forth—in its attempt to reveal the hidden levels of oppression experienced by people with mental health problems. The book will develop strat-egies and understandings that can contribute to bringing about justice and the development of forms of community that are critical centers of rehumanization in a world that can be profoundly dehumanizing. To this end, the book assumes a bias toward the poor, in this case people with long-term mental health problems. It assumes that the Christian God is a God of love, justice, and fairness who will inevitably champion the rights of those who are downtrodden and oppressed by unjust relational, social, political, or spiritual attitudes, values, and systems. Liberation theologies seek after a movement toward justice and faithful change. This book will take this proposition as a fundamental premise and strive to reveal and effectively tackle the very real poverty and oppression that is experienced by people with mental health problems.

Critical Solidarity

However, while drawing on insights from the liberationist tradition, *this book is not an exercise in liberation theology*. Liberation theology is a theological expression that springs from the grass roots of a community that is experiencing injustice and oppression.[12] It is a revolutionary, political, and communal movement by oppressed peoples against the oppression and injustice they are experiencing. While it involves cooperation and solidarity with others, it is not something that can be done *for* a group of people *by* an "outsider." To do this would simply be to reinforce the type of imperialist and paternalistic interventions that lie at the heart of the liberation theologian's critique of Western theology and culture. An authentic liberation theology could be written only by people who themselves have or have had mental health problems. Such a theology would begin with the experience of "survivors," and from there work out a critical theology that could empower people with mental health problems to rise above their oppression toward liberation. While there is a very real need for a liberation theology that emerges from the experiences of people with mental health problems, this book is not intended to fulfill such a need. I have never experienced mental health problems. I am not a survivor, and I do not have the unique insights that people with mental health problems have to bring to the practical theological discussion. However, as a former mental health professional, a practicing pastor, an educator, and a member of a society that views people with mental health problems in a very poor light, I have been a witness to—and at times a participant in—the unjust and oppressive forces that act against people with mental health problems. My experience has raised my consciousness to the injustices and acts of degradation that people with mental health problems are frequently forced to accept and endure. Thus, while it may not be possible for me to write a liberation theology of mental health problems, it *is* possible for me to adopt a stance of *critical solidarity* with people who have mental health problems.[13] Inspired by the prophetic tradition of the Christian faith and the groundbreaking ministry of Jesus, I intend in writing this book to stand alongside people with mental health problems and to show critical solidarity with them, as together we struggle against oppression.

Pastoral theologian Stephen Pattison highlights the importance of clergy, academics, and pastoral workers with access to intellectual skills and knowledge becoming "organic intellectuals," who are prepared to use such skills in the movement toward liberation. "As educated professionals, clergy and other pastoral workers have considerable resources in terms of understanding and the ability to use and manipulate information. This can be of use to those who may have little access to tools for understanding and changing their situation in the face of the ideological and other forces ranged against them."[14] As someone who fulfills all of these roles, I intend to use these skills and my access to particular forms of knowledge and interpretation to work toward enabling the Christian community to discover ways of showing critical solidarity with people experiencing enduring mental health problems. Through an exploration of the role of friendship within the contemporary church, my aim is to help provide a context within which psychological and spiritual liberation can become a meaningful possibility.

The Centrality of Liberation

This book may not be an exercise in liberation theology, but it is, nonetheless, a book about *liberation*. Primarily, it is about the liberation of people with enduring mental health problems from relational deprivation, false ideologies, stigmatizing attitudes, social marginalization, and material, relational, and spiritual poverty. However, as will become clear, it is also a book about the liberation of the church from many aspects of its life and ministry that prevent it from faithful participation in God's continuing mission. Fundamental to the book's argument is the proposition that effective care for people with enduring mental health problems is not an option for the church, but is in fact a fundamental mark of its identity and a vital indication of its continuing faithfulness. The book will suggest that while the church may have many roles within the process of caring for and being with people experiencing mental health problems, above all else the church is called to a ministry of *liberation*. A truly faithful church will be a liberating church that seeks to remain true to the ideals of its founder as it attempts to eradicate poverty and dehumanization in all of its manifestations, and implement justice for and with the poor.

Gutiérrez describes the word *liberation* as expressing "the inescapable moment of radical change."[15] In a real sense liberation and metanoia (conversion/seeing the world differently) are intricately connected. Liberation essentially means freedom, primarily freedom from some form of injustice, captivity, or oppression.[16]

> Oppression is perhaps best understood as a power or force that prevents a person from becoming fully human and thus fully reflective of the image of God. Forces of oppression are precisely forces that rob human dignity because they rob human freedom, human community, and human creativity. To oppress others is to dehumanize them.[17]

This being so, liberation will primarily have to do with enabling people to live humanly. Liberation is a force for *rehumanization*. As the book proceeds, it will become clear that the value systems, social structures, and personal attitudes within Western societies seriously oppress and dehumanize people with mental health problems. The ways in which people are conceptualized, stigmatized, alienated, and caricatured, in a very real sense rob them of their essential human dignity and freedom and often exclude them from meaningful participation within society. The process of dehumanization is subtle, but when revealed, frightening in its depth and intensity. As such, there is a desperate need for liberation from the oppressive forces that bind people to the margins of our thinking and of our communities.

Likewise, this process of liberation includes the liberation of the church from false priorities and escapist theologies. Liberation theologians have argued forcefully that the purpose of the biblical narrative is not simply personal salvation *but the rehumanization of the nonperson*, a task that involves total, sacrificial commitment to the social, spiritual, and emotional welfare of the poor. They suggest that we need to reframe the theological questions we ask of scripture and tradition in order that our theology and praxis can fully embrace the experience of the poor and the nonperson within our societies. The important theological questions should be posed by those who are considered to be "nonpersons, the marginalized, those for whom society has no place, those pushed away from the responsibility of a fully human existence."[18]

Within contemporary Western societies, people with mental health problems fall precisely into this category. As Pattison correctly observes: "Those regarded as mentally disordered (a substantial, if often unnoticed, minority in the population) can be seen as the poor in our society. They should be regarded as the poorest of the poor."

They are poor in economic terms, certainly. The movement toward de-institutionalization has left many people with mental health problems homeless and in extreme poverty.[19] But poverty is more than simply a lack of material possessions. Poverty also has to do with personhood, fulfillment, and enabling individuals truly to reflect the image of God as free beings, able to love, to make choices, and to develop to their potential. Poverty in all of its dimensions denies a person these opportunities.

A truly liberating church that seeks to remain faithful to its founder will necessarily see the quest for the eradication of poverty and the implementation of justice as a primary focus. In encountering, recognizing, and committing itself to people with mental health problems, the church will be liberated from a false individualism that seeks after personal salvation to the exclusion of commitment to the poor.

In calling the church to a form of friendship that images the radical friendships of Jesus, this book challenges the church to refocus its priorities, remember the centrality of its commitment to the poor, and accept their contribution to the process of understanding who God is and what it means to be a faithful community. The book also implicitly calls upon the church to liberate itself from its overconcentration on specifically therapeutic relationships such as counseling and psychotherapy, and regain a vision for those who require different forms of pastoral relationship. It calls upon the church to liberate itself from the fear and stigma of mental health problems and to begin to explore the real people who lurk behind the diagnostic labels that often hide their humanity, people who long for the liberating experience of acceptance and love. In doing this, the church will be freed to be the church in a real and meaningful way.

The Politics of Mental Health

Within the context of mental health problems, the task of liberation has important political implications. Richard Warner has highlighted that there is a vital, but often unnoticed, economic dimension to the development and maintenance of many forms of mental health problems, particularly schizophrenia. He points out that the recovery rates from schizophrenia are considerably higher in third world countries than in industrialized Western capitalist economies. Warner suggests this has to do with social cohesion and the ability of families and extended families to offer a closer, less stressful, and more accepting environment, which is conducive to recovery.

Coming from a specifically pastoral perspective, Stephen Pattison has ably explored the significance of the radical praxis-based approach of liberation theology for uncovering the important political aspects of mental health problems and mental health care. Pattison's analysis "exposes the situation of mentally ill people as being broadly one of injustice, exploitation, powerlessness, and oppression in society as a whole, and within the various contexts in that they are 'cared' for. . . . There are links between the social order and the situation of mentally ill people today. Mental disorder is not an arbitrary personal affliction. The context and care that surrounds it are also integrally linked to wider social factors."[20] Using a critical Marxist/liberationist approach, Pattison presents a model of pastoral care that calls for the church to take a proactive political stance in its care of people with mental health problems. Both Pattison and Warner show clearly that social and political factors impinge on mental health problems to a significant extent.

However, oppression and liberation are not confined to the political dimensions of human life. Nancy Eiesland, in discussing the various ways in which people with disabilities are oppressed and discriminated against, highlights the vital "micro" interpersonal dimensions of oppression, exclusion, and injustice: "Group oppressions are enacted in this society not primarily in official laws and policies but in informal, often unnoticed and unreflective speech, bodily reactions to others, conventional practices of everyday interactions and evaluations, aesthetic judgements, and the jokes, images, and stereotypes pervading the mass media."[21] Here Young points toward the oppressive power of common everyday behavior. Oppression and poverty occur on the interpersonal, as well as the social levels of society, when individuals and communities create a relational, communicational, aesthetic, and linguistic atmosphere that causes the exclusion and stigmatization of those who are perceived to be different. As Tom Kitwood observes in his discussion of the psychodynamics of exclusion: "Many cultures have shown a tendency to depersonalize those who have some form of serious disability, whether of a physical or a psychological kind. A consensus is created, established in tradition and embedded in social practices, that those affected are not real persons."[22]

It is through the myriad of unnoticed social gestures and negative assumptions that people with mental health problems find their sense of self-worth and personhood constantly being eroded. It is through that same process that they come to be perceived, consciously or subconsciously, as "nonpersons" (by society and, sadly, often by themselves), and consequently excluded from meaningful participation within society. As Rebecca Chopp correctly states: "Until we change the values and hidden rules that run through present linguistic practices, social codes, and psychic orderings, women, persons of color, and other oppressed groups will be forced—by language, discourses, and practices available to them— into conforming to ongoing practices, to babbling nonsense, or to not speaking at all."[23]

This critical interpersonal dimension to the process of oppression and liberation has not gone unnoticed by liberation theologians themselves. Gutiérrez suggests that the central vision that guides his conceptualization of liberation theology is the biblical vision of *shalom*.

> The praxis on which liberation theology reflects is a praxis of solidarity in the interest of liberation and is inspired by the gospel. It is the activity of "peacemakers"—that is, those who are forging shalom. Western languages translate this Hebrew word as "peace" but in doing so, diminish its meaning. Shalom in fact refers to the whole of life and, as part of this, to the need of establishing justice and peace. Consequently, a praxis motivated by evangelical values embraces to some extent every effort to bring about authentic fellowship and authentic justice. . . . This liberating praxis endeavors to transform history in the light of the reign of God. It accepts the reign now, even though knowing that it will arrive in all its fullness only at the end of time.[24]

According to Gutiérrez, the primary focus of liberation theology is the earthly manifestation of signs of God's coming reign of *shalom*. The understanding of the word *shalom* within scripture, has specific theological meaning and intention, as John Wilkinson has pointed out.

> The root meaning of the word *shalom* is *wholeness, completeness* and *well-being*. . . . It does however have several secondary meanings, encompassing *health, security, friendship, prosperity, justice, righteousness* and *salvation*, all of which are necessary if wholeness, completeness and well-being are to come about.[25]

The meaning of the word *shalom* is to express opposition to any disturbance in the well-being of a person, society, or nation.[26] *Shalom* does include the vital political dimensions of human existence, but it is not defined by them. While in reality, all of these aspects are inextricably intertwined, here it is important to note that issues of health, security, and friendship are of equal importance to issues of politics and social action within God's coming reign. Gutiérrez suggests that the praxis of liberation is not reducible to "social aspects" in a narrow sense:

> The complexity of the world of the poor and lowly compels us to attend to other dimensions of Christian practice if it is to meet the requirements of a total love of God . . . The struggles of those who reject racism and machismo . . . as well as of those who oppose the marginalization of the elderly, children, and other "unimportant" persons in our society, have made me see, for example, the importance of gestures and ways of "being with" that some may regard as having little political effectivenes."[27]

This is an important observation. Pattison has outlined a helpful model of pastoral care that might effectively address the wider social and political aspects of liberating mental health care.[28] However, useful as his model is for addressing this macrodimension of liberation, his focus on politics and public policy issues does not allow him to address liberation in its microinterpersonal dimensions. Yet, it is this dimension that Eiesland has pointed out is of critical importance for the life experience of people who are perceived to be different. This being so, my intention in writing this book is to supplement exclusively political approaches to the liberation of people with mental health problems with a perspective that explores some of the microsocial and interpersonal aspects that may be overlooked by approaches that focus on politics alone. It is hoped that this book will supplement those works that focus on liberation in its wider social and political dimensions. Taken in conjunction with them, it will provide a holistic liberatory strategy for the Christian community in its attempts to care for people with enduring mental health problems.

The book will therefore take seriously Gutiérrez' suggestion concerning the liberatory significance of "gestures" and "ways of being" that, while apparently simple and nonpolitical, on reflection are profound, radical, and deeply countercultural forms of human action. It is the assertion of this book that the relationship of friendship, as it is worked out within the context of being with people who have mental health problems, is precisely such a "gesture" and a "way of being with" that can initiate and sustain liberation. As such it has the potential to bring about a radical change in the thinking and practice of the church, and in the thinking and practice of all who come into contact with the church. This book hopes to move the church toward liberation, toward that moment of radical change within which it can begin to open its boundaries, reject its prejudices, and develop a community of friends that is truly inclusive and genuinely rehumanizing.

A Community That Notices

This book is an exercise in consciousness raising. This idea is central to liberation theology. By raising the consciousness of oppressed groups, these theologies seek to empower people to re-take control of their lives by equipping them with the tools to recognize and confront oppressive power structures, value systems, distorted theologies, and false ideologies. In this way God's "bias toward the poor" can find embodiment within the life of a transformed, politically active, and socially aware church. Despite the veneer of democracy, freedom, equality, and tolerance that has been laid upon Western society, a deeper, more discerning examination reveals that there are a significant number of people within society who, for various reasons, find themselves on the margins of community. These may include persons who are unemployed, the elderly, women, people of color, those with mental health problems, disabilities or AIDS, gays and lesbians, and others can all experience social isolation and stigmatization. In a very real sense, they can find themselves outcast and downtrodden by a society that neither cares about nor is perhaps even aware of their situation.[28] The problem is that their personal disempowerment coupled with the cultural and political silence that marks their social history means that very often their presence goes unnoticed.

On a recent trip to Los Angeles I was struck by the lack of knowledge many middle-class white people had about the level of poverty and deprivation that existed only a few miles from where they lived. The freeway system meant that every day some of the richest people in the world quite literally drove over some of the poorest people in the world. Daily they came within yards of situations of serious social isolation, exclusion, and poverty and never even noticed it was there (or at least claimed not to notice). Similarly, within the communities of all of the readers of this book there are many "hidden people" whose silent screams pierce the ears of God, yet apparently leave the church undisturbed. People with mental health problems constitute a significant proportion of the hidden poor within present day Western society. When we delve into the lives of people with mental health problems, we discover people who are oppressed at a number of levels. At a material level they often struggle simply to make ends meet. At a relational level they weep silently in the loneliness of their isolation. At a social level these people are deprived of their identity and forced to adopt images and roles that strip them of many of the basics of acceptable human living. At a spiritual level, their experience is often discarded as *nothing but* the product of their illness, and consequently relegated to the realm of symptomatology rather than meaningful human experience. They are stigmatized, alienated, outcast, and—worse than that—without a public voice to defend them. Yet most of us carry on our daily lives as if nothing was happening. This book aims to raise the consciousness of the church to the reality of poverty and oppression in its midst. It calls for the church to regain its identity as a prophetic community that *notices*—a community that notices the sadness, deals with the loneliness, and fights for justice and liberation in the midst of oppressive social values and attitudes; a community that is conscious of the injustice in its midst, and has the willingness and the commitment to do something about it.

A Bias Against the Poor?

While working within the areas of psychiatric nursing and community psychiatric chaplaincy, I was greatly concerned about the lack of emphasis church communities placed on providing care for people suffering from long-term mental health problems. Many churches were very happy to spend large amounts of time and money training counselors to minister to the mental health needs of congregations, yet few were prepared to use resources to address the needs of people living with long-term mental health problems at a congregational level. The churches could offer counseling and psychotherapy to enable people to overcome problems and cope with difficulties, but for those for whom counseling was ineffective, inappropriate, or whose illness was interminable, the church's reaction was at best pastorally limited and at worst openly antagonistic. Certainly some church bodies had specific social work departments and projects that sought to care for people in this situation, but at the level of the local *congregation*, the assumption seemed to be that "these people" were the responsibility of the professional or the specialist, and that the local church had little if anything to offer.

It appears that in becoming overly focused on therapy, problem solving, and cure, the church in her pastoral ministry risks the real danger of excluding the very people for whom Jesus came.[29] The poor, those with interminable mental health problems, homeless people, elderly people with dementia, and people who are intellectually challenged, to name but a few, often find themselves standing on the margins of the church's caring endeavors. This is a disastrous omission. If God does have a preferential option for the poor and for justice, then an understanding of mental health care that risks excluding the poor is wholly unacceptable and dangerously unfaithful.[30]

If there was a bias within the churches that I encountered, it was a bias *against* the poor. It was a bias that led people consciously and unconsciously to exclude some of the poorest people within their communities from any type of meaningful participation within the church community. Yet daily I encountered people who were in desperate need of the type of inclusive community the church is called upon to be—people who, while often requiring professional help, needed much more than medicine and therapy; people with long-term mental health problems who were lonely, isolated and broken, and who were desperate to find a place of belonging where they could encounter relationships that would enable them to find value and hope in what was very often a profoundly hopeless and valueless existence; individuals who needed to learn what it means to love, to be loved, and to experience the love of God as it was expressed within his fellowship on earth, the church. If the church is truly to be the church, and to meet the needs of people in this situation, there is a need for a radical change of perspective.

Understanding as Therapy

One of the central assumptions that lies behind this book is that *understanding is therapy*. Western society, and the church's pastoral care as a reflection of that culture, have been deeply affected by the presumptions of the medical model. Pastoral care has tended to be profoundly activist in its understanding and practices. Even within models of counseling and therapy, that can be very genuinely person-centered, the temptation is to begin with the assumption that the person has a problem that needs to be solved, or a difficulty that has to be overcome. Within the context of mental health problems, this focus on pathology and the definition of health as the absence of illness has meant that the healing power of *presence* and the art of reflective *understanding* have been subsumed in the quest for *explanation* and the battle for the *control* of worst manifestations of illness. Consequently, there are vast areas of human experience that are often omitted from descriptions and understandings of mental health problems and from strategies that attempt to offer appropriate care.

Yet the simple act of sitting with oppressed people can be a radical countercultural, and deeply therapeutic act. "The Son of Man has come eating and drinking, and you say, 'Look, a glutton and a drunkard, a friend of tax collectors and sinners!' Nevertheless, wisdom is vindicated by all her children" (Luke 7:34-35). This book argues that if we are to offer truly person-centered care, then we need a change of perception and a wider understanding of what mental health problems actually are. Such an understanding will strive to move beyond clinical definitions to explore the meaning of mental health problems from the perspective of those who suffer from them and of society at large.

The medical model still has a strong hold on both the research and practice of metal health care. To read some of the literature surrounding this area, one might assume that once one has uncovered the genetic or neurobiological defect that lies behind the condition, one actually knows what the condition is. Its emphasis on specific etiology, a predictable course, describable signs and symptoms, and a predictable outcome modifiable by certain maneuvers offers an alluring model of certainty within an area of human experience that is often chaotic and uncertain. However, anyone who has shared in the lives of people with mental health problems quickly becomes aware that the situation is considerably more complicated than the medical model might suggest. Mental health problems are incredibly complex phenomena that occur to human beings, who are themselves highly complex creatures. Because of this, there can be no such thing as schizophrenia, bipolar disorder, depression, or any other form of mental health problem, apart from the person who is experiencing it. In fact such labels can themselves be deceptive and destructive if they are allowed to define how individuals are understood and treated apart from any kind of relational involvement with them. While people with mental health problems may share certain characteristic symptoms and experiences that, at least from a clinical perspective, make up their particular diagnostic category, the illness experience of people is profoundly affected by their social history just as their psychiatric experience is by their biological history.

Likewise, there can be no such thing as a person apart from the particular communities within which the person exists. Rather than being a fixed entity, as some theories of personhood might suggest, human personhood develops through a dialectical and emergent process, and is wrought out within the personal, social, and spiritual communities in which people live out their day-to-day lives. We become the people we are, we develop our social identities, in and through the types of relationships we encounter in community.[31] Mental health problems, rather than being definable in terms of biology or diagnosis, are an ultimately indefinable combination of *pathology, personhood,* and *community;* the three aspects are inextricably interlinked. If we omit one from our caring equation, we risk misunderstanding the others. Mental health problems are therefore not so much phenomena that need to be *explained*, as human experiences that need to be *understood*.

This being so, caring for people who are living with mental health problems will necessarily involve considerably more than pharmaceutical or therapeutic intervention, symptom control, and the protection of the "innocent public," as common assumptions might suggest. Apart from anything else, when we begin to explore the experience of mental health problems, it very soon becomes clear that the innocent public are not quite as innocent as we might wish to assume. A deeper reflection reveals us all to be deeply implicated within the social history of mental health problems and, as such, profoundly responsible for the situation of those who live with it.

Schizophrenia as a Case Study

The model of care worked out within this book has relevance to all forms of mental health care and indeed in caring for all people who are marginalized. However, while we will explore other forms of mental health problems, I have chosen to adopt a central focus on the condition clinically defined as schizophrenia. This is not an arbitrary choice. Schizophrenia is a very serious and frequently misunderstood form of mental health problem. There is a great need for the church to develop effective caring strategies that will meet the needs of individuals and families who live with this condition. However, I have chosen schizophrenia not because it is necessarily any more serious than other forms of mental health problem. Anyone who has suffered—or who knows someone who has suffered—from any form of psychological disorder, knows that *all* mental health problems are serious for the persons who are experiencing them. What might be viewed as a "mild depression" by a psychiatrist can be a devastating life event for the person who is experiencing it. Similarly, there are many people diagnosed as having schizophrenia or bipolar disorder who function very well with only the minimum of professional intervention. We would do well to avoid developing a hierarchy of mental health problems that takes no account of the persons who are experiencing them.

What makes schizophrenia different from many other mental health problems is not that it is frequently serious, but that it is frequently seriously misunderstood. Unlike some other mental health problems that people seem to be able to understand and to a degree empathize with, schizophrenia presents a challenge that seems to exceed the cognitive and compassionate capabilities of the majority of the population. Schizophrenia seems to epitomize the stereotypical image of madness, with all of the stigmatizing assumptions that accompany such characterization: ideas of extreme dangerousness, two people residing in one body, the complete loss of the person to the illness, profound hopelessness, and a frightening sense of "otherness." All this tends to lead people implicitly or explicitly to think of people diagnosed as having schizophrenia as somewhat less than human. For many churches I spoke to and worked with, schizophrenia was seen very much as the dominant cultural image of madness; the epitome of lost control, degeneration, and fear. When the situation is framed in this manner, it is not surprising that people assume the care of people with schizophrenia to be a purely specialist enterprise that lies within the sole domain of the mental health professions. Schizophrenia seems to bring into particularly sharp focus many aspects of mental health problems that are often hidden from public attention and understanding. As such, it provides an ideal foundational case study on which to develop understandings that may be applicable to the experience of other forms of mental health problems.

There is indeed no such thing as a typical mental health problem. Each person experiences his or her situation in different ways and understands it from different perspectives. However, as one reflects on the lived experience of mental health problems, it becomes clear that there are certain core experiences that mark the lives of many, if not all, people. Experiences such as stigma, social isolation, fear, exclusion from fundamental sources of value, such as work, and the imposition of a negative social identity, frequently mark the experience of people with severe enduring mental health problems. While such experiences are common to all mental health problems, in the case of schizophrenia, because of its enigmatic public profile, the issues crystallize in a particularly forceful way that offers some very important insights into the experience of all forms of mental health problems. A focus on schizophrenia will give us an inroad into the general experience of mental health problems, and will provide a useful foundation for the development of effective mental health care strategies.

A Note on Terminology

The question of precisely what terminology is most appropriate when discussing psychological distress is a difficult one. Some still prefer to use the term "mental illness." However, this is a tricky term. On the one hand, it is useful in that it draws the condition within the medical model and therefore legitimizes it as a genuine illness that is not the fault of the individual or their family. Such destigmatization is, of course, useful. However, one of the intentions of this book is to relativize the power of the medical model, developing a revised framework within which psychological distress can be understood and people living with it can be effectively cared for. Consequently, I shall, wherever possible, use the slightly less evocative expression "mental health problems," to indicate the experiences of people incurring various forms of psychological distress. The term "mental health problem" allows some distance from the medical model and enables us to reflect on forms of care that are not totally the responsibility of the mental health professions.

Chapter 1

Community and Friendship

The Church as a
Liberating Community

Why Bother with Friendship?

The central theme of this book is *friendship*. At first glance, the suggestion that friendship should take center stage in the church's care of people with severe mental health problems may appear to be a rather unusual proposition. In a medicopsychiatric world that places a strong emphasis on therapy, pharmacology, and medical technology, it is difficult to conceive of something as apparently basic as friendship as a serious form of pastoral care for people encountering such difficulties. One might justifiably suggest that this was one area of care that should remain firmly within the domain of the mental health professions. Is it not rather simplistic, one might ask, and perhaps even dangerously naïve, to suggest that such a basic relationship as friendship could be central to the mental health care of people living with severe forms of mental health problems? At one level this is a fair question. Few would want to discard the need for specialist interventions designed to understand and help control the worst manifestations of psychological disorder. As we shall see, mental health professionals can contribute to the enabling of people with severe mental health problems to deal constructively with their conditions and to live lives appropriate to their status as human beings, made in the image of a relational God.

The object of this book, rather than to develop an alternative model of care, is to explore ways in which the church can enter into critical prophetic *dialogue* with current strategies for caring, with a view to constructive collaboration that will enable liberation for all. The concept of dialogue is highly significant theologically, as will become clear as the book moves on. For now it is important to highlight that the art of dialogue depends on the honesty and integrity of the two partners. It is not about developing theologies and practices that simply support caring strategies as they are at the moment. Rather, critical prophetic dialogue involves respecting the position of the other, while at the same time adopting a stance that challenges implicit or explicit biases or injustices. Accepting that conventional strategies may be necessary (although always open to critique), this book argues that they are certainly not sufficient. Medicopsychiatric definitions, understandings, and strategies can be helpful when accepted discerningly. However, they only go so far. It is true that such approaches can help identify particular difficulties and suggest strategies and interventions that can significantly improve the lives of people living with long-term mental health problems. Difficulties arise if we begin to assume that such a way of defining mental health problems is the *only*, or even the most appropriate, way of defining them. The issue is one of power, specifically the power that the perspective of psychiatry has to define the "true" nature of a condition and what the most appropriate strategies are for effective intervention. The important conspirational critiques of psychiatry offered by antipsychiatrists such as Szasz[1] and Laing,[2] though open to serious critique themselves, have offered some challenging insights into the potential that the mental health professions have, implicitly or explicitly, to abuse the power that society invests in them. While this is *not* in any way an antipsychiatry book, it is nonetheless important to bear in mind the level of psychological and social power that the medicopsychiatric community has to define how those with and those without mental health problems perceive psychological distress and react to it.

We in the West belong to a culture that has been profoundly influenced by the medical model of care.

> The medical model assumes that a disorder has a specific aetiology, a predictable course, manifests describable signs and symptoms, and has a predictable outcome modifiable by certain technical manoeuvres. In this model, the illness or problem is understood as an isolated "bad spot" which it is the task of the health professional to excise or control using whatever means are at her disposal. The objective is to return the indi-

vidual to their previously healthy state and to enable them to retake their former position within society. Within this model, health is defined primarily as the absence of disease or infirmity. Ill health is understood in terms of specific pathology that needs to be identified, categorised and eradicated. To be deemed healthy is to be freed from pathology and to experience life as closely to the expected social norm as possible.[3]

It is, therefore, not insignificant that mental health research has increasingly moved toward a focus on science and biology as an explanatory framework within which mental health problems should be understood. Under the influence of the medical model, which the public and mental health professions conceptualize mental health problems primarily in terms of the biomedical model. Current research agendas, for example, predominantly focus on issues of pathology and specific etiology. The objective is to discover the biological roots of each mental health problem and do all that can be done, (a) to normalize and destigmatize it and (b) to seek more effective ways to eradicate the worst manifestations of it.

Of course, these are good aims to have. As will be discussed later, it is proper that we explore the biological roots of mental health problems in order that we may increase public awareness of them and educate the public on how people with these problems should be perceived and treated. Such an approach does much to destigmatize mental health problems and to free people from oppressive attitudes and exclusionary practices. However, the medical model's approach, while perhaps necessary, is certainly not sufficient. Though biology tells us some things about the mechanics of human beings and the technicalities of mental health problems, it tells us nothing of what it means to be human and to live humanly even in the midst of our particular difficulties. The danger with oversomaticizing mental health problems is that it tends to individualize the problem, thus drawing attention away from the critical sociorelational dimension that this book argues is fundamental to the process of oppression in the lives of people with various forms of psychological distress. If the problem is perceived as purely biological, then presumably it belongs to the individual quite apart from the particular social context within which the individual experiences it. This is an error based on the assumptions of the medical model, an error that enables society to abrogate responsibility for the oppression and disablement of people with mental health problems. As such, it requires a liberating counter-understanding.

At best, approaches based on the medical model reveal only a part, and perhaps not even the most significant part, of what it means to live with a mental health problem. Mental health problems are much more than biological defects that require being fixed or controlled by specialist interventions. They are human experiences that happen to unique individuals within particular circumstances. More than that, they are *social* experiences. Whereas the medical model's approach locates the difficulty within the genes or the neurobiology of the individual, this book argues that a major part of the individual's difficulty lies in the society within which a person experiences his or her difficulties. While the medical model's approach may drive us to focus on the eradication and control of pathology, the specific mental health problem may well *not* be of ultimate concern to the individual experiencing it. Frequently one finds that the primary concern of individuals experiencing mental health problems lies with issues of personhood and personal relationships, which, while not unconnected with their particular difficulties, cannot be fully understood by focusing on psychopathology alone.

Yale University professor of psychiatry John S. Strauss in "The Person—Key to Understanding Mental Illness" observes:

> . . . In the process of doing research interviews, conducting rounds and seeing patients in other contexts, it is increasingly striking to me how little I recognise in these people many of the key concepts that dominate the ways we as mental health professionals work. The things patients talk about and the way they talk do not seem to reflect our concepts, or at the very least, our concepts seem to reflect only such a very narrow range of what is going on in these people.[4]

As an illustration he offers the following story:

This 28-year-old man had had the first onset of his schizophrenia ten years previously. He had spent three years in the hospital, and then from the period between seven and five years before my interview had been able to manage outside the hospital. However, five years before my interview he had been readmitted to the hospital and had remained there since. As part of our interviews, we try to delineate the various general levels of illness, at several times in the past. We then determine levels of social relations and work functioning, symptoms and hospitalisation during those times and plot a time line of course of disorder. This line is generated by rating scales of established reliability. In this particular study, we also enquire about the worst year the person has had since becoming ill. I expected that when I asked that question of this young man he would say that it was one of the times when his functioning scores were lowest, his symptoms highest, and when he was in the hospital. He said the worst year was about six years ago, a time when by our scores he was doing fairly well and was not in the hospital. He said that he had been living with his mother and then finally had been kicked out of her house and was living in an apartment. About two weeks after leaving her house he called home. She answered the telephone. He started talking, but when she heard his voice, she said "You have the wrong number" and hung up. He said that was the worst year of his life. My heart sank as he told his story. It was not difficult to understand what he meant, but the worst year according to him and the worst year according to our rating scales were very different. Who was right?[5]

What one has here is a clash of interpretations and priorities and a fundamental difference in situational definition—two narratives revolving around the same situation, one focusing on the person-as-illness, the other focusing on the person-as-person, and both coming to significantly different conclusions as to priorities and life expectations. To the clinicians, from their medicopsychiatric perspective the "natural" assumption was that the "schizophrenic's" (as opposed to person's) worst time was when his illness was at its peak, that is, when his clinical symptomatology was most obvious (when the objects of the researcher's particular area of interest were most obvious). In other words, their position as medical researchers offered them a perspective whereby they defined him, his emotions, his expectations, and his hopes according to their perception of his problem and its implications, that is, as if his illness were inevitably the most important thing in his life. The reality was that what took priority, what had the greatest impact on him was the nature of his personal experiences, in particular his relationship with his mother.

Strauss's final question, "Who was right?" is highly significant. In a sense both narratives are correct from the standpoint of the individuals involved. However, as will become apparent, people with mental health problems are seriously disempowered. When it comes to the question of whose voice will be listened to within such a process of narrative negotiation, the chances are that it will be the voice of the professional who comes through loud and clear. Though Strauss's central interest is in re-centering the person within the process of mental health care, he is not in the majority within the mental health professions. In a medicocentric culture, the narrative of the health professions will almost inevitably tend to take priority over the other narratives. It is vital that we bear these thoughts and propositions in mind as we move on to explore contemporary interpretations of schizophrenia. While acknowledging the importance of the medicopsychiatric view, we must be careful not to allow the power of its voice to prevent us from hearing the voices of those who may be victims of an overly medicalized definition of what mental health problems are and what appropriate responses should be.

Focusing on Friendship

Strauss's vignette suggests that even in the midst of the most profound forms of mental health problems there is a vital relational dimension that is frequently *more* significant, from the perspective of the sufferers, than other factors within their illness. It also suggests that this dimension is often not given adequate priority within standard professional understandings of what psychological disorders are and what they might mean to the people who have them. It is here, within the area of personal relationships, that the Christian community has a vital contribution to make to the care of people with mental health problems. The role of the

Christian community lies not only in creating a context that will nurture relational development and enable people to find wholeness in the midst of their brokenness, but also in actively countering the wider interpersonal and social forces that act to stigmatize, alienate, oppress, and exclude many people with mental health problems from full social inclusion.

The primary conduit through which such a task can be fulfilled is the relationship of *friendship*. Christian friendships based on the friendships of Jesus can be a powerful force for the reclamation of the centrality of the *person* in the process of mental health care. It is within the relationship of friendship that we discover a critical tool of liberation and healing. This can enable the church to fulfill its task of rehumanizing those whom society has dehumanized through its attitudes and its refusal to relate with them in a way that is meaningful and life enhancing. To understand the significance of this proposition, we begin by exploring the relationship of friendship, drawing out precisely why it offers distinctive and unique opportunities for the mental health ministry of the Christian community.

Friendship is a deeply intimate and committed relationship that encompasses people in all their fullness. It is not bounded or dictated by stereotypical presumptions of biological malfunctioning. *The priority of friends is the personhood of the other and not the illness.* As such, a focus on the role of friendship as a primary mode of caring offers a vital counterbalance to the types of positivistic, medicalized approaches highlighted above. It allows us to move beyond pathology, and begin to explore those aspects of *people* with mental health problems that fall outside the boundaries of the medical model. A focus on friendship enables us to ask critical questions that are often not on the agenda of those whose horizons are bounded by the medical gaze of psychiatry and whose focus lies primarily within pathology. A concentration on friendship releases us from an overdependence on technology and allows us to explore issues of human relationships, personhood, spirituality, value, and community, all of which can easily be overlooked or seen as of secondary importance within standard definitions and treatment models of mental health care.

Friendship as a Gift of the Community

Unlike specialist/professional relationships, friendship is a form of human affection that is potentially available to and from the *whole* of the Christian community and from the whole of society. A focus on friendship opens up the possibility that the care of people with severe mental health problems is a communal, lay oriented enterprise rather than an exclusively individualized specialist task, and suggests that the church community may have a specific responsibility within this area. Such a focus on friendship enables the church to offer a *distinctive* contribution to the process of care. Nancy Eiesland suggests that friendship is the distinctively Christian gift that the church offers to marginalized people:

> Whereas we [the church] might like to imagine ourselves as part of the mainstream or "normal" population—Christians have accepted a mission that perpetuates a marginal position. Thus we call to other marginalized individuals for friendship not from the center of society—where we are not either demographically or in terms of political/social power—but at the periphery, where we are because of Christ's radical call to be for the other. Thus the contention is that friendship is the Christian call to all who are on the periphery by virtue of [our] decisions to follow the model of friendship of Jesus; thus we are in no position to worry whether [others], such as people with AIDS, people with physical disabilities, people with learning disabilities, etc., are going to be a "burden" to us.[6]

When the church is truly being the church, it does not sit at the center of power and politics, seeking to establish God's reign through the exercise of power, violence, and exclusion. The task of the church is not to reestablish the reign of Constantine,[7] but rather to live out the rule of Christ, the one who sat on the margins of society with those whom the world deemed to be unlovable. Caring for "strangers" is not an act of charity, but a revelation of the true nature of the church and the true character of the God whom we worship and seek to image. Friendship is necessary, not simply for effective mental health care, but in order for the church to be the church in any kind of meaningful sense. Friendship enables us to take seriously the personhood and social context of marginalized people and seeks to actualize the proposition that all people are made in the image of a relational God and as such, created for loving relationships with God and with one another.

What Is Different About Christian Friendship?

One of the reasons we underplay the healing potential of friendship is that we take for granted that we know what it is. The type of friendship this book will focus on differs from the assumed norm of everyday Western friendship. The form of friendship here is *radical* in that it transcends the relational boundaries that are constructed by contemporary tendencies to associate with others on the basis of likeness, utility, or social exchange. It is radical also in that its primary dynamic is toward the outcast and the stranger, those whom society rejects and marginalizes. It is a profoundly humanizing relationship that reveals something of the coming kingdom of God as revealed in the person of Christ in whom "the possibility of reconciliation and shalom becomes a reality; the enmity between human beings finds resolution and healing and the fragmentation of the human family is swept up and mended by the power of the coming Kingdom. In Christ, servants are transformed into friends, boundaries of prejudice and difference are torn down and the wholeness of the human family is revealed as a genuine possibility.

Such radical friendship is perhaps best described as *messianic friendship* in that, inspired by the power of the Spirit, it takes its shape from the relationships of Jesus the Messiah, and seeks to embody and act out something of his life and purpose. In order to understand and justify such a position, it is necessary to begin by exploring the nature and purpose of the church. In clarifying precisely what the church community is (or at least should be in its ideal form) the shape of the model of friendship that forms the heart of this book will begin to emerge.

Imaging the Messiah: The Church as Sign and Sacrament

Avery Dulles in his book *Models of the Church* identifies five major ecclesial types. He suggests that the church can be viewed as: an institution, as the mystical Body of Christ, as a sacrament, as a herald, or as a servant.[8] For current purposes it will be useful to examine some aspects of Dulles' propositions concerning the sacramental nature of the church. The model of church-as-sacrament emphasizes the present reality of the grace of Christ in the world, with the church being seen as the sign of that reality. "If Christ is the sacrament of God, the Church is for us the sacrament of Christ; she represents him, in the full and ancient meaning of the term, she really makes him present. She not only carries on his work, but she is his very continuation, in a sense far more real than that in which it can be said that any human institution is its founder's continuation."[9] Thus the Christian community as the Body of Christ is seen to be the living continuation of the earthly and messianic ministry of Christ. The church is founded on the historical Christ, sustained and guided by the power of the Holy Spirit,[10] and gathered around and shaped by the biblical narrative.[11]

John Calvin describes sacraments as "effectual signs; the means whereby God leads us to Himself via earthly elements."[12] In like manner, Dulles defines a sacrament as "a sign of grace."[13] By "sign," Dulles means not a mere pointer to something that is absent, but a sign of something really present. "Beyond this a sacrament is an efficacious sign; the sign itself produces or intensifies that of which it is a sign. Thanks to the sign, the reality signified achieves an existential depth; it emerges into solid, tangible existence."[14] The church understood as a sign of grace does not simply point toward an ideal, but actually reveals something of that ideal in its life and ministry. In this sense the church might legitimately be understood as the physical manifestation of God's redemptive love. Thus, the task of the church is to signify the redeeming grace of Christ in a historically tangible form.

> It stands under a divine imperative to make itself a convincing sign. It appears most convincingly when its members are evidently united to one another and to God through holiness and mutual love, and when they visibly gather to confess their faith in Christ and to celebrate what God has done for them in Christ. . . . The church never fully achieves itself as church. It is true church to the extent that it is tending to become more truly church.[15]

40

The church is not a perfect institution.[16] It works out its ministry within the continuing eschatological dialectic between the cross and the Resurrection; what is and what will be. Although it cannot reveal the coming kingdom in all of its fullness, it is charged with the task of revealing signs of how that kingdom will be in the fulfillment of the eschaton. Hodgson explains the paradoxical dialectic that marks the ongoing life of the church in terms of the difference between *basileia* and *ecclesia*, that is, between the kingdom of God and the church.[17] He argues that *basileia* is "an image of a new way of being human in the world in relation to God and neighbour— new community, communion of love, liberation, a new and radical family based not on blood relationships but on human and ethical ones."[18] The church then, as Moltmann correctly observes, is the "anticipation of the kingdom of God under the conditions of history, the vanguard of the new humanity."[19] It is that body which reveals something of the new humanity that has been given to us in Christ (2 Corinthians 4:4). Inevitably the church becomes an institution, an *ecclesia*, that has to maintain itself within history. However, this ecclesia is also "an image, sign, sacrament, and fore-taste of the *basileia*, embodied in the diversity of historical churches. As such it discloses the *basileia* vision unambiguously but actualizes it only fragmentarily."[20] Thus while the church community is called to reveal the coming kingdom in its actions and thinking, it is not an ideal community. It is flawed and struggles to live up to its own identity. Nevertheless, it does contain the messianic vision for the future and reveals something of the coming kingdom if imperfectly.

The Centrality of Christ

Central to the identity of the church is the figure of Jesus. Dulles sees the church as fundamentally centered on the person of Jesus Christ: "God's grace is for all people, but the church is the place where it appears most clearly that the love that reconciles men to God and to one another is a participation in what God communicates most fully in Christ. Christians are those who see and confess Jesus Christ. As the supreme efficacious symbol—the primordial sacrament of God's saving love stretched out to all."[21]

Such a Christocentric view of the church has important implications for the character of the church's caring ministry. Hoekendijk presents a powerful argument for the church to understand itself as a "Messianic community" by following Jesus' example of self-emptying servanthood.[22] He argues that the life of the church must be imitated from the Messiah, which means living the self-emptying life of the suffering servant. Hoekendijk states that the church received her "charter" thus: "Let the same mind be in you that was in Christ Jesus, who, though he was in the form of God, did not regard equality with God as something to be exploited, but empitied himself, taking the form of a slave, being born in human likeness. And being found in human form, he humbled himself and became obedient to the point of death—even death on a cross" (Philippians 2:5-8).

Hoekendijk applies this model, then, to the role of the church: "If someone asks where the church is, then we ought to be able to answer; there, where people are emptying themselves, making themselves as nothing. There where people serve, not just a little, but in total service, which has been imitated from the messiah servant, and in which the cross comes into view. And there, where the solidarity with the fellow man is not merely preached, but is actually demonstrated."[23]

The church is called to embody God's passion for the world that was revealed in the life of Jesus, and to adopt the ethical priorities that were so clearly revealed in his life and death. The truth of the gospel can only be understood when it is manifested in the lives of a people who have experienced and been transformed by the love of Christ. The authenticity of the gospel is always judged by the ability of Christians to live their lives in ways that reflect the truth of the message. The message that in Christ God was reconciling himself to the world (2 Cor. 5:19) only becomes truth as it is embodied within a people whose primary desire is to love and to reach out in compassion to the needy.

The messianic church cares for the world with the passion of Christ and strives to reflect that care in its life and attitudes. This being so, the nature of Jesus' ministry and mission, which is fundamental in forming the character of the church, will inevitably be reflected in the forms of care that the church deems it legitimate to adopt, and the priorities and goals that guide the practice of that care.

Friendship and Liberating Discipleship

As we reflect on the life of Jesus, it becomes clear that the types of relationships he entered into were of a special quality and frequently had a specific focus. His relationships were marked by such things as unconditional acceptance (John 4:5), solidarity with the poor and the marginalized (Matthew 9:10), and total commitment to others, even unto death. The name that he and the other gospel writers gave to this form of committed relationship was *friendship*. It would not be unreasonable to define discipleship as friendship with Jesus: "No one has greater love than this, to lay down one's life for one's friends. You are my friends if you do what I command you. I do not call you servants any longer . . . but I have called you friends" (John 15:13-15).

Sacrificial friendship is the definition of love. Sacrificial friendship, which works itself out as solidarity with the poor, reveals the true meaning of discipleship and faithful living that images the messiah. Bearing in mind what has already been suggested concerning Christ as the pattern for ministry, mission, and the church, we see the importance of such reflections on the centrality of friendship for our understanding of discipleship. By laying down friendship as a pattern for discipleship and a way of being that embodies the coming kingdom, Jesus outlines the specific shape and form that the church's ministry of care should take. Christians are called to be disciples: *friends of the poor.*

Redefining Friendship

Of course, the type of friendship that is revealed in the life and mission of Jesus differs quite markedly from normal Western understandings of friendship. For most of us, friendship is a common relationship of which everyone assumes they know the meaning. Mary Hunt comments:

43

> Friendship is available to everyone, at least potentially. The tiny baby who is befriended by her mother is learning friendship. The elderly person around whom a community gathers when she is dying is capable of teaching friendship. Friendship, by its nature, assumes that persons live in relationships, and that relationships are good.[24]

At one level then, friendships, along with kinships, are the essence of the relational fabric within which all human beings work out their lives. At this level friendship is the most common relationship, available to all and special only in its importance for general human flourishing. Irrespective of its implications for mental health care, friendship is a fundamental and vital form of human relationship. Such an observation should come as no real surprise. For many people, the essence of life, that which makes it worthwhile, is the presence of friends. The prevalence of friendship is a natural extension of the image of God in human beings. Human beings are social creatures, made in the image of a social God who is trinity; a God who *is* love and relationship in essence. God is a community of Father, Son, and Holy Spirit, eternally indwelling one another in a community of love. It is only natural that creatures made in God's image should seek after relationships in all of their various forms.

For most of us, our friendships are based on the principle that like attracts like. We normally assume that making friends depends on sharing common interests and activities and having a shared frame of reference within which we communicate and share our experiences. When we reflect on our own relational networks, we find that the majority, if not all, of our friends are very much like ourselves. This cultural presumption reflects the thinking of Aristotle, whose writings have provided the major philosophical source in Western Christian tradition for dealing with friendship and for making sense of most relationships.[25] This way of approaching human relationships has been deeply influential within Western culture and, by implication, on the church that is embedded within that culture. Aristotle distinguished between three kinds of friendships: friendships of *utility*, friendships of *pleasure*, and friendships of *goodness*. A friendship of *utility* is a

friendship based on usefulness. The friends are friends only inso-
far as they are useful to each other. They are useful to each other as
long as they can provide the goods the other person needs. This
category of friendship would include work-mates, those with
whom we do business, and so forth. Such people are "a necessary
part of our relational landscapes. They provide what is useful to
the common good."[26] Friendships of *pleasure* are based on the
amount of pleasure the participants get from the relationship. They
are friends primarily for the enjoyment they bring to one another.
The third kind of friendship, the highest according to Aristotle, is
the friendship of *virtue* or *goodness*. This kind of friendship is exclusive, in the sense that it can only be between two people, both of
whom are able to actualize the virtue of goodness. "One or two
persons in a lifetime come along who are 'most completely friends,
since each one loves the other for what the other is in himself and
not for something he has about him which he need not have.'
Those friendships are based on mutual goodness and the desire to
respond in kind to that goodness."[27]

Unlike friendships of utility and pleasure, where there can be a
circle of friends, the friendship of goodness is an exclusive and
deeply intimate relationship that takes place between two people,
both of whom *must* share the virtue of goodness. The intensity of
this relationship means that the friends have no love to spare for
other less virtuous friendships.

There are a number of difficulties with such an understanding of
friendship. I will highlight two here. First, for Aristotle, friendship
could occur only between *equals*, that is, two good people serving
to actualize the virtue of goodness within their friendship relationship. In this model, as Sallie McFague correctly observes, "friendship is finally not love of another but of oneself. One needs a friend,
says Aristotle, in order to exercise one's virtue; one needs someone
to be good to in order to be good."[28]

Such an understanding is the antithesis of the types of friendship
revealed in the life and death of Christ.

> In the incarnation, one finds God willingly entering into friend-
> ship with his creatures who could never be his equal. In the earth-
> ly life and ministry of Jesus one finds a continuing picture of a

man entering into friendships not with social equals, but with those whom society had downgraded and considered unworthy of friendship. In the death of Jesus one discovers a man committed to these same friends even unto death.[29]

People with severe mental health problems such as schizophrenia are at times radically different in their outlook, behavior, and attitudes. Friendships based on the principle that like attracts like will inevitably exclude those who for whatever reason are different. Thus, a faithful Christ-centered church cannot accept the premise of "like attracts like" as an adequate foundation for its caring practices.

Second, Aristotle focused primarily on *quality* as opposed to *quantity.* He considered friendship something that decreased in quality as it increased in quantity. However, as we reflect on the friendships of Jesus, we see that the quality of his relationships remained the same, not just for intimates but for all the people he encountered. Certainly the level of intensity of his relationships varied. Jesus had close friends and friends for whom his love was openly expressed in a way that it was not in other relationships (John 19:26). However, though the intensity may have fluctuated, the quality and texture of his friendships always remained the same. While Aristotle retains a hierarchy among friends, Jesus offers a radically new understanding of friendship.

When "respectable society" calls Jesus a "friend of sinners and tax collectors," it wants only to denounce and compromise him. In keeping with the law according to which its ranks are organised, respectable society identifies people with their failings and speaks of sinners; it identifies people with their profession and speaks of tax collectors; it identifies people with their diseases and calls them lepers and the handicapped. From this society speaks the law, which defines people always with their failings. Jesus, however, as the Son of man without this inhuman law, becomes the friend of the sinful and sick persons. By forgiving their sins he restores to them their respect as men and women; by accepting lepers he makes them well. And thus he becomes their friend in the true sense of the word. The denunciatory, contemptuous name "friend of sinners and tax collectors," unintentionally expresses the deep truth of Jesus. As friend he reveals God's friendship to the unlikable, to those who have been treated in such unfriendly fashion. As the Son of Man, he sets their oppressed humanity free.[30]

In befriending those who were cast out by society, and claiming that this is the way of the emerging kingdom of God, Jesus presents us with a model of liberation, an "inescapable moment of radical change" in our perceptions of friendship. In this moment of liberation and revelation, Jesus flattens the relational hierarchy of the Aristotelian model of friendship and presents a new and radically open understanding of friendship—a friendship that is open to those who are, in the perception of society, "not good"—the outsiders, the tax collectors, and sinners, those who are in many respects radically unlike himself. More than that, by moving the status of his disciples from servants to friends, and by suggesting that true friendship demands commitment even unto death, Jesus presents a model of committed friendship that more than transcends the boundaries of utility and pleasure.

Thus, in the friendships of Jesus we find a model of friendship, not as a closed relationship with a single like-minded individual, but as an open relationship focused on "the outsider," a form of relating that should form the template and the core of any church that seeks to follow and to image him faithfully.

> If one takes the friendship of Jesus as paradigmatic of the friendships that are expected of the church, then it becomes clear that the quality of the church's friendships *must* reflect the God whom they image and the messiah they claim to follow. The church community will find its true identity when it comes to understand itself as a community of friends, wholly and selflessly committed to God, one another, and the world.[31]

The church then is a "fellowship of the friends of Jesus,"[32] called to live in the world in a manner that is appropriate to such a status.

Agape and an Ethic of Solicitude

Such a model of friendship is based on a radical ethic of *solicitude*. Stephen Post in *The Moral Challenge of Alzheimer's Disease* argues that the ethical principle of *solicitude*—the anxiety over the good of another—is fundamental for all moral behavior. Drawing on the thinking of Soble, Post suggests that solicitude can take three forms. The first of these is property based, in the sense of being dependent on a person's having certain properties that make him or her attractive or worthy of care in the eyes of another person. In the first model, "the caregiver looks for some comprehensible and explanatory source of his or her solicitude." Such solicitude is property based, that is, "When x loves y, this can be explained as the result of y's having, or x's perceiving that y has, some set (S) of attractive, admirable, or valuable properties; x loves y because y has S or because x perceives or believes that y has S."[33]

A second form solicitude can take is memory based. Faced with a loved one's severe neurological damage and profound loss of memory, caregivers remain solicitous "because that person was near and dear and, no matter how dismantled, continues to be honored in reciprocation." Such a form of solicitude is still property based, but retrospectively so.

While both of these models of solicitude have their place within this study, it is Post's third model that is of particular relevance here. The third is based on a very different principle: the radical *agape* love of God for human beings. This view of solicitude is very much in line with the Christian understanding of *agape* love. Quoting Soble,[34] Post suggests that it "denies the need to be grounded in y's attractive properties (S) or in x's belief or perception that y has S." Such solicitude is not property based, nor is it explicable or easily comprehensible. Such solicitude is a matter of bestowal rather than appraisal, it is unconditional rather than conditional on certain properties in its object, and it is therefore not extinguished by unattractive properties. This solicitude "is its own reason and love is taken as a metaphysical primitive. Such is the structure of agapic personal love."[35]

There is a real danger that property-based solicitude, by definition, is dependent on the continuity of certain properties within the individual. If these are no longer present, then the maintenance of solicitude can be troublesome. Even with memory-based solicitude, there is an implicit assumption that there is a radical discontinuity between the person remembered and the person experienced in the present. If solicitude is based solely on memory, then one is faced with some serious questions as to the nature of the personhood of the person one is attempting to relate with in the present. However, the type of non–property-based solicitude presented in Post's third definition offers a model of solicitude that is grounded in the reality of God's unending and unconditional love for the individual—a love that bestows worth and dignity upon the individual irrespective of context, situation, or any radical change that may occur within particular properties. This kind of solicitude offers a "non-appraisive attitude of radical equality" underpinned by an ethic and an attitude that adopts a position of moral solidarity with the other, irrespective of circumstance. Such a stance is very much in line with the ethical and social position adopted by Jesus—the one who came to reveal God's agapic love in all of its fullness. As such, it offers a powerful ethical underpinning to the model of friendship that has been developed thus far.

Friendship and Virtue

It is, of course, vital to bear in mind that while solicitude may find its ultimate exposition in the life of Christ, it should not be understood as something that is solely the heroic achievement of outstanding individuals. The attainment and maintenance of such an attitude of solicitude-in-friendship requires a community that understands and seeks to live out the implications of taking such a way of being seriously. While there may be legitimate criticism directed at certain aspects of Aristotle's model of friendship, there are dimensions of his thinking that are important to retain. If what has been presented thus far is correct, then Christian friendship is considerably more than simply "another human relationship." Rather it is both a virtue and, as Paul Waddell suggests, "a moral enterprise."[36] It is a way of living that ensures that human beings can be enabled to live their lives humanly. It is a form of praxis (embodied theology) through which we acquire the wisdom necessary and in particular the self-knowledge we require to be people of virtue.

Understanding friendship as a virtue is an important emphasis for the purposes of this book. In *The Nichomachean Ethics*, Aristotle describes virtue as a state of excellence *(arete)* or disposition whose aim is the highest Good *(eudaimonia)*.[37] In essence, for Aristotle the term *virtue* meant "that which causes a thing to perform its function well." *Arete* was an excellence of any kind that denotes the power of anything to fulfill its function. Thus the virtue of the eye is seeing, the virtue of a knife is its cutting edge, the virtue of a horse is running, and so forth.[38] Human virtue is that which causes us to fulfill our function in a way that is appropriate to our status as human beings.[39] Understood in this way, the activity of friendship is that which trains us to be virtuous in the art of being Christlike and, by implication, being fully human.

The suggestion that friendship is an *activity* is significant. Friendship is not a social status or a static human relationship. Rather it is a dynamic activity within which we seek to live virtuous lives worthy of being called truly human. Such a way of living is based on the life of Christ in whom we discover the ultimate definition of what it means to be human (2 Corinthians 4:4). The process of friendship and the process of community development are deeply interlinked. Friendship is not something that we embark upon on our own. Friendship is a skill that is learned in community and in turn contributes to the formation of a specific type of community. Thus we develop the skill of friendship as we encounter one another in friendship and experience the friendship of Christ as he works out his purposes in and through those who seek to follow him. "Friendship is not just a necessity for living well, but necessary if we are to be people of practical wisdom. Through character-friendship we actually acquire the wisdom necessary, and in particular the self-knowledge, to be people of virtue."[40]

From our discussion thus far it has become clear that friendship, like all the virtues, is context dependent—that is, the word "friendship" does not have a universal meaning. The meaning and praxis of friendship can be understood only within the context of the particular community within which it is being practiced, and the specific moral tradition within which it is rooted.[41] The model of friendship previously offered roots itself within the Christian tradition in general and the Gospel narratives in particular, and takes the figure of Christ as the primary exemplar of this form of relational praxis. Virtue-friendships that reflect the friendships of Jesus, the one true image of God, give us a means and a form of self-knowledge that allows us to live life humanly and to begin to move toward the actualization of our status as creatures made in the image of God.

If we contextualize this understanding of friendship within the realm of mental health care, we find that friendship is that virtue which enables us to care with the compassion, humanity, and vision of Christ. The activity of Christlike friendship moves us beyond our socially bound expectations, and opens up new horizons and possibilities for human relationships, community, and mental health care. Christ-centered friendship demands that the church become a community that is deeply committed to those who are, in some senses, "least like us." It demands that we sit with the poor, commune with the marginalized, and sojourn with those whom society despises. In the virtue of friendship as defined by the tradition of the Gospels and the example of Christ, we discover the continuation of the incarnation and the possibility of a radical new vision of both society and church.

Radical Friendship

Reflecting on the discussion thus far, it becomes clear why one might legitimately refer to Christian friendship as *radical* friendship. The *Collins English Dictionary* defines the word "radical" as "favoring or tending to produce extreme or fundamental changes in political, economic, or social conditions, institutions, habits of mind." On reflection, it is clear that one of the goals of the type of friendship described above, rooted in a new way of being human revealed to us in the life of Christ, is to produce just such radical changes within individuals, the church, and the wider community. Such friendships are both *centripetal* and *centrifugal*, reaching inward to contribute to the building of a loving and inclusive community, and outward to embrace and stand with the "outsiders," those who are oppressed and forced to stand on the margins of acceptable society. As such, *messianic* friends are always necessarily pushing against the boundaries of oppressive political and economic systems, ideologies, social conditions, and false epistemologies that might cause the suppression of the *imago Dei* in portions of the community. When Christian friends come together in solidarity and loving commitment, they encounter the world at a different level and see it from a different perspective. It is this radical edge to the friendship relationship that images the friendships of Jesus and enables friends to "see the world differently," and in seeing differently, move toward the initiation of liberation.

As the following chapters will show, people living with severe mental health problems are often defined as essentially "other," and marginalized, discriminated against, and excluded accordingly. Due to the nature of their condition and its psychological and social consequences, they are among the poorest and most marginalized within society. This being so, and in the light of the argument of this chapter, it becomes clear that *caring for the needs of people living with mental health problems is not an option for the church. Rather it is a primary mark of its identity and faithfulness.* The church community cannot simply choose whether it should or should not minister to people with severe mental health problems. Quite the opposite. In order to *be* the church in any kind of meaningful sense, it *has* to seek to minister to people living with mental health problems in all of their diversity. To minister within this area is a confirmation of the church's faithfulness to its calling. If God does have a "bias toward the poor," and if the church truly wishes to image Christ in his ministry of liberation and re-humanization, then the church must take the needs of this group of people most seriously. It is out of a desire to enable the church truly to be the church by developing a new and transformative form of ecclesial praxis that images the relationships and attitudes of Jesus, that this book finds its rationale and its goal.

Chapter 2

Setting the Context
Deinstitutionalization and Care in the "Community"

Recently the care of people with mental health problems has begun to move away from large institutions toward a model of care that focuses on the community. In most Western countries, the last few decades have shown a dramatic fall in the number of hospital beds, combined with modest increases in community resources.[1] In the United Kingdom and in the United States, there has been a major reduction in the amount of available institutional care that has led to a very large and rapid emptying of mental hospitals. It is estimated that "90 percent of the people who would have been in the hospital 40 years ago are not in the hospital today."[2] Within this context there have been fundamental changes in the way in which care for persons with mental health problems should be provided. It is now considered that people with mental health problems should be admitted to the hospital only where this is absolutely necessary for specific treatments. In the field of acute psychiatry this has led to more frequent admissions for shorter periods. Patients already in the hospital who could benefit from community based care have been discharged. Admission to the hospitals has thus been reduced, as have the number of long-stay patients.[3]

It is not possible or necessary here to offer an in-depth critique of the various policies, controversies, and political agendas that lie behind the current emphasis on deinstitutionalization. However, it will be helpful to reflect on some of the implications of this movement as they relate to the model of care that is being developed within this book. The movement from hospital to community has both positive and negative aspects. Positively, there are many long-term patients with various types of psychiatric difficulties who simply should never have been in the hospital in the first place. As one reads through the case notes of people who have been in the hospital for many years, one is struck by the frequency with which one finds loose and often nonexistent diagnostic criteria for admission. Several long-stay patients whose case histories I examined in researching this book were incarcerated for such things as "moral insanity" (having an illegitimate child), or the vague "diagnosis" of "causing a public affray." Many of these people would certainly not be admitted to the hospital today. In fact, Fuller Torrey speculates that the vast majority of all individuals discharged from institutions could live successfully outside the hospital if medication and aftercare services were provided. "In that sense deinstitutionalization was and is a humane and reasonable idea."[4] Despite a good deal of handicapping caused, among other things, by long-term institutionalization, the side effects of pre-atypical neuroleptic medications, and inadequate material or relational support, many live good quality lives and are reasonably well integrated within society.

On the other hand, the reality is that deinstitutionalization has been a disaster for many people with mental health problems. As Stewart Govig observes, for the most part the project of deinstitutionalization as it has worked itself out within the United States has been a notable failure. It has become "a psychiatric Titanic, the largest failed social experiment of twentieth-century America." The ideal may have been to liberate individuals from the bondage of psychiatric institutions, but the reality reveals countless sad, lonely, isolated individuals for whom deinstitutionalization has been a movement away from varying degrees of security and friendship to nothing. A similar tale of lonely, discarded people could be told regarding the consequences of closing the large psychiatric hospitals in Great Britain.[5]

The Problem with Institutions

There can be little doubt that the old psychiatric institutions, many built before the turn of the century, have failed as caring institutions. "Most of them were built for custodial rather than therapeutic care and a lack of resources has prevented many of them from being substantially up-graded."[6] The reality is that, while offering a degree of safety and security, they often created dangerous subcultures that were frequently abusive, sometimes violent, personally destructive, and often fundamentally oppressive. The potentially abusive nature of psychiatric institutions is shown very clearly in Erving Goffman's book *Asylums*. Fictitiously, but no less powerfully, it is described in popular novels such as *One Flew Over the Cuckoo's Nest*,[7] and Paul Sayer's novel, *The Comforts of Madness*, which offers a harrowing account of a man with schizophrenia who is subjected to the regimented and routinized confines of a psychiatric hospital. As McKie comments:

> Until recently care has been predominantly institutional. . . . Too frequently [these institutions] were staffed by nurses (or attendants) who had little training, if any at all, in therapeutic or interpersonal skills. There was little concept of rehabilitation or contact with the outside world. . . . With the use of legal detention. . . psychiatric hospitals were rife during the sixties and seventies with reports of mistreatment of patients, poor staff morale, and crumbling buildings.[8]

Most large psychiatric institutions were physically situated on the outskirts of towns and cities, which compounded the real and perceived sense of difference and otherness which existence in such institutions brought about.[9]

As Browning observes, "When the large psychiatric hospitals were built they were frequently erected in remote areas behind high walls. Those who were admitted for treatment and care were therefore out of sight and when out of sight there was the danger that they were out of mind and forgotten."[10]

More positively, the past few years have seen major changes in the way such institutions are managed and the types of regimes under that they function. Psychiatric hospitals certainly *can* show a more tolerant environment where "basic human needs such as adequate accommodation and nutrition, companionship, social interaction, employment and leisure activity are at least to some extent ensured. Because of their centralization of resources, the hospitals can provide many different types of therapeutic facilities and patients are not confined to treatment by medication or other physical methods alone."[11]

Hospital care encompasses both positive and negative aspects. On the one hand, psychiatric hospitals *can* provide a safe place for troubled individuals, an asylum in the positive sense of the word. Well-organized multidisciplinary teams can bring effective holistic care to individuals and genuinely enhance their life opportunities. However, hospitals can also be highly oppressive places, particularly for those suffering from severe and chronic mental health problems. The nature of such impairments means that people are very vulnerable and open to various forms of abuse and exploitation, both by members of staff and by their fellow patients.

Oppressive Institutions

The vulnerability of people within psychiatric institutions is an important point to reflect upon. Due to the nature of their conditions and the types of depersonalizing social forces that they encounter on a daily basis, people with long-term mental health problems are among the most vulnerable within our societies. However, within the confines of the institution, their vulnerability is increased manyfold.

Total Institutions

In his book *Asylums*, Erving Goffman develops the concept of "total institutions," such as prisons or psychiatric hospitals.[12] A total institution is a place of residence that contains a large number of persons who, for whatever reason, have been isolated from wider society for lengthy periods of time. Such an institution is closed, insular, and runs according to an enclosed and formalized administrative regime. All aspects of life within the institution are conducted within the same location and all activities are determined by the regime of the institution, taking place according to a strict timetable that is dictated by the power of the regime. In situations such as these, inmates have little or no moment-to-moment powers of decision making. On admission they abandon, or have forcibly taken from them, their right to agree or disagree to specific actions. There is a strict demarcation between staff and inmates, and staff attitudes toward inmates tend to be narrow and marked by hostile stereotypes. The institution is total in the sense that it forms an insulated subculture that differs greatly from the culture at large. Within such a situation, the potential for explicit and implicit degradation and abuse is high. Patients have no power, and no control over what happens in their lives. Any signs of autonomy or "rebellion" are pathologized and dealt with through medication or physical restraint.

I remember as a trainee nurse being ordered to tell thirty patients to strip and line up in the bathroom in rows of ten, in order that they could be shaved and bathed by nursing assistants. On reflection, this was not an act of care but a method of control. Simple acts of personal hygiene became tests of willpower and evidence of the total control that nurses had over patients. Any dissenters would be isolated, and if they became "violent," held down and injected with powerful sedatives. The medication was not for the benefit of the patient; rather it was a means of control used by nursing staff to ensure that the regime carried on without challenge or interruption. Routine almost always took precedence over people. Total institutions not only strip all power from patients, they frequently effectively disempower and dehumanize staff as well. It is true that within this situation, I did have a choice: either I rebelled against the system and threw away my career, or I conformed and threw away something of my humanity. Sadly, and to my shame, when you are nineteen, altruistic needs often take second place to career needs.

We may not want to take on board all of the critiques of psychiatry presented by the antipsychiatry movement; nevertheless, there are within institutions serious issues of power and control that we ignore at our peril. While technically holding onto their basic rights such as the right to shelter, protection from the law, decent food, appropriate healthcare, and so on, in terms of *meaningful* citizenship, patients within institutions can be deeply oppressed. What use is the right to free speech when everything you say is assumed to be the product of your "madness"? What is the point of thinking of yourself as a citizen when those around you often may not even see you as a person? What use is it to have a right to buy property when the stigma that surrounds your illness means that you have very little chance of getting employment when you are released?

Such difficulties concerning citizenship and mental health problems are not unique to the asylum system. Many people with mental health problems living within the community suffer similar forms of abuse and deprivation of human rights.[13] However, within the confines of the subculture of the institution, such abuse can be concentrated and exacerbated in a highly destructive manner.

The Problem of Community

Caring for people with mental health problems within the community also has much to be said both for and against it. Potentially it offers a much wider range of possibilities for the individual to build relationships, become a member of a faith community, develop interests and find useful forms of employment, all of which are obviously beneficial in terms of self-esteem, acceptance, general life enhancement, and mental health development. In the philosophy of policies of deinstitutionalization, "the ideal is that people should live a normal life in normal circumstances, and not be unnecessarily distinguished as mentally ill."[14]

In a very real sense this philosophical ideal is in line with one of the primary objectives of this book, which is to enable those whose personhood is threatened by negative societal attitudes and values to live their lives as fully valued human beings. However, there is a huge gulf between the *ideal* of a caring community and the *reality* of the situation on the ground. Apart from the financial difficulties that policies of deinstitutionalization have created, there is another more significant dilemma faced by community care policies: within an individualistic culture such as is found within Western societies, there is really no such thing as community in the sense of a cohesive moral community that strives to offer care and attention to others. When official policies speak of "community" they are really only talking about life outside the institution. The term "community" is seen as designating a geographically or administratively defined area as opposed to a close network of positive, sustaining, human social relationships. In other words, the concept of community is understood in terms of *location* rather than of actual social or moral content. The word "community" used in this context is a morally neutral term that says nothing about the potential quality of life that an individual might expect to experience upon entering it, or the types of difficulties he or she will encounter. As Peter Barham astutely observes, "Community conceived as a mere site, without reference to the forms of social relationship that are embodied there and to the constraints of those relationships, certainly offers no guarantee whatsoever of any improvement in the form and quality of our moral relationships with psychiatric patients."[15] It doesn't take much reflection to realize that there is a general uncertainty over what the concept of community actually means, and by implication what "caring-in-community" might consist of in practice.

> To the politician, "community care" is a useful piece of rhetoric; to the sociologist, it is a stick to beat institutional care with; to the civil servant it is a cheap alternative to institutional care which can be passed to the local authorities for action (or inaction); to the visionary, it is a dream of the new society in which people really do care; to the social services departments it is a nightmare of heightened public expectations and inadequate resources to meet them. We are only just beginning to find out what it means to the old, the chronically sick and the handicapped.[16]

This being so, there is no guarantee that deinstitutionalized care carried out within the "community" will be any more life enhancing or less abusive than institutional care, though it holds the potential for being so.

One major difficulty with all policies of deinstitutionalization is that it is notoriously difficult to assess their success. Little exists in the way of hard facts and figures on which to base a proper assessment. This is a highly unsatisfactory situation. The danger is that while community care policies have indeed enhanced the lives of many people and, given proper funding and planning, do have much to offer in terms of mental health care, the only thing that the public hears about is the high profile and mainly negative cases when community care has gone wrong. This simply confirms and propagates negative stereotyping and makes the possibility of creating *real* community for persons with mental health problems even more problematic. Although all of the implications of these observations cannot be drawn out here, it is necessary to point toward the need for a thorough assessment of deinstitutionalization policies and an accessible way of communicating that knowledge to the general public. In this way public perceptions of how people with mental health problems *actually* function within the community (as opposed to how they are perceived to be functioning) can be given the opportunity to be shaped in an authentic and more positive manner.

Caring for "Strangers"

Community and institutional care both have much to be said for and against them. Yet the continuing emphasis on policies of deinstitutionalization and community care means that people with mental health problems inevitably form a significant part of our social landscape. The need for genuine community is perhaps the most pressing need in the process of caring for those individuals. If there really is no meaningful community, then it is the task of the church as a community of friends to create communities within which people can genuinely be cared for and find a place of solace, acceptance, and hope in the midst of loneliness and frequent experiences of hopelessness. A church that takes seriously its ministry to the poor *must* be prepared to offer a positive and constructive response to the presence of people with mental health problems within society. *Community care is considerably more than governmental policy. Community care is a fundamental responsibility of the community-of-friends.*

Chapter 3

What
Is
Schizophrenia?

Having set the context for the investigation, we now begin to explore the nature and experience of mental health problems by developing a holistic model of schizophrenia. By holistic model, I mean one that not only seeks to *explain* the technicalities of schizophrenia, but also to give full consideration to what it *means* for a person within the context of his or her whole life. In working through some of the complexities of this phenomenon, it will be possible to uncover some of the hidden injustices and forms of oppression that infiltrate the lives of people diagnosed with enduring mental health problems. As we explore schizophrenia, the subtle ways in which individuals are moved from the status of persons to nonpersons by the social and relational structures of Western societies will become clear. Along the way, we will point beyond the boundaries of schizophrenia in order to illustrate how the experiences of people with this particular disorder might apply to other mental health problems.

Interpreting Illness

It is worthwhile to begin by reflecting on some of the complex dynamics involved in understanding mental health problems. Current research strongly suggests that many forms of mental health problems have some kind of biological cause. However, it is crucial to recognize that mental health problems, while quite possibly biological in origin, are also human experiences that happen to real people within specific social contexts. As such, they are open to a multitude of different understandings and interpretations, all of which have implications for the ways in which they are perceived and the forms of treatment approaches deemed legitimate for dealing with them.

Medical anthropologist Z. J. Lipowski points out that there are a number of different ways in which people can conceptualize particular illnesses. Lipowski argues that illness can be conceptualized as *irreparable loss or damage*, a *value*, an *enemy*, a *challenge*, a *strategy*, a *relief*, a *weakness*, or a *punishment*.[1] His theory is outlined below by the author in diagrammatic form.

The Meanings of Illness

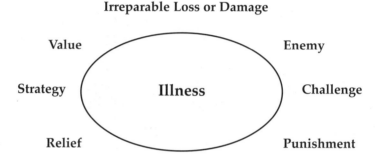

Irreparable Loss or Damage

Value		Enemy
Strategy	**Illness**	Challenge
Relief		Punishment

Weakness

This model shows some of the ways in which people can define situations and attribute meaning to illness experience. For example, from the perspective of the family of people with severe mental health problems, the narrative is often one of irreparable damage or loss. From their viewpoint, the person they knew and loved, along with the dreams, hopes, and expectations that they may have had for that individual, are shattered and destroyed by the illness. In their eyes, very often the person—that is, the person they knew—is lost to the illness. Alternatively, some might see the illness as a relief, a strategy, or even a mystical experience. Some Christian writers such as Jay Adams see mental health problems such as schizophrenia as strategies that people embark upon to avoid the admission of personal sinfulness.[2] In the midst of all of these competing interpretations of the illness, the person with the problem may well have a radically different perception of what it means and the types of priorities and responses that should be deemed appropriate.

The question of which interpretation of illness experiences is correct was raised in chapter 1. Within a social context where the medical model reigns supreme and the power of the mental health professions exceeds the power of the individual, the possibility of the medicalization of illness experiences (that is, an interpretation of an illness that places primary emphasis on issues of pathology and control as opposed to personhood and growth) is very real. It is difficult to talk about conditions such as schizophrenia, depression, bipolar disorder, and so forth, without beginning with issues of pathology rather than people. The ways in which militaristic metaphors are frequently used in defining treatment approaches in medical and psychiatric textbooks are interesting and highly suggestive. From this perspective, illness and disease are seen as *challenges* to be *overcome*, or *enemies* to be *battled against*. However, the approach of the medical model, while highly influential, is only one, and not necessarily the most appropriate, interpretation of what mental health problems actually are as human experiences. Nevertheless, its powerful diagnostic and treatment approach along with its concomitant emphasis on *cure* rather than *care* retains a powerful hold on public and professional expectations. As we progress, it will prove useful to bear in mind the significance of the interpretative context of the subject being explored, and the possibility that our own Enlightenment worldview might blind us to some fundamental truths.[3] As we proceed to reflect on the nature of schizophrenia, we would be wise to bear in mind these underlying power dynamics. As the various issues are addressed, we should be aware that our own thinking may well have been conditioned by cultural expectations and assumptions that stem from an interpretation of mental health problems that is bounded by the assumptions of the medical model.

Clinical Perspectives on Schizophrenia

Schizophrenia affects about one percent of the world's population. It is a condition that appears to affect the most basic mental functions that give people their sense of personhood, individuality, uniqueness, and direction. It is primarily a thought disorder that presents itself in the form of disordered thinking and feelings, that in turn leads to disordered activity. Schizophrenia is classified as a psychotic disorder. As such it is characterized by a distortion in the person's perception of reality, giving rise to misinterpretations of the environment in such a way that logical responses appear to fail.

Contrary to common assumptions, *schizophrenia is not a split or dual personality.* There is a condition called multiple personality disorder in which a person's personality is split and the person takes on different personas, but this is *not* schizophrenia. Rosenhan and Seligman note that a common misconception about schizophrenia is

> that it involves a split personality of the Dr. Jekyll and Mr. Hyde sort, with its attendant unpredictability and violence. This error arises from the origins of the word schizophrenia: schizo = split, phreno = mind. When the Swiss psychiatrist Eugene Bleuler (1857–1939) coined the term in 1911, he intended to suggest that certain psychological functions, ordinarily joined in normal people, are somehow divided in schizophrenics. When non-schizophrenics perceive, say, a horrifying incident, they immediately have an emotional reaction that corresponds to their perception. But, according to Bleuler, this does not happen to schizophrenics, for whom thought and emotion are split. Bleuler never meant to imply that there were two or more alternating personalities residing in the schizophrenic.[4]

The split that the term schizophrenia implies is between the way a person *perceives* reality and the way that reality actually is. Because of this, people going through acute periods of schizophrenia, in some senses "do not inhabit the same world" as others. Consequently, and understandably, the primary outcomes of schizophrenia are *alienation, dislocation,* and *incomprehensibility,* both on the part of people with this mental health problem and on the part of those around them.

The Experience of Schizophrenia

Put briefly, the main ways in which persons diagnosed as having schizophrenia experience their condition are as follows:

Hallucinations   Hallucinations are false sensory perceptions that have a compelling sense of reality.[5] Persons with schizophrenia may hear, see, or smell something that in reality does not exist, such as voices telling them what they should or should not do. Barbara Turner offers a powerful and personal example of the impact hallucinations can have on both the sufferers and their relatives and friends. She wrote about the continuing voices:

> "Hurt yourself!" "You're so stupid!" "You'll never be any good!" I was crouched sitting up in the corner of the living room. I had to make them stop! Leaning forward I rocked back and slammed my head against the wall. The voices got a little quieter, so I did it again. And again and again. Through the hubbub of voices berating me, I heard a small voice. "Mommy?" I opened my eyes and saw my four-year-old son, Travis, standing there in his rumpled pyjamas. He clutched his Big Bird doll to his chest. "Mommy, are you OK?"[6]

Delusions   Delusions are false beliefs that are not subject to reason or contradictory evidence and are not part of a person's culture. Delusions can involve themes such as persecution, religious mysticism, and grandeur. In the fascinating autobiographical monograph *Wild Haemorrhages of the Imagination*, this experience is described in the following terms.

> Paranoia is one of the most difficult frames of mind to live with. For one thing I find that I have absolutely no means of privacy as I am under the illusion of people—friends, relatives and worst of all, strangers—who can see into my mind and determine what my innermost thoughts are. With their eyes they can bore into the top of my head (and at times I often feel as though the top of my skull has been opened up) and somehow my thoughts are reflected into their brains and that their very worst ideas are being transmitted into my brain ending in total turmoil and confusion.[7]

Disordered Thinking   Often the person's thinking is affected by the disorder. Consequently, the person may speak in a way that others cannot easily follow.

> There is difficulty keeping to the point and separating the rele-
> vant from the irrelevant. The person's thinking may be slow, or
> skip from one subject to another often going off at a tangent. . . .
> Thoughts may be jumbled and disjointed. It is difficult for the
> person to organize his thinking in any way at all.[8] . . . My
> thoughts race and don't seem to connect in a rational way. They
> are disjointed and because I cannot remember what they were
> seconds previously, I therefore cannot construct a sensible con-
> versation, action or deed.[9]

Because of this disruption of thought and perception, the sense of
self that normally gives people a feeling of individuality, cohesion,
uniqueness, and self-direction is frequently disturbed in schizophrenia. This is sometimes referred to as a loss of ego boundaries,[10]
and frequently is evidenced by extreme perplexity about a person's
identity and the meaning of his or her existence, or by some of the
specific delusions described above, particularly those involving
control by an outside force.[11] In the words of pastoral theologian
Charles Gerkin, the person diagnosed as having schizophrenia has
lost a "sense of story line," and therefore lost the sense of self.[12]
Their personal story no longer holds together, and the ravages of a
broken narrative shatter their sense of personal identity.

Withdrawal and Loss of Initiative, Energy, and Motivation

It is important to understand that there are *two* sets of symptoms
that persons diagnosed as having schizophrenia may experience at
some points in their lives: positive and negative.

Positive Symptoms Positive symptoms are those described
above—hallucinations, delusions, thought disorders—all of which
might normally be associated with profound mental disturbance.
These symptoms are primarily associated with the acute phases of
the illness. Some people experience these symptoms all or most of
the time, whereas others experience them intermittently. However,
with schizophrenia there is a second, and often unacknowledged
or misunderstood, set of negative symptoms.

Negative Symptoms The term "negative symptom" is descrip-
tive of the sufferer's general attitude toward self, others, and life.

People diagnosed as having schizophrenia are often emotionally withdrawn with respect to self and others, and generally suffer from some degree of impaired functioning interpersonally, vocationally, and academically. Enjoyment of normally pleasurable leisure activities is destroyed. Failure to acknowledge the importance of negative symptoms leads to misunderstandings, interpersonal friction, and accusations of laziness and unsociability. These negative symptoms can have a profound impact on a person's life and, although not as obvious to the outsider, can be equally as devastating.

> The worst thing about this illness is that it tears out your soul. You know? If I could just find the strength I could beat it, but I am always so tired, so lethargic I just can't move against it. I was . . . still am I suppose, a student . . . studying Geography. But I think I am going to have to pack it in. I can't concentrate on a book for two minutes. If I do manage to read anything I can't remember . . . its gone before I finish the page! I just want to sleep. If it wasn't for my mother constantly hassling me I would just sleep all day! I once slept for 22 hours! Even then I was knackered when I woke up. I hate it when the voices start, but at least then I feel like I am alive. Just now I think I'm dead, but I just don't know it yet!

Abnormal Emotions   Abnormal emotions occur when a person reacts emotionally in a way that is deemed to be inappropriate to present circumstances. For example, a person may laugh at a funeral, or cry when receiving good news.[13] However, the most common manifestation of this symptom is simply the blunting of emotions, whereby a person cannot feel any kind of emotional response, no matter how happy or sad a particular event might be.

Lack of Insight   Despite the apparently bizarre and inappropriate nature of their behavior, these people with schizophrenia do not recognize that anything is wrong with their feelings or their behavior. Lack of insight is considered to be one of the primary identifying features of psychotic illness.

It is important to bear in mind that schizophrenia varies greatly in type and intensity from person to person. People will vary in the symptoms they experience, with a minority experiencing most or all of them for most of the time and others experiencing some symptoms intermittently while managing to function reasonably normally for large portions of their lives.

The Course of Schizophrenia

The average age of onset of schizophrenia in men is between 20 and 25, whereas the average onset for women is between 25 and 30. "Before the illness is recognized there is often a prodromal phase in late teenage with social isolation, interest in fringe cults, social withdrawal (e.g., living alone in their bedroom with minimal contact with family and no friends)."[14] Therefore, symptoms and signs may predate sometimes by many years the next phase that is the "active" phase of the illness, characterized by positive symptoms such as hallucinations, delusions, and so on. Through the use of antipsychotic medication, this active phase can be aborted, but this is not always the case. Although something like a fifth of people suffering from their first episode of schizophrenia may make a reasonable recovery, the majority have multiple episodes, and about half have long-term impairment of function affecting their ability to form relationships and to work.[15]

The actual course and severity of the illness and its accompanying symptoms are extremely variable, with some people living their lives constantly in, or moving in and out of, acute psychiatric hospital wards and others functioning reasonably well (sometimes very well) within a community context. Due to this variability of outcome and the diverse possible life trajectories that accompany this illness, it is important to bear in mind that there is "no such thing as schizophrenia," understood as a universal phenomenon which has a fixed course and an inevitable outcome. Schizophrenia is something that happens to unique individuals in particular personal, social, and cultural circumstances, which can have a profound impact on a person's coping skills, the course of the illness, and the possibility and definition of recovery.

The Treatment of Schizophrenia: Pharmacological Interventions

Antipsychotic medications, or neuroleptics, have been available since the mid-1950s and have greatly improved the outlook for many people diagnosed as having schizophrenia. These medications reduce the psychotic symptoms of schizophrenia and allow people living with it to function more effectively and appropriately.[16] Such drugs do not *cure* schizophrenia or guarantee nonrecurrence of psychotic episodes. Rather, they seek to control the symptoms and allow the person to have a better quality of life.

The Problem with Neuroleptic Medications

One of the main difficulties with neuroleptic medications is that they have extremely unpleasant side effects such as *akathisia*—restlessness; *Parkinsonianism*— muscle weakness, tremor, stiffness, and a shuffling gait; *dystonia or dyskinesia*—involuntary muscle spasms, especially of the eyes and neck. *Tardive dyskinesia* may also appear after a long period on continuous medication. This disorder is characterized by involuntary movements most often affecting the mouth, lips, and tongue. Although these side effects are extremely unpleasant, they can be controlled to some extent with other medications. Nevertheless, one of the major causes of psychotic relapse for people diagnosed as having schizophrenia living in the community is not taking medications, and one of the reasons people stop taking them is because of these unpleasant side effects.[17]

Atypical Antipsychotic Medication

During the 1990s there were important advances in the pharmacological treatment of schizophrenia with the introduction of the so-called atypical antipsychotic medications. These drugs are called "atypical" antipsychotics because they are not thought to work primarily on the dopamine receptors in the brain in the way that typical antipsychotic medication does. These new medicines offer the benefits of the older (typical) antipsychotics, but have a reduced propensity to cause extrapyramidal motor symptoms. A number of recent studies have suggested that these newer forms of medication may offer important clinical advantages compared to the forms of antipsychotic medication that have been used in the past.[18] Generally, the evidence seems to suggest that they are more effective over a broader range of symptoms with fewer side effects.

One of the reasons that people stop taking forms of medications that have the potential to improve their quality of life is that extremely unpleasant side effects accompany them. One major advantage of atypical antipsychotic medications is that people are more likely to stay on a medication if it is not worse than the illness itself! In reducing the number of side effects, while at the same time maintaining their therapeutic efficacy, atypical antipsychotics have made a significant contribution to enabling people to retain the motivation to continue with their drug regime.

The rare but significant incidences of violence carried out by people with schizophrenia are often tied in with the person's refusal to take any form of medication. In terms of violence to self, family, or others, if atypical medications mean that the person is more likely to continue willingly with a drug regime, and consequently more likely to avoid the circumstances that lead to violent outbursts, then this can only be beneficial. The jury is still out concerning the consequence of the long-term use of atypical medications. Nevertheless, atypical antipsychotic medications currently provide a significant source of hope for people diagnosed with schizophrenia.

However, I make these points with extreme caution. In juxtaposing schizophrenia and violence in this way, I am *not* suggesting that there is an inevitable connection between the two. As I will argue more fully later, people diagnosed with schizophrenia are no more prone to violence than other members of the general public. While atypical medication may help reduce violence in certain people, this is *not* to imply that *all* people diagnosed as having schizophrenia are inevitably violent (despite the fact that schizophrenia's media profile frequently suggests otherwise). This is an important point that I will highlight here and develop more fully as we progress. Likewise, I would not wish to suggest that atypical medication is the magic bullet of psychiatric care. It is not. Medication can be useful, but, as we shall see, schizophrenia is not something that can be dealt with through medication alone.

The Meaning of Medication

While pharmacological interventions may well have an important role to play in improving the quality of life experienced by people diagnosed as having schizophrenia, it is important to be aware of the full implications of having to take medication. If we simply focus on issues of biology and correct chemical intervention—that is, the perspective of the medical model—we risk missing what is of fundamental importance to the *person* taking the medication. For the persons taking the medication, it is considerably more than a technical maneuver designed to control the worst manifestations of their condition. Taking medication is a deeply meaningful experience that has a profound psychological and social impact on the lives of those who have to take it. In order to understand what I mean by this, it is necessary for us to focus specifically on what we might describe as the *social hermeneutics* of pharmacological intervention. By the term "social hermeneutics," I refer to the ways in which taking medications is understood and interpreted within the social experience of individuals, and the specific *meanings* that are ascribed to it.

The question of the meaning of medication is one that needs to be taken very seriously. While there has been a proliferation of research exploring what medication *does* for and to individuals, there is a paucity of research that seeks to explore what medication *means* to individuals. Medications and the act of giving and receiving medications are filled with meaning. These meanings differ according to context and circumstance, and frequently according to lay and professional perspectives. Put baldly, and at the risk of caricaturization, schizophrenia, understood in terms of the medical model, is a biological, chemical, and/or genetic condition that responds favorably to certain kinds of pharmacological intervention. The mental health professional is the healer, and schizophrenia is the target that needs to be dealt with without any necessary reference to the specific context or life-experiences of the patient. Medication primarily means the provision and administration of an effective, safe, clinically tested pharmacological product, aimed at controlling the particular set of signs and symptoms that makes up the diagnostic category of schizophrenia. The act of medicating is part of the role of the professional and can be interpreted in varying terms as a therapeutic act of care and compassion. It is viewed as an action carried out for the benefit of the individual and the wider society.

However, from the perspective of the *person* with schizophrenia, or any other long-term mental health problem, the meaning of medication is often very different. While one might assume that a person would be glad to take medication if it relieved the worst manifestations of the condition, this is not necessarily so, even with those newer drugs that have fewer disturbing side effects. The mental health professions frequently pathologize the non-taking of medication, labeling patients who behave in such a manner "awkward" and "noncompliant," yet the reality of the situation is often much more complex.

Peter Barham and Robert Hayward in their fascinating study of people diagnosed with mental health problems who have returned to the community after many years in psychiatric institutions, note that there are numerous pressures on individuals to take on the primary social identity of "community mental patients." By this they mean that people tend to become highly stigmatized by their experience of mental health problems and their previous residence within an institution. When they re-enter society, there are a variety of ways in which their identity as persons is eroded by the strength of their unwanted social identity as "mental patients." Within such a context, the taking of medication assumes a very specific meaning. Barham and Hayward suggest that "the pressure to accept a definition of oneself as a community mental patient emerges most forcibly in relation to medication. It is here that awkward questions about the capacities of people with a history of mental illness to exert control over their own lives, and to make rational judgements about matters that concern their own well-being, are brought into sharp relief."[19]

Thus we have here an important power struggle revolving around the interpretation of medication. On the one hand we have the "mental patient," who has now been "released from the asylum," and is struggling to find a new identity and a sense of meaningful citizenship. Within this context medication can become a powerful symbol that can be perceived as a sort of rite of passage between the social state of "mental patient," and that of "citizen/person." Patients do not have the choice of taking or not taking their medication. Citizens do. On the other hand, we have the mental health professions who have multiple responsibilities: to the patient, the psychiatric institution, society, and governments, who view medication as a way of ensuring that the patient does not relapse and can remain within society. Preventing destructive symptoms is, of course, not in itself a bad goal. However, unless the dimension of meaning is addressed, there is a real danger that what may be a genuinely therapeutic gesture becomes a context for misunderstanding, contradictory interpretations, and social control.

The Meaning of Medication in Depression

In order to clarify and develop this point, it will be helpful to draw on the work of sociologist David Karp on the social dynamics of depression. Karp argues that the problem with taking medication for depression (and by implication other forms of mental health problems) is that the act of taking it, and the acknowledgment that one needs it, is a profound statement about what one is and how one's social identity is to be understood. The process of taking medications involves "a complex and emotionally charged interpretative process in which nothing less than one's view of self is at stake."[20] The act of taking medication for mental health problems is a clear affirmation that the person has a stigmatized emotional disorder, and as such, requires a dramatic redefinition of his or her concept of "self." "In this respect, a willingness to begin a regimen of psychiatric medications is far more than a simple medical decision. It is a decisive juncture in one's self-definition as an emotionally ill rather than merely troubled person."[21] One of Karp's interviewees puts it thus: "I didn't want to be told that I had something that was going to affect the rest of my life, and that could only be solved by taking pills. It was sort of definitive. I had a label and it was a label that I thought was pejorative."

Thus, even if medication does reduce symptoms and allow a person to achieve a better quality of life, this does not necessarily mean that the person will perceive the medication in a favorable way. In my experience this deeper meaning to the process of taking medication, highlighted by Karp, is highly significant with regard to the care of people with mental health problems. I have encountered a number of people who have seen the act of stopping their medication as a highly symbolic gesture that, from their perspective, redefines their self-concept from "mental patient" to "normal citizen." In a sense, ceasing taking medication is seen as a rite of passage or an act of self-liberation, a movement from "mental patient" to "citizen." When, after a period on medication, they have felt better, the next step for them is to free themselves from the symbolic as well as the real bond of medication. By stopping their medication they are enabled to move away from their identity as "mental patients," who will be on medication for the rest of their lives, toward a new identity as "normal persons," whose quality of life is not dependent on drugs. Of course, the consequence of such actions can be disastrous, with relapse and violence—normally self-violence, but occasionally directed toward others—being a not infrequent result.

It is critical that we acknowledge this "hidden" dynamic that is embedded within the process of drug taking and the refusal of medication and think through the consequences of the hopelessness of having a social and personal identity as a "mental patient." There may well be a strong link between issues of personhood and self-esteem and issues of consuming medication that is overlooked or smothered by clinical and slightly polemic terminology such as "noncompliance," "difficult patient," and so forth. It may well be that the problem of the person not taking medication has not simply to do with awkwardness, lack of insight, or delusional activity. Within a community context, it may be that a vital component of their behavior concerns the way in which their mental health problem is defined by themselves and by society, and the consequences of this definition for their experience of self and self-value.[22]

Medication? Yes, but it's not the only thing.

I am not saying that medication is a bad thing and that people should stop taking it. What I am saying is that taking medication is much more complicated than it often appears to be, and that mental health professionals, families, and all who are involved must seriously address the issues of meaning that I have highlighted here. Barham and Hayward found that the majority of people did not object to taking medication. What they *did* object to was the suggestion that medication was *all* there was to treating their mental health problems, that is, understandings that confined their situation within the boundaries of the medical model of understanding. They note that

> most [of the interviewees] did not object—in the short term at least—to taking medication, and indeed many of them found it beneficial, but they were intent upon ensuring that medication did not interfere with what they held to be the main priorities in their lives. And it was here that conflicts with the medical profession arose. What participants looked for from psychiatrists was an approach in which—to put the matter in more formal terms—the prescription of antipsychotic drugs was an adjunct to a psycho-social understanding of their predicaments rather than a substitute for such understanding.[23]

This is an important observation. There is considerably more to the care of persons living with mental health problems than simply prescribing drugs. As we shall see in chapter 4, there is a strong movement within psychiatry and also within some organizations that offer care and support for people with mental health problems and their families, toward understanding schizophrenia in biological terms. Within such a context, psychosocial intervention is often seen as secondary or even epiphenomenal to dealing with and developing an understanding of the biological and genetic aspects of schizophrenia. Thus the treatment and understanding of schizophrenia is encapsulated within the structure of the medical model, with psychosocial intervention being understood as secondary to biological intervention. Barham's subjects reverse the dynamic of this assumption by suggesting that schizophrenia should be reframed and understood primarily from its social and interpersonal aspects, with medication being understood as the secondary, supportive process within that context. Thus medication is seen to be necessary but certainly not sufficient as a response to schizophrenia. Even if schizophrenia were found conclusively to have organic origins, from the perspective of people's lived experience, the focus of care has a critical interpersonal and social aspect that is at least equal to, and—in Barham's interviewees' opinion—surpasses pharmacological intervention. In order to understand why such a reframe should take place, and what the therapeutic implications of such a shift in emphasis might be, it is necessary to explore something of the social experience of people diagnosed as having schizophrenia. It is to such a critical exploration of the experience of schizophrenia that the following chapter turns.

Chapter 4

Beyond the Medical Model

Schizophrenia as a
Neurobiological Disorder

There is increasing evidence to suggest that schizophrenia has some kind of genetic and/or neurobiological component. While there is a growing body of literature surrounding this area, the precise nature of the biological malfunction that causes schizophrenia remains open to debate. Various theories have been put forward suggesting that it is caused by such things as chemical imbalances, obstetric complications, neurological damage, or influenza.[1] Others suggest that schizophrenia is genetic in origin, with social factors acting as exacerbants of a genetic predisposition. Cardno and McGuffin make a strong case for the primacy of genetics in the etiology of schizophrenia:

> The best established aetiological component in schizophrenia continues to be the substantial genetic liability. In most individuals, this is likely to be caused by the collective action of multiple genes. In addition, one or more major genes may be inherited in a proportion of families. Environmental aetiological theories are less well established. If an environmental factor is clearly delineated it is likely to be of relatively small effect and to interact with the genetic liability.[2]

While none of these theories is conclusive, taken together, they do present persuasive evidence for attributing the etiology of schizophrenia to some sort of neurobiological defect. It may be that it is a combination of some or all of these factors that come together under certain circumstances to form the syndrome of schizophrenia. "It is possible that the people who have schizophrenia are a heterogeneous group with different areas of their brains affected to varying degrees by neurochemical imbalances, neurodevelopmental problems, genetic defects, viral infections, or perinatal damage among other causes."[3]

It is beyond the scope of this book to assess critically the complex scientific arguments put forward in support of each of the above biological explanations. For current purposes it will be sufficient to say that there is a growing body of evidence that appears to point toward neurobiology as being a significant contributing factor in the genesis of schizophrenia, even if the precise mechanisms remain unclear. If this is so, then it is important that research continue within this area. Cardno and McGuffin correctly point out that "A treatable cause for a percentage of patients is worth hunting for. Prior to this century, between 10 and 30 percent of schizophrenia-like patients probably had neurosyphilis. Without the knowledge of neurosyphilis that we now have, this group of treatable patients would merely be a sub group of an even larger population of undifferentiated schizophrenia."[4]

If it is possible for people to be spared the very real pain and distress that this condition can bring about, then it is important that time and resources be allocated to research into the etiology of schizophrenia.

A good deal of the information coming from the major agencies dealing directly with schizophrenia in Britain and the United States reflects this emphasis on the neurobiological roots of schizophrenia.[5] These groups are firm in their conviction that schizophrenia should be understood as a neurobiological disorder. Analogies are frequently drawn between forms of chronic physical illness and schizophrenia, the quite correct implication being that one would not blame or stigmatize someone for having diabetes, so why blame or stigmatize a person for having schizophrenia. The following extract is typical of this literature:

> Schizophrenia is a brain disease, now definitely known to be such. It is a real scientific and biological entity as clearly as diabetes, multiple sclerosis, and cancer are scientific and biological entities. It exhibits symptoms of a brain disease, symptoms which include impairment in thinking, delusions, hallucinations, changes in emotions, and changes in behaviour. And, like cancer, probably has more than one cause.[6]

The reasons for this major emphasis on biology are partly an attempt to normalize and destigmatize mental health problems and partly a response to the work of people like R. D. Laing and Gregory Bateson, who developed theories of schizophrenia that essentially sought to blame the parents of people with schizophrenia for their condition. According to these theories, schizophrenia is seen primarily as an *interpersonal* disorder within which the family is viewed as the primary cause in its development. Bateson and his colleagues at the Mental Research Institute in California studied the communication patterns of adult patients suffering from schizophrenia. The result of their explorations was the *double-bind* hypothesis that they outlined in their 1951 paper entitled "Toward a Theory of Schizophrenia."[7] Waldron-Skinner helpfully summarizes this position.

> They suggested that schizophrenia resulted from a person being placed in an untenable position in relation to someone who was of primary emotional significance to him. Two contradictory messages are received at once, so that there is no way in which the loved person can be pleased or obeyed. For example, a parent holds out his arms to his small child in welcome but his facial expression indicates anger or hostility. The child perceives both love and hostility in the parent's non-verbal messages and is left confused.[8]

Building on this notion of the double bind, the Scottish psychoanalyst R. D. Laing developed the idea that certain types of family were *pathogenic institutions* in that the child is surrounded by overwhelming psychological and social stress. Miles summarizes Laing's thinking thus:

> The experience and behaviour that is called schizophrenic is a special strategy by which a person can live in an unliveable situation. The parents destroy the individual by mystifying him and he responds by counter-mystifying them. Thus Laing's position is that the only difference between the persons called schizophrenic and everybody else is that impossible demands were laid on the former who in turn responded with appropriate, though irrational seeming behaviour. Thus one person in a schizophrenic family becomes the scapegoat on whom all stresses are concentrated. Psychiatry for Laing is coercive and repressive; diagnosis

and treatment are used as means of controlling people who make nuisances of themselves. By calling a person a schizophrenic the psychiatrist is colluding with the family in blaming the patient for the faults of the parents and that much damage is done by consigning a person to a mental hospital. Laing does not accept schizophrenia as a pathological state—such a diagnosis he describes as ascribing stigma in order to suppress.[9]

As one thinks through the implications of this theory, it is obvious why families of people diagnosed as having schizophrenia would be unhappy with it. This model of schizophrenia blames the parents for their child's condition, with psychiatrists taking the role of co-conspiritors against the patient. This interpretation of schizophrenia is firmly rejected on both sides of the Atlantic by many of the major agencies dealing with people with schizophrenia and their families.[10] They highlight the fact that there is no empirical evidence to imply that such a suggestion is anything more than mere speculation.[11] It is certainly true that there is a relationship between stress in families and *relapse* in schizophrenia.[11] However, this does not necessarily lead to the conclusion that family stress *causes* schizophrenia. While Laing's theories may be alluring, imaginative, and undoubtedly evocative, there is no real evidence to suggest that his propositions concerning the etiology of schizophrenia are anything more than speculation.

Nevertheless, such thinking has had a detrimental effect on the lives of people living with schizophrenia and their families. The type of neurobiological explanation that is currently popular is, in many respects, very useful. Though difficult to substantiate, theories that implicate families in the etiology of schizophrenia have been no less influential, and as such require to be taken seriously and addressed thoughtfully. By providing strong, empirically based evidence that points toward a cause that lies primarily within the individual rather than the family, one is provided with an effective counter to such family blaming.

Destigmatizing Mental Health Problems

Another gain that the neurobiological model of schizophrenia offers is with regard to the destigmatization of mental health problems. Drawing analogies from biological medicine "normalizes" the person's condition and thus brings it within the boundaries of the medical model. When this happens it becomes a socially acceptable illness, thus freeing the person from unnecessary stigmatization. This not only offers an effective challenge to the types of family blaming theories we have looked at, it also acts therapeutically in locating the illness firmly within the medical model, thus presenting a person's mental health problem within a framework that is deemed to be acceptable and legitimate within Western societies. By pointing toward concrete, empirical evidence that mental health problems are not the fault of the individual or their families, schizophrenia can be reinterpreted in a way that is acceptable to the individual, the family, and the wider society. Such an approach is thus of great importance in terms of rehumanizing people who are frequently dehumanized by particular negative interpretations of their illness.

More Than Biology

Important and potentially therapeutic as this movement has been, as mentioned previously, it brings with it its own set of problems. The medical model provides a powerful interpretative framework within which diseases can be understood and modes of treatment can be worked out. However, while it might appear to offer a comprehensive picture of disease and illness, the picture, though useful, is incomplete. The danger is that the interpretative power of the medical model comes to dominate all other understandings in such a way as to blind us to some of the highly significant realities that surround the lived experience of schizophrenia. These realities fall beyond the gaze of the medical model, but are nonetheless fundamental for a therapeutic understanding of what schizophrenia is. An overemphasis on the biological aspects of mental health problems tends to locate the persons' difficulties primarily within the boundaries of their own bodies. The persons' problems are *theirs*, and the treatment is focused on specific, neurobiological defects within individual people. However, bodies do not operate in a vacuum, and mental health problems are considerably more than technological problems that need simply to be solved through the development of greater neurological knowledge and improved pharmacological intervention.

One of the difficulties in attempting to conceptualize schizophrenia primarily in terms of neurobiology or genetics is that it abrogates the wider society from its responsibility in *causing* people with this and many other forms of mental health problems to become seriously disabled. The disability rights movement has taught us to distinguish between *impairments* and *disabilities.* Impairments are "the discrete functional limitations that are present within individuals that cause some manifestation of physical, mental or sensory impedance. Disability relates to the loss or limitation of opportunities to take part in the normal life of the community on an equal level with others due to physical and/or social barriers."[12]

It is true that persons' biological impairments may profoundly affect their lives in certain respects. However, I would argue that much of the disablement experienced by people with mental health problems has to do with the social context within which they experience their difficulties, and the destructive web of attitudes, false assumptions, and negative interpretations that people bring to their situation. Critical reflection on the lived experience of people diagnosed with schizophrenia reveals society to be as "ill," "disoriented," and "deluded" as the individual with the mental health problem.

If we assume that schizophrenia is *nothing but* a neurobiological disorder, and that once we have identified the particular biological defect within the individual we will know what schizophrenia is, we risk missing the vital social dynamics of this condition that are at least as important as any neurological or genetic dysfunction. I am *not* suggesting that a person's social experiences *cause* him or her to develop schizophrenia (although they may contribute to the exacerbation of symptoms and relapse). What I *am* saying is that a person's experiences within society are as much a part of the illness as the hallucinations, delusions, and other symptoms that make up the clinical diagnosis. As such they should be taken as seriously as biological factors when we are considering what effective care might mean. Likewise, simply normalizing schizophrenia by bringing it within the medical model, on its own, will not change public opinion. Simply treating an individual's symptoms is not enough. If we are truly to care for people with schizophrenia, then there is a need to "treat" the wider social dimensions of the condition with the same critical rigor we assume to be normal in the treatment of the individual neurobiological dimensions. Useful as the clinical and biological explanations of schizophrenia are in telling us *some* things about schizophrenia, there is much more to this condition than can be captured within standardized psychiatric definitions and treatments. The identification of biological factors is only a beginning in our understanding of what mental health problems *really* are, and neurological interventions are only *one* aspect of caring for people experiencing them.

Professional Care

Another significant difficulty with drawing schizophrenia within the boundaries of the medical model is that, if it is seen to be a purely medical condition, then obviously the care of people diagnosed with it will be assumed to lie primarily with mental health care professionals. The danger is that even if the individual is sent back into the community, the perception remains that she is the responsibility of the specialist. Such a way of framing schizophrenia often means that the primary form of relationship that is open to a person diagnosed with this form of mental health problem is with the "specialist," the professional who is *paid to relate to them*.[13] While it is true that many professionals do all that they can to ensure that their relationships with their clients are personal and meaningful, they are there because they are paid to be there. One young man who had been institutionalized since he was eight years old with a schizophreniform illness told me that he had just been allocated a befriender. To his absolute delight, he had found that he had been able to strike up a good relationship with both her and her boyfriend. "I've never had a friend before who wasn't either a patient or a mental health professional," he told me. Bearing in mind that this man was twenty-four years old, this is a tragic situation. What must it feel like if your only friends are people who are paid to be your friends! As one social services manager astutely observed, "If your only friends in the world are a psychiatrist, a general practitioner, a community psychiatric nurse, and a social worker, how would your mental health be?"[14] Such limiting of relational possibilities can only be detrimental to an individual's mental health.

Thus, while a neurobiological approach to understanding schizophrenia may be a necessary part of the overall care of persons with this form of mental health problem, it is certainly not sufficient. In order to understand and effectively deal with people diagnosed with schizophrenia, we must take seriously what it means as a social phenomenon, and begin to explore the role of the wider community in creating and sustaining many of the difficulties that people experience.

A Natural History of Schizophrenia

While there may be certain signs and symptoms which together form the criteria for the clinical definition of "schizophrenia," there is no such thing as schizophrenia, understood as a universal phenomenon that manifests itself in the same way irrespective of person, context, or circumstance. Schizophrenia is *always* a human experience that is lived out and interpreted by unique individuals within specific social contexts, contexts that can profoundly influence the course of the condition. However, this diversity is not always acknowledged either within the perceptions of the general public or by the mental health professions. For many, schizophrenia is assumed to have a natural history, that is, a fixed and certain course along which the condition will progress *irrespective* of person, culture, or context. John Strauss notes that historically

> . . . one of the basic hypotheses about schizophrenia was that it embodied and was validated by a uniformly bad outcome. The notion that diagnosis is related to outcome or that "diagnosis is prognosis," is one of those apparently simple ideas that is extremely powerful and goes back at least to the time of Hippocrates. A diagnosis should reflect a pathological process, and a pathological process should have some reasonably predictable evolution over time, some kind of natural history.[15]

There is a danger in using analogies of cancer and multiple sclerosis to illustrate the nature of schizophrenia. While such examples function effectively to normalize the perception of the illness, they can serve to confirm the common public misperception that schizophrenia is necessarily progressively degenerative and that somehow the person is totally enslaved by their neurobiology and consequently "lost" in the midst of their illness. As we shall see, this is not the case. Nevertheless, as W. I. Thomas astutely observed: "If men define a situation as real, they are real in their consequences.... In other words, the subjective 'definition of the situation' is just as important as the objective situation in its social effects."[16]

The potentially devastating consequences of such a misperception are well illustrated in the case of Genine, a young woman I recently met, who had just been diagnosed as having schizophrenia. Her psychiatrist presented her with an explanation of her illness in biological terms similar to those highlighted previously. She told me how she immediately went home and took an overdose of sleeping tablets. She simply did not want to live with the hopelessness this particular form of illness definition instilled in her. Certainly her problems had been normalized, but they were normalized in such a way that she perceived no hope for a normal life. As she saw it, in the same way a cancer sufferer is faced with a series of grinding encounters with radiation or chemotherapy and the ever-present possibility of slow and painful death, she was faced with the prospect of a lifetime of medication and the permanent identity of a "schizophrenic," a social and self-identity that, for her, spelled social death. She saw no point in carrying on.

The Loss of the Person

The thinking of many people, including many people with schizophrenia, is still influenced, consciously and unconsciously, by the impact of Emil Kraeplin's 1896 description of the syndrome of behaviors and experiences which later became known as schizophrenia, as *dementia praecox*—literally, early or premature deterioration.[17] For Kraeplin dementia praecox typically occurred in young people and induced a general tendency toward emotional and intellectual deterioration.[18] More positive conceptions were developed by Kraeplin's successors, Bleuler and Schneider, both of whom acknowledged the possibility of recovery by some people. Yet vestiges of the deteriorative definition still remain within the perception of mental health service users, the general public, and mental health professionals (for example in such commonly used terms as "burnt out schizophrenic," to describe persons who no longer show the acute symptoms of schizophrenia). Undoubtedly there is often a profound and distressing change in the individual who develops this mental health problem. He or she may appear profoundly different during times of acute disturbance, as the descriptions of schizophrenia presented previously have suggested.

Yet it is certainly *not* the case that the person is wholly lost to the illness, at least not in the way that is commonly assumed. There is a good deal of convincing evidence, some of which will be examined as we proceed, pointing toward the fact that, contrary to such historical and contemporary assumptions, schizophrenia does not have a fixed, irreversible course that will *only* respond to specialized clinical interventions.[19] Even if schizophrenia is finally proved to be a genetic or neurobiological disorder, it remains a very personal experience that is open to and affected by the wider social context within which the individual experiences it. As Barham and Hayward observe, the "evidence from a number of studies shows that outcomes in schizophrenia quite heavily depend not so much on factors intrinsic to the disorder itself as on how former patients come to evaluate themselves and their situations."[20] Schizophrenia can be influenced, positively and negatively, by such things as economics,[21] culture,[22] self-motivation,[23] hope and personal relationships,[24] spirituality,[25] and other social factors that are not immediately apparent within the medical model of understanding. While there may be a neurobiological entity that clinically can be described as "schizophrenia," when that entity enters the social arena it is open to numerous social forces and varied interpretations, all of which deeply affect the course of a person's illness experience.[26] This being so, even though there may be shared biological deficits and malfunctions it is inaccurate to talk about schizophrenia as having a *natural* history in the sense of a fixed and inevitable course that will replicate itself in the experience of all people.

The Social History of Schizophrenia

However, although there may not be such a thing as a *natural* history of schizophrenia, there is what we might describe as a *social* history, that is, a particular set of social experiences and a specific life trajectory on which people diagnosed as having schizophrenia are launched. This social history constitutes the *lived experience* of schizophrenia and society's reaction to it, including the reaction of people with mental health problems themselves. It is here, within the social history, that the person experiences disablement, oppression, and a variety of forms of injustice.

In order to clarify what I mean by the idea of the social history of schizophrenia, it will be helpful to draw upon the thinking of medical anthropologist and psychiatrist Arthur Kleinman. Kleinman highlights the importance of the ways in which one conceptualizes disease processes. In his research he points to the distinction between the concepts of *disease* and *illness*. A person's *disease* refers to the organic, viral, or other physical basis of the condition. Cancer, influenza, and measles would constitute diseases and disease processes. Likewise, the types of biological defects and malfunctions that it has been suggested are instrumental in the development of schizophrenia would come under this banner of disease. The concept of *illness*, however, when applied to a diseased state, refers to the *social consequences* of the disease. "Illness refers to the ways in which the sick person and the members of the family or wider social network perceive, live with, and respond to symptoms of disability."[27] While *disease* may be a biological state existing independently of (but not apart from) human knowledge and interpretation, *illness* is a *social status* directly created and formed by human perception and interpretation. The idea of the social history, as it is used in this book, comes close to Kleinman's concept of illness. Irrespective of the biological basis of schizophrenia, there is a particular illness experience (social history) which is common to many if not most people diagnosed as having schizophrenia. As we will see, this social history includes a history of oppression that manifests itself in material and relational poverty, depersonalization, limited possibilities, rejection, exclusion, marginalization, and stigmatization. I argue that it is the individual's experience within society, his or her "social history," which primarily dictates the person's quality of life, and his or her ability (or inability) to attain and maintain a positive sense of personhood, and ultimately some degree of mental health.

While there is strong evidence to suggest that there are neurological and genetic factors involved in the etiology of schizophrenia, these should not be understood as acting deterministically, but rather should be viewed as significant contributing factors within a complex biopsychosocial and, as we shall see, spiritual phenomenon. Schizophrenia may have certain biological aspects to it, what we might call a *neurobiological narrative* (disease processes) running parallel to this and with equal importance for our understanding. But it is a *personal or relational narrative* (social history) that has an equal, if not more profound, impact on the overall life trajectory of individuals. It is within this second narrative—the social history of schizophrenia—that people experience various forms of poverty, oppression, and marginalization.

Chapter 5

Creating Nonpersons
The Poverty of
Schizophrenia

By simply excluding someone from the human group — by which I mean a group that is held together by the needs of survival — we can destroy their possibilities of self-realization, i.e. prevent them becoming a full person.[1]   —Rex Ambler

Creating Nonpersons

Terms such as "oppression" and "poverty" may not immediately be seen to relate to the situation of people with mental health problems, yet on a more critical examination, their appropriateness becomes clear. The social history of people with schizophrenia is marked by poverty, exclusion, oppression, and lack of opportunity that bestows upon them the status of nonpersons within society. However, the oppression is subtle. As Tom Kitwood observes in his discussion of the psychodynamics of exclusion: "Many cultures have shown a tendency to depersonalize those who have some form of serious disability, whether of a physical or a psychological kind. A consensus is created, established in tradition and embedded in social practices, that those affected are not real persons."[2]

When individuals and communities create a relational, communicational, aesthetic and linguistic atmosphere that causes the exclusion and stigmatization of those who are perceived to be different, their oppression is deeply damaging and thoroughly destructive of the humanity of a significant section of the population. It is through the myriad of unnoticed social gestures and negative assumptions that people with mental health problems find their sense of self-worth and personhood constantly being eroded. It is through that same process that they come to be perceived, consciously or subconsciously, as "nonpersons" (by society and, sadly, often by themselves), and consequently excluded from meaningful participation within society.

Poverty of Personhood

Roy Porter notes that the voice of people suffering from mental health problems "is one deeply conscious of having been made to feel different. Generally they complain that 'alienness' is a false identity thrust upon them, or indeed a non-identity, a sense of being rendered a nonperson."[3]

In the light of the current movement toward deinstitutionalization, Porter's observation is highly significant. Barham and Hayward note that:

> As historians of madness have shown, we have inherited from the last century a "deep disposition to see madness as essentially Other."[4] The transformation of Victorian asylums into gigantic custodial warehouses hastened the "decline of dialogue between society and psychiatrist on the one hand and the disturbed on the other (increasingly 'shut up' in both senses)" and irretrievably established their differences.[5] In crucial respects this custodial history is recapitulated in the traditional account of schizophrenia as a narrative of loss in that the pre-illness person goes missing, seemingly abandoned by the force of the disorder. On this view schizophrenia "is more than an illness that one *has*; it is something a person *is* or may *become.*"[6] (Italics added)

Barham and Hayward's comments emphasize two points that are important for present purposes. First, historically (and in a slightly different way, contemporarily) society's response to people with mental health problems has been to isolate them, to shut them away from the rest of the population. Consequently, the majority of society has had little or no contact with them, apart from what is very often a distorted and caricatured picture presented through the media. As a result the "public identity" of persons living with schizophrenia has been defined as essentially "other," that is, not belonging to society proper.

Second, those who have emerged from asylums have emerged with a very uncertain personhood and identity. If schizophrenia truly does destroy the person, as "natural history theory" would suggest, then one is left with the perplexing question as to what these "schizophrenics," these "nonpersons" are who are emerging from the mental hospitals into our communities, and accordingly, how they should be treated.

In highlighting this confusion over the nature of the humanity of people with schizophrenia, Sue E. Estraff emphasizes that schizophrenia is what one might describe as a *totalizing* condition. Schizophrenia "is an I am illness—one that may overtake and redefine the identity of the person."[7] Unlike measles, the flu, or any other common ailment, a person does not simply *have* schizophrenia, they actually *become* schizophrenia. The tendency in public and professional perception is to regard persons ontologically in terms of their illness, that is, as "schizophrenics." Schizophrenia becomes central to the way in which others identify persons, (their social identity) and how such persons themselves build and understand their own identity (their personal identity). Schizophrenia becomes their primary identifying role, and the mental health services their primary reference group. In this way, these persons *are* indeed "lost" to the illness, but not because of any inevitable natural process of deterioration. These persons are lost to the illness because a particular form of social identity is formed around them, an identity that is created by negative societal negotiation and that subsequently becomes a public persona that people with schizophrenia then internalize and build into their own self-conception.

Once again, it is *not* being suggested that social pressures in some way cause or are responsible for the development of schizophrenia. What *is* being asserted is that these persons' life history and the development of their social self, the personal identity, is adversely affected by the cultural ascription of a negative social identity that confuses the person with the illness. It is in *this* way that schizophrenia becomes a social construction, and it is in *this* way that the "schizophrenic" is created, stereotyped, and marginalized. In a very real sense, people diagnosed as having schizophrenia become *nonpersons.*

People living with schizophrenia are deprived of some of the fundamental social experiences necessary for the development of healthy human personhood. Basic social opportunities that are foundational for the positive development of personhood are simply not available to people who are perceived in the ways outlined above. The following are rarely available to people with schizophrenia: the opportunity to find one's "true self"—who one is as a unique individual; the chance to discover a valued social identity; the opportunity to feel that one has an accepted and acceptable place within society; the possibility of developing a positive personal and social identity; and the opportunity to develop meaningful relationships with self and others. This deprivation is not simply a result of their clinical condition (which does contribute to their social isolation); rather it is the result of fundamental flaws and false assumptions within society's perception of them and the nature of their condition, which leads to their social definition as fundamentally "other." What greater poverty can there be than to be deprived of the circumstances and forms of relationship that enable persons to live humanly and to be themselves? This enforced poverty of personhood oppresses and alienates people with schizophrenia and confirms them in their status as "nonpersons" who are forced to stand on the margins of acceptable society.

Poverty of Opportunity

Carpenter notes the social ambiguity of schizophrenia when he observes that schizophrenia

> strikes at the very heart of what we consider the essence of the person. Yet, because its manifestations are so personal and social, it elicits fear, misunderstanding, and condemnation in society instead of sympathy and concern. Schizophrenia remains unparalleled as a stigmatizing [disorder] with all the societal consequences of personal shame, family burden, and inadequate support of clinical care, research, and rehabilitation. It is ironic that in a society with pride in individual freedom and achievement, the response to a person whose personal capacity is being eroded. . . . is the withdrawal of opportunity.[8]

One of the results of the process of depersonalization is the withdrawal of opportunities to participate meaningfully in society and to gain access to many of the sources of self-respect and self-esteem that are available to others. Poor self-esteem and hopelessness in people with schizophrenia is not simply the product of the disease process; it is also connected to the exclusion from many of the normal relational and material sources from which the majority of the population gain their sense of value, self-confidence, and worth.

For example, within present day capitalist societies, where work is viewed as fundamental to popular understandings of worthwhile human existence, a person's employment is a major source of value, self-worth, and economic sustenance.[9] People with the diagnosis of schizophrenia are often excluded from this primary source of value and income. The positive and negative manifestations of the illness, coupled with destructive public perceptions, attitudes, and stigma, mean that it is very difficult for people with this diagnosis to gain any form of meaningful employment.[10] The condition itself places major barriers to employment, but there are many people who are capable of holding down employment who simply do not get the opportunity because of particular assumptions about their condition. This exclusion from primary sources of value leaves many people with schizophrenia feeling there is no future for them. Consequently, life appears profoundly hopeless and meaningless. For many, the social experience of schizophrenia is one of material deprivation, meaninglessness, hopelessness, and constant devaluation, with no possibility of a hopeful future and no power to alter the trajectory of their lives. This factor may contribute to the 10 percent of people with schizophrenia who commit suicide.[11] It would appear that people diagnosed as having schizophrenia are destined to be dependent persons in a world that values individualism, competitiveness, independence, productivity, and financial prosperity. For those who are in any way dependent, who cannot compete or are not productive, there are few alternative sources of value within a society that no longer understands the meaning of mutual responsibility and "community." As Genine's story suggested, within such a social context it is difficult for an individual to accept his or her illness without acknowledging that it entails a necessary element of hopelessness and disempowerment accompanied by a withdrawal of opportunity to participate in that which is valued within society.

Poverty of Relationships

The most painful thing for people with schizophrenia is the level of relational poverty they encounter. Certainly some of this is the product of the disease process itself, but schizophrenia seems to provoke society into displaying a particularly negative, impersonal, and at times openly hostile reaction toward those who live with it. These reactions, assumptions, and stereotypes make it extremely difficult for people to find and maintain positive interpersonal relationships—*the* most important source of value and self-esteem available to human beings.

The processes involved in bestowing someone or something with value bear consideration. Things do not have a value in themselves, but only become valuable according to the meanings that are ascribed to them. Thus, for example, "a family portrait may be invaluable to the family concerned, but have tantamount to no value outside of that family. A friendship ring may be of inestimable value to a friend and of absolutely no value to a jeweler. The value of the picture or the ring stems from and depends upon the attitude/relationship of others toward it."[12] David Pailin suggests that a similar principle is appropriate for an understanding of how human beings should be valued: "The fundamental worth of a person is to be seen to lie in the love of others for that person. Worth is not something that belongs to a person as a solitary individual. It is given to each person by the way that others, including—and ultimately—God, regard him or her."[13] This is not to suggest that if a person has no friends or relatives, he or she is not of value. *All* human beings are of ultimate value, and that status is sustained by God's gracious gift of relationship toward them.[14] Nevertheless, on a temporal level, if we gain our sense of value from our human relationships, then we are forced to ask what is the "worth of persons who justifiably consider that no one cares about them? A person who finds herself or himself in such a position is justified in feeling worthless. Furthermore, because no one at all cares about them, they may regard any affirmation of their own dignity as persons as practically impossible as well as pointless. Self-esteem is the product of being of worth to others."[15]

The primary way in which we gain and experience self-worth is not through social achievement, material wealth, or an ability to compete in the market place, but through others' love for us. If such relationships are unavailable, or if we perceive ourselves not to be worthy of them, this can lead to a catastrophic loss of self-esteem and deep feelings of being devalued. People diagnosed as having schizophrenia frequently are justified in assuming a lack of love from others.

The Social Isolation of Schizophrenia

In order to understand fully the social processes that are at work in creating the forms of poverty that have been highlighted, it is necessary to develop a deeper understanding of the complex social and interpersonal processes that underlie such forms of social behavior and negative reactions to mental health problems. It is clear that there are particular difficulties inherent within schizophrenia as a clinical condition that make communication and relationship building very difficult. Poor ego boundaries, bizarre speech and behavior, and an inability to maintain eye contact are just some of the features that interfere with the normal process of relational interaction. Because individuals with schizophrenia do not remain within the unwritten codes of social intercourse, other people often do not understand what is going on when they encounter such an individual. The normal characteristics that are necessary for the development of successful interpersonal relationships—mutual symbolic exchange and interaction, common situational definitions, and adequate communication of shared meanings—at times appear not to be present within such encounters. Because of this, one of the major barriers that separate the person with schizophrenia from the rest of society is the fundamental *incomprehensibility* of their condition. Schizophrenia is confusing and disorienting for those experiencing it *and* for those whom they encounter. As such, it is open to being ascribed a number of different meanings and interpretations. As Van Den Bosch points out, "schizophrenia is a severe psychiatric disorder of the inner world which proves difficult to understand by the outside world. . . . Schizophrenia is probably the most incomprehensible disorder of the mind."[16]

The incomprehensibility of schizophrenia makes it difficult for people with it to relate to others, and for others to relate to them. It also leaves open the possibility of misrepresentation, misunderstanding, and stereotyping. Consequently, schizophrenia poses a major challenge to the normal framework of shared meanings and reciprocal interaction upon which the communication process is built and on which the cultural norm of friendship, based as it ordinarily is on the "principle of likeness," inevitably depends.

Horwitz, commenting on this distortion of communication, which he notes is present in a number of mental health problems, points to the fact that

> any piece of behaviour is made intelligible either by attributing a socially recognisable motivation to the behaviour, e.g. "he murdered his wife out of jealousy," or by locating the action as an instance of a typical social category, e.g., that man is chopping wood. When observers assume that actors know what they are doing and are guided by rules in their behaviour, social behaviour appears to be meaningful. It is when observers cannot find meaning or comprehensibility in behaviour that they are likely to apply labels of mental illness.[17]

According to Horwitz, when individuals step outside the socially accepted norms of communicative behavior, their action becomes incomprehensible to the majority of the population. It is this incomprehensibility which is then used as a defining line between what is normal and what is abnormal behavior.

The attribution of meaning to any social action is a fundamental requirement of all social interactions. No meaningful communicative interaction can occur unless each participant can understand, at least to a mutually acceptable extent, what the other is doing. Horwitz goes on to argue that *intelligibility* is what marks out mental health problems from other forms of behavior within society.

> All societies need some category to designate behaviours that fall outside the boundaries of comprehensibility. The notion of men-

tal illness is rooted in the basic requisites of social interaction: that persons be able to find each others' behaviour mutually comprehensible. Labels of mental illness are applied to behaviour when the categories observers use to comprehend behaviour do not yield any socially understandable reasons for the behaviour.[18]

The failure of observers to find any meaningful purpose in behavior Horwitz calls *incomprehensibility,* and he considers this to be the essential quality at the core of behaviors that are labeled "mental illness." This is not to suggest that mental health problems do not exist, or that they are simply a construction of society. Rather, what we are considering here are the *consequences* of the specific behaviors (illness experience) that tend to accompany particular forms of mental health problems. These consequences are the social products of particular conditions, rather than things that are inherent within the condition itself.

Horwitz' proposition is interesting: According to his analysis it would appear that, contrary to the conflict theories of mental health problems proposed by antipsychiatrists such as R. D. Laing, the identification of mental illness is *not* a power-oriented conspiracy whereby the psychiatrist abuses his power by labeling "innocent persons" mentally ill with concomitant negative social and emotional consequences. In fact the identification of mental health problems is fundamentally a *lay* enterprize.[19] Individuals are primarily marked out by the general population as having mental health problems when they find themselves unable to participate in social interaction according to the tacit rules of comprehensibility that guide all human social interaction. Once marked out, they are brought to the attention of the mental health professionals, who in turn provide an official diagnosis.

Barriers to Love

The incomprehensibility of mental health problems makes it difficult for the "normal" person to relate with the "other." The tendency *then* is to engage in an "I-It" relationship toward the incomprehensible individual and assume him or her to be incapable of entering into authentic relationship, to withdraw one's own relationship, and to pass responsibility for the individual on to the professional.

These observations are important with regard to schizophrenia. The behavior, experiences, and ways of communicating associated with schizophrenia often strike at the basic properties of normal social interaction and comprehensibility. People find it difficult to *empathize* with the experience of schizophrenia. Empathy is a communication skill that lies at the heart of all interpersonal relationships. Most counseling theories would suggest that the counselor's ability to empathize accurately with the client is foundational for the development of a successful and health-bringing counseling relationship. For example, Truax and Carkhuff suggest that

> accurate empathy involves more than just the ability of the therapist to sense the client or patient's "private world" as if it were his own. It also involves more than just his ability to know what the patient means. Accurate empathy involves both the therapist's sensitivity to current feelings and his verbal facility to communicate this understanding in a language attuned to the client's current feelings.[20]

If Horwitz is correct in asserting that incomprehensibility is a fundamental constituent of any understanding of mental health problems, and if Truax and Carkhuff are correct in asserting that empathy is basic to the development of health-bringing relationships, then it becomes clear that schizophrenia itself may well cause many people with schizophrenia to become isolated and friendless. It is not simply that their illness, in itself, makes them less desirous of relationships.[21] The problem seems to be that the particular symptoms and experiences that the person encounters make normal communication and relational interaction extremely difficult, thus engendering a negative relational response from those with whom they come into contact. Consequently the person is experienced as somehow "other,"[22] and lines of communication and relationship collapse.

Not only is the individual experienced as essentially "other," he also experiences himself as alien and different. The individual internalizes this social definition of "otherhood," which then becomes a part of his social identity, that is, part of the way in which he perceives himself and is perceived in the world. If one

perceives oneself as fundamentally different from the rest of society, it will be very difficult to form any kind of stable and meaningful relationships. If one is perceived by others as fundamentally
different, the task can become quite impossible. In this way the
"schizophrenic" is created, and defined by self and others as fundamentally different. Under such circumstances, any friendship
that is grounded only in the "principle of likeness" is destined to
fail both from the perspective of the sufferer *and* the potential
friend.

Images of Madness

However, important as these inherent communication difficulties may be, there is a wider social dimension that is inextricably
connected with the interpersonal one. It is not only the incomprehensibility of *actual* behavior that causes relational difficulties.
There is also a major problem in the way in which an individual is
perceived in the eyes of the general public, irrespective of her *actual*
behavior, speech, or mental state. The tag of "mentally ill" in itself
brings about alienation and relational disconnection. Human
beings act toward things as they are perceived, interpreted, and
defined, and not necessarily as they are. As David Karp puts it,
"All objects, events, and situations derive their meanings through
human interpretation. We are ultimately free to define anything we
choose, including illness."[23] This suggestion is important for developing an accurate understanding of the social history of schizophrenia. The inherent incomprehensibility of schizophrenia is
compounded by a socially constructed incomprehensibility that
manifests itself in inaccurate, stereotypical, and distorted public
images of what schizophrenia is and what a person suffering from
it is *actually* like. These images in turn profoundly affect the ways
in which schizophrenia is interpreted and understood, and the
type of treatment that persons diagnosed as having it will receive.

While such images may not be accurate or truthful, they are no
less real in their consequences. Sociologist Agnes Miles, in her
research into the public perceptions of mental health problems,
found that

... studies have consistently shown that people evaluate mental illness negatively, reject and discriminate against mental patients, and base their views on traditional stereotypes.[24] ... Overall the public image of a person suffering from mental illness is considerably more gloomy than that of a person suffering from physical illness, and in certain respects it appears to be closer to the public image of a criminal.[25]

Miles concludes that there exists a stereotype of mental health problems and of persons who suffer from them that is negative and widely held by the lay public. A good example of this type of distorted caricature is to be found in media and public juxtapositions of schizophrenia with violence. According to MIND:[26]

The public's perception of mental disorder is of the raving lunatic or homicidal maniac. ... In fact the vast majority of murderers have no history of mental disorder—they are as "sane" as you or me—and the vast majority of mentally disordered people pose no threat whatever to anyone except themselves. Violence is a rare occurrence even in acute schizophrenia and is by no means as common as people perceive it to be. ... The vast majority of patients are in practice more likely to be victims than offenders.[27]

Thus, although there may be a propensity toward violence among some people with schizophrenia (as there is within certain members of society at large), in reality it tends to be directed toward the persons *themselves* rather than toward others. This of course differs from the general perception of schizophrenia that tends to paint a picture of extreme violence as inherent within the condition. Greg Philo highlights this distorted public perception in his research into media images of mental illness.

Beliefs about schizophrenia were related by group members to images from both factual and non-factual sources. This description from a woman in Motherwell combines both of these: "A lot of things you read in the papers and they've been diagnosed as being *schizophrenic*. These *murderers*—say Donald Neilson, was he no schizophrenic? the *Yorkshire Ripper* . . . on Brookside that man who is the *child-abuser* and the *wife beater*—he looks like a schizophrenic—he's like a *split personality*, like *two different people*.

First he gets like self-pity and he brings flowers and works his way back into the house and you could feel sorry for him, then he's a child abuser and a wife-beater."[28] (Motherwell Group, Interview, emphasis added)

This statement contains truths, half-truths, and misinformation, and vividly illustrates the general confusion there is over what schizophrenia is and how people diagnosed with it are assumed to behave. Thus people with mental health problems find themselves criminalized and considered socially unacceptable, not because of what their condition actually *is*, but because of the way it is *perceived* within common folklore. Such false perceptions necessarily lead to disempowerment and the closing down of possibilities for acceptance and a valid and valued place within society.

Disabling Images

Otto Wahl, in his extensive investigation into public perceptions of mental health problems, highlights a study that was done to compare the attitudes of people to cancer and schizophrenia. In this study, undergraduates were read vignettes that portrayed a person as having either cancer or schizophrenia. They were then asked to rate the persons according to a series of traits. Wahl records that "the person identified as having schizophrenia was perceived as less desirable as a friend, less acceptable as a club member or neighbor, and less able to function in the community than the cancer patient."[29]

In the light of Miles' observations concerning the negative attributions that are ascribed to mental health problems, this in itself may not seem too surprising. However, when one takes into account that the vignette descriptions were *exactly the same*, apart from the name of the disorder, one begins to realize that there is indeed a major problem in the public's perception of mental health problems in general and schizophrenia in particular. Wahl's point is of critical importance. It is not so much bizarre behavior or speech to which people react as the particular images of mental illness which they hold.

> It is the public's negative image of mental illness and not the person or specific disordered behaviour to which they respond with discomfort and rejection. They are responding not to what they observe directly about the person with a mental illness, not to the actions or emotions of the psychiatric patients they encounter, but to stereotypes, their expectations, their acquired images of people with mental illness.[30]

People do not respond to the *person as person*, but to the *person as illness*. The fundamental form of relationship that a high proportion of the lay public offer toward people with schizophrenia is grossly ill informed and profoundly *impersonal*. The person living with schizophrenia is thus seen to be highly *stigmatized* in the perception of the public, and almost completely subsumed to their illness.

Understanding Stigma

The observations presented by Miles, Philo, and Wahl make it clear that stereotyping and stigma lie at the heart of the experience of all mental health problems and are intricately tied in with the social isolation that many sufferers experience. Because of the debilitating nature of schizophrenia and its enigmatic public image, people living with this illness are particularly prone to becoming stigmatized. Kirkpatrick and his colleagues in their research into the rehabilitation and social integration of persons with schizophrenia, discovered that "the primary external obstacle [to rehabilitation] identified was stigma, from both society and professionals."[31] Although one might at first consider stigma to be epiphenomenal to the central syndrome of schizophrenia, in fact it is a central part of the experience of people with schizophrenia and is a fundamental blockage to authentic understanding and the possibility of meaningful relationships.

Erving Goffman describes stigma as "the situation of the individual who is disqualified from full social acceptance."[32] The term "stigma" is used to refer to "an attribute that is deeply discrediting."[33] Goffman suggests that when a person is stigmatized because of some defect of character, behavior, or appearance, he or she is "thus reduced in our minds from a whole and usual person to a tainted, discounted one."[34] Goffman suggests that

> by definition, . . . we believe the person with a stigma is not quite human. On this assumption we exercise varieties of discrimination, through which we effectively, if often unthinkingly, reduce his life chances. We construct a stigma theory, an ideology to explain his inferiority and account for the danger he represents, sometimes rationalizing an animosity based on other differences, such as cripple, bastard, moron typically without giving thought to the original meaning. We tend to impute a wide range of imperfections on the basis of the original one.[35]

Miles makes a similar point concerning the subtle ways in which a person is stigmatized through jokes and everyday conversation:

> Such phrases as "Are you crazy?" or "It would be a madhouse" or "It's driving me out of my mind" or "We were chatting like crazy" or "He was running like mad" and literally hundreds of others occur frequently in informal conversations, and the discussants do not mean to refer to the topic of insanity and are usually unaware that they are doing so.[36]

Through the process of stigmatization a particular form of social identity is created and bestowed upon the stigmatized individual, a social identity that is fundamentally spoiled.

More than that, stigmatization acts to devalue and dehumanize those who become stigmatized. To stigmatize someone is to take one part of a person and make that the definitional point for the whole person. Thus people suffering from depression become "depressives," anxious people become "neurotics," and people with schizophrenia become "schizophrenics." Once persons are stigmatized and set apart by the attribution of a negative social identity, it is much easier for others to think of them as somehow less than human and to treat them as objects rather than persons. When persons become stigmatized, once again, in a very real sense they become nonpersons, a designation that, as we have seen, has profound social consequences.

Significantly, this stigmatization comes not only from others; the stigmatized individuals are also part of the society that stigmatizes them and as such shares in the social expectations and norms that, when broken, cause an individual to become stigmatized. Thus, "shame becomes a central possibility, arising from the individual's perception of one of his own attributes as being a defiling thing to possess, and one he can readily see himself as not possessing."[37]

From Mental Patient to Former-Mental Patient

Central to the situation of the stigmatized individual is his or her inability to feel or to experience *acceptance*, either by oneself or by others. "Those who have dealings with him fail to accord him the respect and regard which the uncontaminated aspects of his social identity have led them to anticipate extending, and have led him to anticipate receiving; he echoes this denial by finding that some of his own attributes warrant it."[38] Even if individuals are able to correct the "blemish" that has caused them to become stigmatized, they are seen as simply having undergone "a transformation of self from someone with a particular blemish into someone with a record of having corrected a particular blemish"[39]—a shifting of the negative emphasis of their social identity from "mental patient" to "former-mental patient," from "schizophrenic" to "schizophrenic in remission."

Conclusion

It has become clear why people with schizophrenia can quite justifiably be considered nonpersons and why effective ministry within this area is fundamental for a faithful, liberating church. The types of relational and social poverty highlighted in this chapter have important implications for a church that seeks to take seriously its ministry of liberation and justice for the poor and the oppressed. Given the nature of the situation and the life experiences of many people with severe mental health problems such as schizophrenia, it is absolutely unthinkable that the church could simply sit back and assume that other agencies should be responsible for the care and welfare of people living under such circumstances. Now that our consciousness has been raised to the lived experience of schizophrenia, we have no choice but to take prophetic action that will tangibly reveal our critical solidarity with a group of oppressed human beings. It is for such persons that Jesus came, and for them that he has entrusted responsibility for their care to the church that is his body on earth.

Now we need to move on from our social analysis and begin to draw out the implications of the previous discussions for a revised form of praxis for the church community. However, before doing that, it will be helpful to reflect on whether it is possible to generalize the findings of our case study on schizophrenia to other forms of mental health problems.

Chapter 6

Stories
from
Dark Places

One form of psychological disorder that shares much in common with the social history of schizophrenia is the condition known as bipolar disorder. While the clinical conditions of schizophrenia and bipolar disorder are different, on a closer examination, it becomes clear that they share a social history that is remarkably similar.

Bipolar disorder (otherwise known as manic-depressive illness) is a form of mental health problem that manifests itself in extreme swings of mood. Persons with this disorder will fluctuate between periods of extreme elation and deep troughs of depression. During the periods of elation, people may exercise poor judgment that can be quite destructive to their lives. For example, they may spend excessively, which can have a catastrophic economic and social effect on themselves and their families. During the depressive phase, people suffer extreme sadness. Prior to the advent of lithium therapy about 15 percent of people with this disorder committed suicide.[1] Thus, this condition is profoundly disabling socially, emotionally, and spiritually. Because of the high profile of its manic phase, it is a difficult disorder to keep hidden. Consequently, people with this condition are vulnerable to the types of stigmatization and alienation that have been highlighted. The social history of this illness is one marked by humiliation, exclusion, and a serious loss of credibility and respect in the eyes of the wider public and the individuals themselves. Like schizophrenia, this form of mental health problem has an ambiguous public profile.

A good example of the difficulties incurred by people living with this condition is seen in the experience of film star Margot Kidder, who was found wandering and distraught in Hollywood. Kidder, best known for her role as Lois Lane in the Superman movies, had silently struggled for many years with bipolar disorder. As one considers how devastating this condition can be for individuals and their families, one might expect that when her condition came to the attention of the public, she would have received compassion and understanding. This was not the case. Voyeuristic pictures of her in serious distress were flashed across the world, media images that bore little compassion for the real pain she was experiencing. The news items reporting on Kidder's situation presented a strong message that becoming mentally ill is not viewed with compassion; it is sordid and tawdry—a process within which one's dignity is not retained.[2] People appeared fascinated by pictures of Kidder's pain, and large sums of money changed hands for the rights to pictures and information about her plight. Likewise, Kidder's situation quickly became fair game for high-profile comedians who took delight in developing "humorous" anecdotes and stories exploring the "funny side" of her situation. It appears that being diagnosed with a mental health problem gives society the right to disrespect individuals, publicly humiliate them, and discard the possibility that what "the world is watching" is not entertainment, but a tragic life experience of a real human person.

The negative reaction received by Kidder stands in stark contrast to the heroic reception that Christopher Reeve, who played the role of Superman alongside Kidder, received when he addressed the Academy Award ceremony and the Democratic Convention from his wheelchair.[3] Reeve, who was paralyzed from the neck down in a riding accident, has been enabled to maintain the public profile of "hero" and "survivor." Kidder on the other hand, was forced into the tragic position of having publicly to confess that she'd rather be thought of as an alcoholic and drug abuser than a person with manic depression. As she told Barbara Walters in a televised interview, "Mental illness is the last taboo. It's the one that scares everyone to death, and I have had to include myself in that until the last few months."[4]

Meaningful Citizenship

The negativity of the public profile of bipolar disorder is profoundly disempowering. It not only serves to stigmatize and alienate people with this disorder, it also effectively excludes them from some fundamental human rights, as well as the social and legal processes that all of us depend upon for our protection and sustenance. It is true that in theory, people with the types of mental health problems we are discussing here hold the status of full citizens. However, in practice this is often not the case. Put simply, the concept of citizenship encompasses a set of basic expectations, rights, and obligations that are to be accessible to all people, not just to some. Such rights would include the right to appropriate medical care; the right to have the protection of the law, the right to participate in the political process; the right to health; the right to education, a healthy environment, and so forth. While people with mental health problems may have such rights on paper, in reality they are often unable to exercise them in any kind of meaningful sense. The following story will illustrate some of the reasons for this.

Jack is diagnosed as having bipolar disorder. Many times, during a "high," he has spent all of his family's savings on totally unrealistic ventures that, at the time, appeared to him to be sound, but on reflection were disastrous for all concerned. Jack tends to have more highs than lows, but when he goes down, he plummets into the depths of depression. When he becomes depressed, Jack withdraws from his family and friends and spends a large amount of time in his room by himself, sleeping or gazing out of the window and ruminating incessantly on the foolishness of his previous behavior. Jack is on permanent medication, and it seems to keep him sufficiently stable for him to hold down a good job as an assistant manager at a local superstore.

Recently he told me of an incident that had caused him great concern. He had gone along to a local town council meeting. The topic of the discussion was recent increases in local taxes, a subject that was obviously evocative. As the meeting went on, the atmosphere became more and more heated. All around him people were shouting, gesticulating wildly, throwing their fists in the air, and making all sorts of bizarre threats to the committee. He suddenly became aware that if he were to behave in the same way as those around him, he would almost certainly be ejected from the hall, and might even find himself institutionalized! Even though his behavior would have been exactly the same as those around him, because of the stigma of his illness, everything he did tended to be pathologized and attributed to his mental health problem. Consequently, in this situation he was effectively excluded from the political process. Jack was forced to sit and listen to the arguments and discussions without truly being able to participate. He was "in the meeting, but not of it."

Such experiences of disempowerment and the discrediting of normal behavior are a constant pattern in Jack's life. Time and again he finds his opinions severely limited and his perspective disregarded by people who while always polite and apparently caring make it clear that his illness means that he can be tolerated but never taken seriously. Once again we find the totalizing effects of mental health problems. Though Jack's bipolar disorder is a significant part of his life, it is not the *whole* of his life. He is a bright, intelligent man who has much to offer. However, his potential is frequently crushed by the constant attribution of his behavior, thoughts, and ideas as *nothing but* the product of pathology. In the same way as schizophrenia was seen to subsume the person to the illness, so also has Jack's life become totally "lost" to his diagnosis, with devastating effect.

Justice? What Justice?

Another story pertains to the ways in which people with mental health problems are frequently excluded from the legal process, and as such become vulnerable to various forms of abuse without meaningful recourse to the law.

Jan is thirty-two years old and self-abusive. Her diagnosis is unclear. Some psychiatrists have suggested that she has a personality disorder, others suggest that she has a form of anxious depression. Either way, Jan experiences long periods of sadness from which she struggles to emerge. In addition to being self-abusive, she has extremely low self-esteem. Jan is also an alcoholic, and has been for ten years. She is thus seen to be a highly stigmatized individual. Jan has three children, whom she loves deeply. Sadly, they are all in care and she sees little of them. In fact, she is rather afraid to see them, as she is never quite sure how she will react or behave in their presence. Once, three years ago, she attempted suicide in front of her eldest son, an act that severely traumatized both her and her child. Since then she has tended to avoid contact, apart from birthdays and Christmas. It is, of course, difficult to get to the root of her difficulties, but from her perspective, and from the perspective of her therapist, they stem back to when, between the ages of six and nine, she was systematically sexually abused by her uncle. The uncle has never been taken to task, despite the fact that he also abused her brother at various points when his nephew was younger. While Jan's condition is complex, the pattern of self-abuse and self-hatred that is manifested in her life would support the possibility of some form of abuse in her early life.

Recently Jan and her brother decided that they should take their uncle to court. While her brother was deemed to be a good witness, in that he had no history of mental health problems and held down a good job as an office clerk, the legal authorities refused to proceed with the case because, in their opinion, Jan's psychological condition would mean that the case would almost inevitably be thrown out of court. If it did come to court, the prosecutor reckoned that Jan would be unable to stand up to the inevitably aggressive questioning of the defense lawyers. The authorities offered to go ahead with the prosecution only if Jan would withdraw her complaint and allow the focus of the case to fall on her brother. Jan and her brother, deeply upset by the attitude of the legal authorities, decided not to proceed with the case. Jan went home and made yet another attempt on her life. What was the point in carrying on when her status as a noncitizen and, as she saw it, a mere "sexual object" at the disposal of men to do with what they will, had apparently been legitimated by the powers that be? In her perception, she was now open to being abused by any man who wished to do so, and there was absolutely nothing that she could do about it. The sad fact is that she might well be correct.

Now at one level, such a decision not to prosecute is understandable. Within the system as it stands, Jan would indeed make a bad witness. Her history would inevitably be brought into the case, and she would be forced to answer some unpleasant questions in a public setting that would be highly distressing for her.

She might well not be able to withstand the pressure. However, by not being allowed to proceed with this case, she was stripped of a fundamental human right—the right to legal redress and protection under the law.[5] It is true that her unstable emotional state and the fact that the accusations were being made retrospectively complicated Jan's situation. However, the real problem does not lie with Jan, or her particular mental health problem. The real problem lies in a system that by its very nature disadvantages some of the most vulnerable people within our societies. Likewise, people with developmental disabilities, elderly people, and people who have poor linguistic skills encounter similar difficulties with the legal system and are consequently quite vulnerable to various forms of abuse. Jan's story reveals clearly the vulnerability of persons with mental health problems within a community that, far from being caring, may well be threatening and exploitative. Within a legal system that by its nature excludes certain vulnerable sections of the population from its protection, who will listen to her voice and the voices of others in similar situations? Who will be their advocate in the face of powers that seek to silence them and ignore their pain in the face of injustice? One of the tasks of prophetic Christlike friendship will be to stand in solidarity with people like Jan and to strive for justice in the face of gross injustice.

Clashing Discourses, Personhood, and Dementia Care

Before closing this chapter, there is one further area to which it will be useful to apply the analysis that has been worked out thus far. In the previous discussion on schizophrenia, the idea of the double narrative was developed, that is, the suggestion that there are two stories that surround mental health problems, one medico-psychiatric, the other personal. The vignettes that we have explored thus far have begun to illustrate this idea. It will be helpful to probe one final area that, while initially appearing to be wholly neurobiological, on a more critical reflection turns out to have a social history that is not dissimilar to that of people diagnosed as having schizophrenia. The area of dementia and dementia care provides an excellent example of the double narrative.

Oliver Sacks relates the story of a man, Jimmy, whose memory had been destroyed by Korsakov's syndrome. Korsakov's syndrome is the product of long-term alcohol abuse that leads to irreversible degeneration of the brain. One of its central features is profound memory loss. The loss is so extreme that sufferers become people without a past or a future, interminably trapped in an eternal present and bound permanently within one period of time. People with this form of mental health problem are in a very real sense lost and unable to establish roots. Sacks, from his position as a neurologist, assumed that Korsokov's syndrome had "de-souled" Jimmy. However, while Sacks conceived of Jimmy as being absent in a way that was fundamental to his humanity, those close to him saw something else. Sacks recalls how one of the nurses drew his attention to a hidden dimension of Jimmy's existence: "Watch Jimmy in chapel and judge for yourself." Sacks continues:

> I did, and I was moved, profoundly moved and impressed, because I saw here an intensity and steadfastness of attention and concentration that I had never seen before in him or conceived him capable of. . . . Fully, intensely, quietly, in the quietude of absolute concentration and attention, he entered and partook of the Holy Communion. He was wholly held, absorbed, by a feeling. There was no forgetting, no Korsakov's then, nor did it seem possible or imaginable that there should be—clearly Jimmy found himself, found continuity and reality, in the absoluteness of spiritual attention and act.[6]

Sacks's medical gaze revealed only pathology and assumed hopelessness. Yet, when he was "forced" to listen to Jimmy's lived experience, the voice of spirituality transformed his understanding, resurrected the person behind Jimmy's problems, and opened up new possibilities for care that reached beyond the definable and into the mystery which is human life. Likewise for Jimmy, his encounter with the Holy provided him with an anchor and a sense of self that was otherwise missing from his life. In the realm of the spiritual, Jimmy seemed to function in ways that transcended the expectations of the medical profession and offered him relief and purpose in the midst of a world of profound meaninglessness.

Those who have worked with people experiencing other forms of dementia will be able to identify with this story. Time and again I have been struck by the impact that worship can have on people with dementia. People who appear to have little contact with reality for the vast majority of their lives, can suddenly spring into life when they hear the Lord's Prayer, or particular hymns and Bible readings. Now, there are some who would reduce this simply to residual memory, the last vestiges of the person that was, the assumption being that the neurological damage caused by the dementing processes has destroyed the person that was. While they might *appear* to be there in times of lucidity, these people would say, in reality they have been destroyed by the dementing process.

However, not unlike schizophrenia, dementia also has a double narrative that takes us beyond the boundaries of fading neurology and into the hidden mysteries of personhood and what it means to be human and to live humanly. In order to understand this, it will prove useful to explore something of the work of Tom Kitwood and Stephen Post and their attempts to reconceptualize dementia by drawing the focus away from pathology and toward the person. It is true that—unlike schizophrenia—dementias, in all their varied forms, do appear to have a natural history that is inevitably marked by cognitive and neurological decline. However, that is not the whole of the story. The work of English psychologist Tom Kitwood on Alzheimer's disease has shown clearly that while dementia may be organic in origin, the actual life course of people with this condition is not as determined by fading neurological activity as was once presumed. Kitwood argues that, not unlike our understanding of schizophrenia, our understanding of dementia has been constructed by a cluster of discourses, of which the dominant one is grounded in medical science.[7] Within this interpretative framework, persons with dementia are totally subsumed to their neurological condition, even to the point where, linguistically, they are frequently referred to as "dead." The possibility that the person may remain, despite the ravages of the condition, is often not even considered. Thus dementia has become so medicalized that other ways of interpreting the person's condition are subsumed to the power of the medical interpretation.

Throughout the many debates on the causes and treatments of senile dementia and indeed in much of the literature on dementia care, certain questions are very rarely asked. Who is the dementia sufferer? What is the experience of dementing really like? How can those who have a dementing illness be enabled to remain persons in the full sense? That they are experiencing subjects, with cognitions, intentions, desires, emotions, there can be no doubt. In the dominant discourse, however, and in some of the subordinate discourses also, dementia sufferers are present largely as an absence. Those who are recognizable as persons are the carers. The dementia sufferers themselves are not; rather, they are defined out of the world of persons, even to the extent of it being claimed, almost literally, that those in the later stages are already dead.[8]

Thus, due to the power of the medical interpretation of dementia, the *person* behind the label, has been "lost" from the debate about what dementia is and what constitutes effective dementia care.

However, while dementia may be neurological in origin, the suggestion that this understanding necessitates a view of the human person with dementia as essentially "dead" is seriously mistaken and reveals a misinformed understanding of the way that the brain functions. In an attempt to reframe our preconceptions of brain functioning, Kitwood argues that the process of dementing can be radically reframed if it is explored on three levels.[9] At the first level we have the structural condition of the brain that is established over the lifetime of the individual. This level of brain functioning is open to the rigors of time and disease processes and is necessarily deteriorating throughout a person's life. It is degeneration within the physical structure of the brain that causes the process of dementing. The second level is hypothetical. "It is the highest level of mental functioning that is possible when a person's brain is in a particular structural state . . . the upper limits to mental functioning are set by the structural state of the brain."[10] The third level comprises the *actual* mental functioning of the person. Kitwood points out that the actual functioning of all people is considerably lower than their potential functioning. None of us ever achieves maximum brain function. Consequently, the human brain has a depth of reserve functioning that is rarely if ever used. Such a schema has important implications for the ways in which we choose to care for people with dementia. First, there is no necessary correlation between level one and level three. If we assume that we can understand and define Alzheimer's simply by exploring level one, we make a grave error. However, "in fact this error is made repeatedly, and the findings of medical science are called in as a testimony to its truth."[11] Second, if we accept that there may well be regions of the person's brain that remain undeveloped despite the ravages of Alzheimer's, this opens up space to explore ways in which the person's brain functioning may be enhanced or diminished through nonneurological factors.[12]

Kitwood calls for the development of an alternative discourse that focuses on such things as personhood, interpersonal relationships, and spirituality.[13] He presents convincing evidence to suggest that given an appropriate sociorelational environment, a degree of *rementing* can take place. For example, Sixmith and colleagues in a study of "homely homes" where the care was of a very high quality found "clear examples of 'rementing,' or measurable recovery of powers that had apparently been lost; a degree of cognitive decline often ensued, but it was far slower than that which had been typically expected when people with dementia are in long term care."[14] While research within this area is in its infancy, the point to note here is that there is significant doubt being cast on traditional medicalized understandings of dementia and how it should be treated. Such reframing of the central features of dementia and the injection of the possibility of hope and relational intervention opens up real possibilities for the types of solidarity friendships that have been described thus far to play a critical role in the care of person's with this form of mental health problem.

The Poverty of Dementia

A closer reflection on the life experiences of people with this condition also reveals that they are deeply in need of the type of liberation that has been a focus of this book. Stephen Post, in quoting E. T. Lucas writing on the moral context of Alzheimer's disease, notes that people with dementia have heterogeneous disabilities that confer on them a preferential moral significance based on the magnitude of their needs. They are the socially outcast, the unwanted, the marginalized, and the oppressed. A remarkable amount of elder abuse and neglect falls upon people with dementia, not just because caregivers are exhausted or ignorant, but because they are defenceless and easily victimized.[15]

Because Alzheimer's disease offends the basic moral principles and social assumptions upon which Western societies are built, people with this disease will inevitably come to be ranked among the poor within our societies. Post astutely observes that:

we live in a culture that is the child of rationalism and capitalism, so clarity of mind and economic productivity determine the value of a human life. The dictum "I think, therefore I am" is not easily replaced with "I will, feel, and relate while disconnected by forgetfulness from my former Self, but still, I am." Neither *cogito* (I think) nor *ergo* (therefore), but *sum* (I am). [16]

To have Alzheimer's disease, or any other form of dementia, is to have a form of neurological malfunctioning that stands in stark contrast to cultural assumptions that define the very nature of human personhood. People with dementia are particularly *vulnerable* within a society that worships the very thing that they are losing. In a society that prizes reason and autonomy and assumes the primacy of the "self-made individual" and economic productivity, those who are lacking or challenged within these areas are particularly vulnerable to the types of depersonalizing forces that push them into the social status of nonpersons.

As such, they are vulnerable to the possibility of being forced to accept forms of care that can be fundamentally depersonalizing. Post draws an analogy from the work of Stanley Hauerwas on mental retardation:

People with retardation can receive "oppressive care," a kind of care based on the assumption that the retarded are so disabled that they must be protected from the dangers and risks of life.[17] Their capacities and agency are easily underestimated, so that

117

they are to some extent trained to be retarded. Societies have struggled to receive people with retardation in ways that will allow them to flourish. The key to good care is not only to "do for" people with retardation, but to "be with" them, for a readiness to be with bridges a gap between us and them that is "not unbridgeable."[18] Many of us feel repulsed by people with retardation if we have not been around them much; experience and acculturation can help. *We fear them, because we do not know them.* Can we be morally rich enough as a society that the well-being of people with retardation is enhanced? In religious traditions, of course, it is exactly the concern with the downtrodden and weak that is a special mark of moral excellence, and people with retardation fit that description.[19] (Italics added)

While there are obvious differences between retardation and Alzheimer's disease—one is a narrative of loss, while the other is a narrative of failing to meet socially defined norms—the parallels between the two related to the possibility of oppressive forms of care are obvious. Likewise Hauerwas's observation about the fear of the stranger, and the healing power of opening oneself to the strangeness of the other, is highly relevant for the effective care of all people who, for whatever reason, are perceived to be different. In light of the oppressed state of people with dementia, Post calls for a position of *moral solidarity* with people experiencing Alzheimer's disease. Such a stance is very much in line with the type of critical solidarity that underpins this book in that it "calls for a critical reflection on cultural attitudes towards people with dementia, especially on the attitude that nothing can be done for them. *Solidarity, comfort, and reassurance are not 'nothing'* "[20] (Italics added).

From this it can be seen that the types of theoretical discussions that have been presented thus far are not epiphenomenal to the process of hands-on caring. If the focus of dementia research remains on issues of brain pathology and the ways in which a person is damaged by the disease, rather than on issues of personhood, spirituality, and the significance of personal relationships, then we risk perpetuating injustices on one of the most vulnerable groups within society.

While the previous discussion may appear strange and theoretical, in fact the points presented are of vital significance for the day-to-day care of people with dementia. A simple but moving example of the importance of demedicalizing our perceptions of dementia is offered by Margaret G. Hutchison in her paper "Unity and Diversity in Spiritual Care."[21]

> An elderly lady suffering from dementia, paced the corridors of the nursing home restlessly—repeating over and over, just one word. The staff were disconcerted, but no one seemed quite sure how to calm her and put her mind at rest. In fact they were at a loss to understand the reason for her distress. The word she repeated over and over again was God—and that was all she said. One day a nurse got alongside her and walked with her up and down the corridors until eventually in a flash of inspiration she asked the lady, "Are you afraid that you will forget God?" "Yes, Yes!" she replied emphatically. The nurse was then able to say to her, "You know even if you should forget God, He will not forget you. He has promised that." For this lady who was forgetting many things, and was aware of it, that assurance was what she needed to hear. She immediately became more peaceful, and that particular behavior ceased. She was responding positively to care which extended beyond the needs of body and mind—care of the human spirit. . . .[22]

Several things emerge from reflection on this story. The fact that the staff were at a loss to understand this woman's distress would support the research that strongly suggests that there is a serious lack of awareness to the spiritual dimensions of care among the mental health professions.[23] It also reflects the types of negative, medicalized assumptions about the nature of dementia that have been highlighted thus far. Because of the aforementioned negative assumptions about people with dementia, the woman's predicament could very easily have been drawn within the boundaries of the medical model, defined as disruptive behavior due to neurological deterioration, and dealt with through the use of physical or pharmacological restraint. However, in recognizing the personal and spiritual nature of the problem, the nurse was able to reframe the woman's situation in a way that enabled her to conceptualize it not as a nursing *problem* to be *solved*, but as a *human experience* to be *understood*. In doing this she was able to focus on that which was fundamental to the patient-as-person—her fading spiritual awareness. A person's spirituality provides the framework within which he or she interprets the world and locates themselves within it. This being so, forgetting about one's spirituality will be a devastating blow to a person's sense of self-in-the-world that will inevitably bring about anxious and disturbed behavior.[24] If this woman's experience had been misinterpreted and simply drawn within the parameters of the medical model, the health professionals would have failed to care for her in a fundamental way.

Significantly, the resources of the Christian tradition enabled the nurse to affirm within herself that this woman would remain a person wholly loved by God irrespective of the degenerative nature of her condition. This spiritual knowledge allowed her to take seriously the woman's situation and to offer precisely the type of response that enabled her to find solace and a degree of peace even in the midst of her inevitable decline. This woman had little need for the technical knowledge of pharmacology, psychiatry, or psychotherapy. What she required was the practical knowledge of spirituality as it manifested itself in her personal relationship with the nurse. It was that which enabled her to hold on to God sure in the knowledge that God would hold on to her. The nurse offered her friendship, understanding, and a comforting presence, and in so doing opened up fresh possibilities for healing, liberation, and rehumanization. This short but poignant vignette embodies and reveals the possibilities of the model of friendship that has been developed thus far. While there is still much work to be done, even at this stage we can begin to see the potential that friendship has for the development of a liberating pastoral community.

Similar examples of the significance of the double narrative for the care of persons have been highlighted with regard to mental retardation,[25] depression,[26] AIDS and cancer,[27] and even premenstrual tension.[28] The critical thing to recognize is that in all of the mental health problems that have been discussed, while biology may be significant, even when neurological damage is profound, *people are not wholly at the mercy of either their brains or their genes.*[29]

There is a whole dimension of human experience that falls beyond the gaze of the medical model, but which is fundamental to the experience of people with mental health problems. Human problems are always also human experiences and as such are multidimensional phenomena that affect the *whole-person-in-the-whole-of-his-or her-world*. People living with mental health problems are not merely passive victims of disease processes who need to be fixed by the appropriate application of medical technology. While biology may well be the initiating factor, each subsystem of the person—physical, mental, emotional, and spiritual—interacts to produce the person's experience of illness, disability, and distress.

Chapter 7

Memory, Resurrection, and Hope

Within Western societies, people with mental health problems might justifiably be described as poor, marginalized, and oppressed. The lives of people with mental health problems have been problematicized, caricatured, and stigmatized to such an extent that the fact that they are real persons who are fully human in every respect is frequently forgotten. Toward the end of this chapter, I will draw out three themes that emerge from theological reflection on the concepts that have been presented thus far: *memory, resurrection*, and *hope*. In exploring these three themes, I will develop the central theological theme that runs throughout this book: *the church must maintain critical solidarity with the poor and the oppressed*. A firm practical theological foundation for the revised forms of ecclesial praxis will be developed in the final chapters.

Remembering as Caring

The previous exploration of dementia highlighted the pastoral and personal significance of remembering and being remembered. For people whose memory is being destroyed by the ravages of neurological disease, the knowledge that they remain remembered and loved by others is of ultimate importance. However, the significance of memory for pastoral theology is not confined to the area of dementia care. John Patton proposes that memory and the act of remembering is a central theme in our understanding of what pastoral care is and how it should be done.

> Human care and community are possible only because we are held in God's memory; therefore, as members of caring communities, we express our caring analogically with the caring of God by hearing and remembering one another. God created human beings for relationship and continues in relationship with

creation by hearing us, remembering us, and meeting us in our relationships with one another . . . [pastoral care is] a ministry of the Christian community that takes place through remembering God's action for us, remembering who we are as God's own people, and hearing and remembering those to whom we minister.[1]

The church is a community of remembrance, called into existence by the memory of the acts of God in history. It exists only because it remembers the story of what God has done and, in remembering, seeks to live out the meaning of that story in its life, worship, and structures of care. Throughout Scripture, memory and being remembered are of great significance. The Psalms, for example, are filled with cries asking God to remember human beings in the midst of their joys and tribulations. In Psalm 119:49-50, the writer recalls the promises of God in his time of distress: "Remember your word to your servant, in which you have made me hope. This is my comfort in my distress, that your promise gives me life." Again, in Psalm 105:5-9 the psalmist recalls the things that God has done in the past, and uses them as assurances of what God will do in the future:

Remember the wonderful works he has done, his miracles, and the judgments he has uttered, O offspring of his servant Abraham, children of Jacob, his chosen ones. He is the LORD our God; his judgments are in all the earth. He is mindful of his covenant forever, of the word that he commanded, for a thousand generations, the covenant that he made with Abraham, his sworn promise to Isaac.[2]

For the psalmist, the knowledge that God has not forgotten God's people, and that the covenant promises remain secure offers comfort and hope in the midst of suffering, confusion, and chaos.

God's remembering is not an act of sentimental retrospective reflection, but rather a powerful act of affirmation and commitment to his continuing involvement with human beings in history. Memory and action are inextricably intertwined within the process of divine remembering. Patton argues that there can be no dichotomy between God's thought and God's action. God's remembering always implies God's movement toward the object of God's memory. As Brevard Childs puts it, "The essence of God's remembering lies in his acting toward someone because of a previous commitment."[3] Thus acknowledging that God remembers presupposes that God will act on that memory in the same ways as God has acted in the past. Walter Brueggemann, as quoted in Patton, makes a similar point when he suggests that "the gospel of this God that he remembers. . . . His remembering is an act of gracious engagement with his covenant partner, an act of committed compassion. It asserts that God is not preoccupied with himself but with his covenant partner, creation. It is the remembering of God, and only that, which gives hope and makes new life possible (see also 1 Samuel 1:11, 19; Judges 16:28; Psalms 8:4; 10:12; 24:1-3; Jeremiah 15:15). Above all, Job 14:13 articulates the conviction that God's memory is the last ground of hope in the realm of death."[4]

Thus, remembrance, hope, and faithful action are inextricably intertwined. In recognizing that God remembers us, we are inspired to believe that God is with us and for us in the same way God has revealed Godself as being with and for humanity throughout history, and ultimately within the incarnation and death of Christ.

Remembering Jesus

The incarnation, death, and resurrection of Jesus provide continuing evidence that God has not forgotten human beings, and that God continues to desire relationship and justice. Jesus' presence with the poor and the marginalized reminds the world of the nature and focus of God's actions in the world. God is a God of love, who hates oppression and unfairness and demands justice for those who are the victims of history. However, and of equal importance, the presence of Jesus among the poor reminds those who sit on the margins of acceptable society that God has not forgotten them; that God is with and for them, in sacrificial love that knows no limits, and transcends even the barrier of death. It is this challenging memory of Jesus ministering to the poor that dictates the shape and texture of the caring practices of the church. The task of a liberating church is to reveal signs and pointers to remind the world that the way it *is*, is not the way that it *should be*, and that loving "the outsider" is not an act of charity, or a function of "specialist ministries," but is, in fact, a "new" way of being human. In remembering God's actions in history and in the life, death, and resurrection of Christ, the Christian community is drawn into a new way of living and of seeing the world. This way refuses to forget the pain of the oppressed, or the degradation of those who are excluded and fragmented by the types of social forces that seek to provide a picture of "normality" that bears little resemblance to the coming kingdom. Such a community embodies the fact that God has not forgotten the world. The church as a community of friends is charged with the task of reminding people with mental health problems that God has not forgotten them, and reminding those who would oppress them, wittingly or unwittingly, that God is with and for those whom they reject and marginalize.

Dangerous Memories

Johan Baptist Metz talks about the Christian church as a community of remembering and storytelling that passes on and nurtures dangerous memories.[5] Dangerous memories are stories of the "other"—the victims of history who have been forgotten by society, but who remain at the forefront of the memory of God. In raising our consciousness to the reality of the lives of the oppressed, such stories become dangerous because they radically intrude upon and call into question, our complacent and comfortable present.[6] When taken seriously, the stories surrounding the lives of people with mental health problems constitute dangerous memories. They reveal forms of deep oppression, and processes of dehumanization that call the church to adopt a countercultural stance of critical solidarity with them, regardless of the cost. In listening to such stories and in sojourning with people with mental health problems, the church is forced to adopt a marginalized position. No longer can it accept "the ways of the world," or stand by silently as people's lives are undermined by social and interpersonal forces that deny the humanity of people with mental health problems and force them to become their illnesses. These stories call the church to a radically new stance of critical solidarity that is difficult and deeply challenging. Such a stance makes little sense in the eyes of the world, but forms the essence of the coming kingdom. As the Christian community listens to the types of stories that have been recited in this book, and as its consciousness is raised and its memory stimulated, it can do nothing other than give itself fully in commitment to those who are rejected and marginalized. Thus, in remembering and listening to the dangerous memories of people with mental health problems, the church is called out of its apathy, näiveté, and amnesia, and drawn into dangerous new ground.

Remembering the Person

Memory is of fundamental importance in fostering the type of pastoral care that this book hopes to inspire. The lives of many are marked by the experience of being forgotten and discounted by society. We find a process within which the person-as-person is gradually dislocated from society and separated from his or her personhood. This separation happens to such an extent that one's illness takes precedence over one's status as a human being with profoundly negative social and relational effect. Persons with mental health problems may exist as "objects" in the minds of media and public; the fact that they are human beings—made in the image of God, and loved by God beyond all measure—has somehow been forgotten. This being so, the first task of effective liberating care is to *remember* them.

It is clear, from the perspectives of Scripture and common experience, that human beings need to be remembered. This is particularly so for those people with mental health problems who struggle to make sense of life in a "community" that finds it easy to forget about them. To be remembered by God is to realize that we are of eternal worth and value in God's sight. In remembering someone, we acknowledge the person as worthy of memory, and acceptable as a full person. It is easy to forget that the word "remember" means re-member, that is, to put back together that which has been broken. The opposite of remember is not to forget, but to dis-member; to take something apart.[7] We have already seen the ways in which people with mental health problems are forgotten and dismembered by assumptions, images, and attitudes that reduce them from persons to illnesses, seeking to identify their whole being by only one aspect of their experience. Rather than being seen as whole persons with holistic needs and expectations, they are seen as nonpersons whose needs are rarely taken seriously. Thus, their identities are fragmented, as are their relational structures and life opportunities. This being so, the first pastoral action of the Christian community, as it seeks to image Jesus' mission of liberation and hope, will be to participate in God's continuing action of remembering those who have been cast aside and forgotten by society. In remembering people with mental health problems, the Christian community participates in the process of re-membering those who have been broken. By drawing them together in our understanding, thinking, and caring, "the person behind the illness," will be re-membered and the Christian community enabled to take a crucial initial step in the process of resurrecting and liberating those whom society considers to be "dead."

Resurrection and Hope

Theological reflection on the pastoral significance of memory leads us into our second motif, that of *resurrection*. If it is true that people with severe mental health problems are forgotten, and often assumed to be "missing" or even "dead," then remembering will necessarily lead to a second pastoral task for the Christian community: to "resurrect" the people who have been lost to their illness. But precisely what do we mean by "resurrection"? Obviously, the primary meaning of resurrection refers to the bodily resurrection of Christ that provides the ground for all hope and new possibilities for the future. But the motif of resurrection also permeates our way of being in the world, as it extends to address all forms of death. Gustavo Gutiérrez notes that the "resurrection of Jesus is never called, in the Bible, a miracle; it's so much more. The Resurrection of Jesus, if I may be permitted to express it this way, is the death of death."[8] Gutiérrez' point is an important one. In the Resurrection of Christ, we do not simply find a miracle or a parable designed to point us to a higher truth. In the Resurrection of Christ, we discover that creation has entered a new era that is radically different from the way things were previously, an era within which God has overcome death in all of its variant forms, and that there is hope, even in the midst of apparent hopelessness. The question of hope, and its relationship to the Resurrection, is an important one to which we now turn.

A Community of Hope and Revelation

Jürgen Moltmann points toward the critical tension between what is and what will be, a tension that marks the life of the Christian community. The Christian community exists within the dialectical tension between the pain and suffering of the cross and the hope and new possibilities of the Resurrection life. In the cross, we find God adopting a stance of critical solidarity with the world, as God enters into the suffering of humanity in all of its fullness. On the cross, God does not simply acknowledge or inactively remember the pain of the poor, the marginalized, the oppressed, and the rejected. Rather, the cross reveals God proactively entering into the pain of human existence, opening up Godself to the experience of suffering, and sitting in critical solidarity with those who suffer in the face of apparent hopelessness. Thus, the cross reveals God's continuing affirmation that God is with us even in the midst of the most horrendous forms of pain and injustice.

The Resurrection is God's powerful statement that the way things are is not the way they should be, or always will be. The Resurrection informs us that evil has not triumphed, and that God's reign will prevail in the eschatological scheme of things. The Resurrection is "God's great protest against death," and against all the manifold forms of evil and suffering that death takes already in the midst of life.[9] It is the turning point for creation, and the beginning of a process of redemption that is present now in part, but is still to come in all of its fullness.

Such a revelation of the nature and purposes of God has important implications for the church. The Christian community exists in the tension between the pain and chaos of what is, and the fresh and radically different possibilities of what will be, when the Resurrection life becomes the natural life of creation. The task of the church is to reveal pinpoints of resurrection light in the present and, in so doing, inspire hope and meaning in a world that struggles to find both. Thus, to return to Gutiérrez' point, in the

Resurrection we truly discover the death of death, but not only physical death. The light of the Resurrection signals the end of death in all of its forms, including the types of social and spiritual death that are central to the experiences of many people with mental health problems. The Resurrection contains God's cry of assurance to people with mental health problems that they are not forgotten, and that God desires to "resurrect" them in the here and now, to call them to experience the fullness of life within the kingdom of God, where there is neither Jew nor Greek, slave nor free, male nor female (see Galatians 3:28) black nor white, nor schizophrenic, nor depressive—only whole people loved and cared for by God beyond all measure. The Christian community is called to reveal the firstfruits of this resurrection life and to participate in the process of resurrection that begins now, and finds its fulfillment in the eschaton.

A Community of the Resurrection

But, what do we mean when we speak about "resurrecting persons" in the here and now? Marcella Althaus-Reid asks the question: "How do people resurrect? In a future moment outside history and with trumpets and angels coming from heaven? Or in the tension of the present, but 'not yet among us,' reign of God?"[10] The answer is probably both. At one level, it is obvious that the Resurrection is a once-only historical event that cannot be repeated. It is the historical truth of the Resurrection that inspires hope and new possibilities for the present in the light of the future. However, at another level, the Resurrection, understood as the "death of death" reveals it to be a continuing, eschatological process within which the Christian community is called to adopt a critical stance against all forms of oppression that lead to death, whether physical, spiritual, relational, or social death. Therefore, resurrection has a threefold meaning. At one level it is a historical event within which God acted decisively to raise Christ from the dead, and in so doing, set in motion a redemptive process that is the ground of all human hope and realistic expectation. At a second level, the Resurrection contains the promise of an eschatological event within which human beings will be raised to life in the new kingdom. At a third level, the

Resurrection is a continuing process, a way of being, wherein the Christian community is called to live in such a way that death, in its wider sense, is recognized and the reality that it has been overcome lived out in its continuing praxis in the world.

Resurrection and Community

The historical resurrection of Christ was a multivocal and communal event. While hope was inspirited into the human condition by the revelation of the resurrected Christ, the inspiration was both a personal and a communal event that led to the Resurrection of a community to a new life of hope and fresh possibilities. Thus, the Resurrection can be understood as *both* a personal event within which Christ was raised by God in the power of the Spirit, *and* a corporate experience within which a community was brought back to life by the radical revelation of the risen Christ.

> The fact is that Jesus' resurrection was also a community event: women and men witnessed how he came back from death, walked among them and continued the dialogue that existed before his crucifixion. . . . So it is legitimate to think that, starting with Jesus' resurrection, a whole community of people who suffered his loss when he was crucified came back to life again. Their eyes were opened in the sense that death took on another meaning; the Resurrection became the paradigm showing us the durability and indestructibility of life and justice.[11]

If that was so at the time of the Resurrection, so it is also true for the church today. Resurrection, in the wider sense that is being explored here, is a personal and a communal event that occurs when the bonds of death are broken, and the blindness that has kept the community from recognizing the signs of death is healed through the process of remembering. When the Christian community remembers the poor and acknowledges and seeks constructively to address those elements of death that scar their existence, it finds itself resurrected from a form of spiritual, social, and relational death within which it remains ignorant to issues of suffering and injustice. It is resurrected into a new life within which the purposes of God and the coming kingdom provide a radical new horizon and a transformed set of goals. Such a resurrected community is called to a ministry of memory, resurrection, and hope, as it seeks to develop forms of relating and ways of being with the poor and the "nonpersons," who have been forgotten and "buried" within the corporate psyche of present day Western societies. It is called to remember those whom the world has forgotten; to participate in the Resurrection of people whose personhood and relational possibilities have been destroyed by the social forces that have been outlined in the previous chapters; and to inspire hope in those whose lives at times appear to be profoundly hopeless. The church is called to initiate such a community of resurrection.

Chapter 8

Resurrecting the Person

Friendship, Hope, and Personhood

We have laid down a reasonably full and critical analysis of what mental health problems are, both as clinical diagnoses and as social experiences. We have also reflected theologically on how the situations of people experiencing them might be understood, and how that theological knowledge might function in shaping the identity of the Christian community and the focus of its caring actions. Schizophrenia provided us with a central focus for analyzing the experience of mental health problems. In this chapter, we will begin to explore ways in which we can develop effective pastoral strategies that will deal with the experience of people with mental health problems. The question is: *How might the major barriers to relational development be overcome, and ways found to enable individuals living with mental health problems to fulfill their personhood, and to live lives worthy of creatures made in the image of a God who is love?*

In the light of the totalizing tendencies of mental health problems, perhaps the most appropriate place to begin is by examining the relationship between the person and his or her particular mental health problem. We have seen that people with mental health problems tend to become totally identified with their disorders. This leads to their developing a social identity as "schizophrenic," "dementia victim," "manic depressive" and so forth—forms of identity that can be highly destructive of opportunities to develop healing relationships with God, self, and others. This leads to a form of social death that demands the full attention of a community that is seeking to live out the Resurrection life. A first step is to explore whether it is possible to separate a person from his or her illness, conceptually and psychologically, in such a way that, in line with Kitwood's emphasis in dementia care, "the person comes first." If this can be done, then it may be possible to develop ways of ensuring the healthy development of persons-as-persons, while taking their mental health problems seriously and offering appropriate care. One possible way of achieving such a goal is to reconceptualize mental health problems in order to acknowledge the seriousness of a person's problems while remaining focused on the person-as-person, rather than the person-as-illness.

Many people living with mental health problems are relatively symptom free at times, and at other times are deeply troubled and disturbed.[1] This being so, in many important respects a person may be deemed "insane" at one moment in time, but at other times be regarded as completely sane.[2] If this is the case, it may be more appropriate to think in terms of pathological thoughts and actions, rather than pathological people. In other words, a more appropriate way of conceptualizing and understanding the actual experience of people with mental health problems is to *separate the person from the illness*.[3]

Separating Mental Health from Mental Illness

The important thing about such a change in conceptualization is that it allows us to develop an understanding of mental health quite apart from mental *ill* health. In other words, it allows us to focus on the person, quite apart from the illness. In terms of "resurrecting persons," such a conceptual shift is of great significance. Keith Tudor notes that "it is commonplace to view the relationship between health and illness—and, therefore, mental health and mental illness—as two ends of the same continuum."[4] Within such a model, health is defined in opposition to illness with individuals being more or less healthy, depending on their position between the polarities. According to this model, people with long-term mental health problems will always be understood as mentally ill. Any conception of mental health care will primarily have to do with symptom control and the administration of appropriate medication. However, this is only one way of conceptualizing mental health and ill health. Tudor suggests that a more appropriate way of defining the relationship between mental health and illness is by "viewing each one as a separate continuum: the one, a mental disorder continuum; the other a mental health continuum."[5] This conceptualization enables one clearly to separate health from ill health and in so doing, focuses attention on issues of mental *health*, rather than simply mental *ill health*. It also enables one to conceptualize and experience being in different places on the two continua at the same time.[6] In this way, it is possible to consider mental health, apart from ill health and disorder, and to consider what it might mean in practical terms, to talk about developing the mental health of the people with long-term mental health problems. This understanding resonates with the "two narrative" theory of mental health problems highlighted earlier in this book. We might suggest that the maximal to minimal health continuum, with its primary emphasis on *illness,* represents the primary focus of the traditional psychiatric biomedical narrative. The specific training, research techniques, and forms of practice typical of mental health professionals result in a tendency to understand and define mental health according to the absence or presence of pathology. However, to persons living with a mental health problem, their primary concern frequently revolves around the maximal to minimal *health* continuum. This level focuses on meaningful personal relationships, spiritual direction, the quest for meaning, a valued place within society, and so forth. Within this continuum, mental health can now be understood in terms of growth and personhood, rather than by the person's illness experience, which affects, but does not define, the person. It is then possible to define mental health in terms of the whole person, rather than simply one aspect of the person, or his or her experience. Mental health can thus be understood as a complex process of psychosocial and spiritual development, that may or may not involve the eradication of specific mental health problems. Mental health involves a complex and reciprocal relationship between the physical, psychological, social, and spiritual domains within an individual, so that the health and illness status of each domain affects and is affected by the status of the other domains. Understood in this way, mental health is viewed in terms of a person being provided with adequate resources to enable him or her to grow as an unique individual and to live humanly as persons-in-relationship. As such, mental health inevitably incorporates such aspects as the capacity for growth,[7] adequate sources of meaning,[8] and hope for the future.[9] Additionally, mental health includes a sense of empowerment;[10] an ability to accept challenges and to grow in the midst of them;[11] adequate resources to ensure the possibility of sustaining healthy interpersonal relations with self, God, and others;[12] and an experience of feeling there are possibilities for the future, regardless of one's circumstances.[13] All of this contributes to enhancing the personhood of the individual and allows development of the strength to live humanly, even in the midst of profound mental health problems.[14] Seen from this perspective, mental health is a considerably more open and positive construct than might otherwise be thought.

According to this understanding, a person with a mental health problem may be relatively free from the major symptoms of the illness, and yet still be mentally unhealthy, in that relational opportunities are poor or nonexistent, and opportunities for constructing a hopeful future are minimal. Similarly, a person with chronic, unremitting mental health problems may still be able to develop some degree of mental health. If they are given the opportunity to experience appropriate supportive relationships, situations, and experiences, these may enable them to develop confidence, self-esteem, and a sense of possibility for their lives. There is, of course, an inevitable overlap between the two continua. Nevertheless, this structure offers a constructive approach to mental health and ill health by opening up new vistas of hope and possibility for those whose mental health problems are interminable. While the primary focus of the mental health professions is often on illness, this model opens up the possibility of effective interventions from other sources, such as the Christian community, who can find a strong focus on the development of *mental health.* In this way, a clear *collaborative* role for the Christian community can be delineated, and possible avenues opened up for supplementing and enhancing the current caring strategies carried out by the mental health professions.

Most important, this understanding allows one to focus on the *person* rather than the manifestations of the mental health problem. Instead of working according to specific pathology or cultural stereotypes, this reconceptualization of mental health problems allows us to consider questions of personhood and the possibility of mental health, even in the midst of interminable difficulties. If there is a separation of illness from person, then there can no longer be such a thing as a "schizophrenic," or a "manic depressive"— only whole persons who, at various times and to differing degrees, live with the symptoms of particular forms of mental health problems.[15] As a first step toward resurrection, such reconceptualization is invaluable.

Defining the Person Apart from the Illness

This focus on the person, rather than on the illness, in the care of people living with mental health problems, is an important one. This view has strong precedent within present day psychiatric research literature. John Strauss, a professor of psychiatry at Yale University, in his research into the subjective experience of schizophrenia hypothesizes that

> . . . the role of the person in mental disorder is not peripheral, merely as a passive victim of a disease to be fixed by medicines. . . . My hypothesis [does not] agree with the view that the person and the disorder are the same, as is implied by much psychoanalytic theory. Rather, I propose that clinicians consider the person and the disorder as separable for the purposes of understanding both more adequately.[16]

Strauss suggests that when one conceives of an individual who suffers from a mental health problem, one must think in terms of the individual as a *person* who also has a disorder, rather than a person who *is* a disorder.[17] He goes on to make a number of observations that are significant for the purposes of this book: "In a series of interviews with persons who had improved after ten years or more of severe mental disorder, several suggested that a key turning point for them was a change in attitude. . . . Somehow, after an extended period, they found themselves wanting not just to live with their illness but to have a life along with it or in spite of it."[18] Thus, in stark opposition to the view that mental health problems have a natural and determinative history, and that "diagnosis necessarily equals prognosis," Strauss's research suggests that, given the correct circumstances and support, persons with mental health problems can gain a particular attitude that can enable them to view their situation and themselves from a more positive and constructive perspective. From there these individuals begin to develop some degree of mental health, and hope for a possible future.[19] Strauss continues:

> Some stated that they came to accept their disorders. But this was not the kind of giving-up acceptance or resignation that often seems generated by the attempts some professionals make at helpful teaching (e.g., "You have an illness like diabetes and will have it all your life. You'll need to stay on medication and there are certain things you'll never be able to do."). The acceptance described by these subjects was one that involved hope for a better life and the resolve to work for it. In several instances subjects noted that symptoms—even delusions or hallucinations—then started to become less dominating and often faded considerably.[20]

To suggest this is not to imply that medication is necessarily inappropriate or unhelpful, only that—on its own—it is not enough. There is considerably more to the process of recovery and rehabilitation than simply controlling symptoms. Strauss suggests that particular circumstances and events within a person's life can help him or her reframe the situation, and define it in a way that may be totally different from the way it is seen by others, such as family, friends, mental health professionals, and society at large. By reframing his or her situation, the person can be enabled to accept the illness in a proactive, constructive, and potentially health-bringing way.

Recovering Friendship as a Mode of Liberation

How then might such an attitude be initiated? How can one suffering from profoundly demoralizing difficulties be enabled to reframe one's situation in a way that will allow for the possibility of hope and healing? The final chapters of this book will argue that a key to such reframing of illness experience and the instillation of hope lies in friendship. The model of friendship presented in the life and work of Christ offers real possibilities for therapeutic change. Committed friendship that reaches beyond culturally constructed barriers and false understandings and seeks to "resurrect the person"—who has become engulfed by their mental health problems—is a powerful form of relationship. It offers hope and new possibilities to people with the types of mental health problems that are the focus of this book.

Foundational to a person's experience of mental health problems are feelings of hopelessness, worthlessness, and poor self-esteem. While biological and biochemical factors may contribute to this, one of the main factors underlying poor self-esteem and hopelessness is the exclusion of people with mental health problems from many normal relational and material sources from which the majority of the population gain their sense of value, self-confidence, and worth. For many, the type of acceptance Strauss describes, which is marked by "hope for a better life and the resolve to work for it,"[21] seems unrealistically idealistic. Nevertheless, it is by no means an impossible ideal.

Finding Hope in the Midst of Hopelessness

One of the primary ways in which hope is inspired within human beings is through personal relationships. Helen Kirkpatrick and her colleagues echo the line of thinking we have been pursuing, in observing that many long-term studies are challenging the traditional view that severe mental health problems necessarily have a chronic deteriorative course.[22] Studies suggest that from one-half to two-thirds of people with schizophrenia show significant levels of recovery.[23] In line with Kitwood's observations of dementia, such research suggests that "the possible causes of chronicity may be viewed as having less to do with any inherent natural outcome of the disorder and more to do with a myriad of environmental and other psychosocial factors interacting with the person and the illness."[24] These researchers argue that the literature, and their own research, strongly suggest that the ability of the sufferer to develop some degree of *hope* is fundamental to the recovery process. The primary way in which hope is engendered within an individual is in and through *personal relationships*. Drawing on the definition offered by Judith Miller, they describe hope as:

> . . . anticipation of a continued good state, an improved state, or a release from a perceived entrapment. The anticipation may or may not be founded on concrete, real world evidence. Hope is an anticipation of a future which is good and is based upon mutuality (relationships with others); a sense of personal competence; coping ability; psychological well-being; purpose; and meaning in life as well as a sense of the "possible."[25]

In line with what has been suggested thus far, they argue that mental health problems are marked by "a cycle of disempowerment and despair that leads to symptoms of learned helplessness, including apathy, resignation, anger, submissiveness, depression, anxiety, withdrawal and compliance."[26] However, they present convincing evidence to support the thesis that hope, as it is manifested through interpersonal relationships, can break through this cycle and enable the individual to get "a foot on the rung" of the ladder back into society.

Byrne and colleagues in their paper entitled "The Importance of Relationships in Fostering Hope,"[27] also acknowledge the centrality of personal relationships in the development of such a hope that heals. They argue that personal relationships seem "to be the catalyst that allows hope to develop exponentially. The 'sense of the possible' expands when two individuals in a trusting relationship can work together."[28] This being so, as Kirkpatrick and Collins point out, mental health problems "may not affect psychological well-being to the extent that psychic energy cannot be mobilised to maintain hope."[29]

An important point that can be drawn from such research findings is the suggestion that the sufferer's ability to hope and to cope with their illness seems to inspire hope in the carer, *and* be inspired by the hope that is present within the carer. Several of the respondents within a research project conducted by Byrne and her colleagues referred to what they describe as a "contagion effect," wherein the carer's hopefulness could positively influence the hopefulness of the cared for. Put simply, *hope inspires hope.*[30]

In terms of pastoral care at a congregational level, this is a very important point. Hope lies at the heart of the message of the gospel—hope for the broken-hearted; hope for the afflicted; the poor; the marginalized; those whom society casts aside. Likewise, hope and the inspiration and maintenance of hope lie at the heart of the *church's* ministry of mental health care. The Christian community, as a community of memory, resurrection, and hope, has the potential to make a valuable contribution to the type of caring strategies proposed by Strauss. If congregations can be enabled to offer this type of hope-bringing relationship, it will not only benefit people with mental health problems, but it will also empower church communities to become hopeful communities that are able to care effectively for "the outcast and the stranger." If we can find some way to initiate such a cycle of hope, we will have moved toward the type of resurrection that is fundamental to effective mental health care.

Friendship and Hope

Byrne and colleagues highlight the central features of healing relationships that inspire hope as *empathy, unconditional positive regard, respect, warmth, commitment and caring.*[31] Kirkpatrick and colleagues emphasize that, from the perspective of the sufferer, vital to the relational process is the ability to listen, to value the individual as a whole person, to understand the sufferer's perspective and to accept the person for who they are. One of the most significant interventions in the treatment of mental health problems is *understanding.* While pharmacology and therapy may well be useful in the treatment of mental health problems, *understanding is a vital form of intervention that is fundamental to the process of rehabilitation.* Thus we find that "support becomes more than an adjunct to the task of treatment; support becomes the task itself."[32] Supportive relationships such as friendship are not secondary to the therapeutic process—they are *fundamental.*[33]

Reclaiming Friendship

It now becomes clear that friendship has great potential for the mental health care of people living with long-term mental health problems. Strauss, Kirkpatrick, and Byrne present evidence of the kind of change of attitude that is needed, and indicate that this changed attitude can be initiated when people are enabled to enter into a particular type of relationship that embodies the qualities of the proposed model of friendship. This type of committed caring that focuses on the person behind the diagnosis is very much in line with the kind of relationally based, committed caring that is revealed in the life of Jesus and in his friendships. Friendships that image the friendships of Jesus "fit the mold" presented by the research reviewed within this chapter. These friendships have the potential to be powerful counters to the dehumanizing forces that have been discussed.

If we reflect for a moment on the friendships of Jesus, one of their primary aims was to enable hope and relational wholeness to those who had been broken, isolated, and marginalized. For example, in his encounter with the Samaritan woman (John 4:7), someone who was heavily stigmatized and outcast by the Jewish people, he begins not with her race, gender, or dubious morality, but with her as a person worthy of relationship and respect. In speaking with her and sharing her drinking vessel, Jesus makes himself marginalized and unclean. However, in doing this he takes her into the community of God, resurrects her personhood, and heals her brokenness.

Likewise, his meeting a Gerasene man who was said to be possessed by demons and whose bizarre behavior had become his social identity shows a profound respect for the man as a person worthy of a valued place within the community (Luke 8:26). He takes time to commune with him and to listen to his story. In doing so he brings a depth of healing that surpasses the simple exorcism of demons. The effect of their encounter is so powerful that this man who has lived alone for many years, suddenly craves the company of Jesus. It is more than a coincidence that Jesus' final act toward this man was to send him back to his community to move him toward a place of integration and acceptance (Luke 8:26-39).

Jesus' friendships were always personal, as opposed to instrumental, primarily aimed at regaining the dignity and personhood of those whom society had rejected and depersonalized. Jesus' friendships reached beyond the socially constructed identity of individuals and, in entering into deep and personal relationships of friendship with them, he was able to reveal something of the nature of God and enable the development of a positive sense of personhood based on intrinsic value rather than on personal achievement or outward behavior. Whether he was calling to Zacchaeus, the much hated tax collector, to come down from the tree and eat with him (Luke 19:2) or preparing for his death while communing with his friends (Matthew 26:26) the friendships of Jesus reached beyond social expectations to reclaim the personhood of the other.

This type of friendship is catalytic.[34] Unlike other more instrumental relationships such as those found in counseling and psychotherapy, which set out specifically to do something, it is a form of relationship that acts as a catalyst that enables health and rehumanization simply by being there. Unlike many agents with whom people with mental health problems may come into contact, the task of the Christlike friend is not to *do* anything for them, but rather to *be* someone for them—someone who understands and accepts them as persons; someone who is *with* and *for* them in the way that God is also *with* and *for* them; someone who reveals the nature of God and the transforming power of the Spirit of Christ in a form that is tangible, accessible, and deeply powerful.

In concluding this chapter, we might conceptualize the function of such friendships within a modification of the model of meaning and illness that was presented earlier.

Friendship and the Redefinition of Personhood

Irreparable Loss or Damage

Value   Possibilities

Redefinition of Self   Person as Unique, Valued, Cared for   Challenge

Relief   Hope

Strength

In this revised model, it is the *person* who sits at the center of our understanding, and it is from that starting point that we begin to learn about his or her mental health problems. Certainly the person's problem may well remain a challenge and an irreparable loss. However, the damage or loss is not the last word. Now there are new possibilities. In and through the development of hopeful relationships, new possibilities are opened up that focus on growth, hope, and a redefinition of the self that can bring value, meaning, and healing.

The role of the Christian community truly must be to become a community of friends who take seriously their ministry of resurrection; a community that acknowledges that relational isolation, social marginalization, and exclusion are not compulsory parts of the experience of mental health problems. The Christian community must strive to overcome death as it manifests itself in the marginalization and oppression of a very vulnerable section of the population. Such a community will be prepared to struggle alongside those who are oppressed and marginalized, in order that they may find a place of value and acceptance within which hopeful relationships can bring healing, hope, and resurrection.

Chapter 9

Enabling Friendship-in-Community

A Ministry of Introduction, Education, and Enablement

Understanding Friendship Formation

In reflecting on the difficulties encountered by people living with mental health problems, one clearly sees that the development of meaningful friendship will not happen of its own accord. Even within the Christian community, there is no readily available pool of friendship that people can tap. The type of friendship this book is calling for will have to be *enabled, nurtured,* and *sustained,* if it is to become a realistic possibility.

Friendship is a learned skill. Friendship is the product of an ongoing process of socialization that continues throughout the life cycle, within which individuals learn the rules of communicating and relating and work out the boundaries that encompass their encounters. One learns how to develop friendships in the process of encountering others in community. As one experiences friendship, one is enabled to share that experience with others. However, there are many groups within our society—men and women who suffer from AIDS, homeless people, people with mental health problems, and people who are cognitively disabled—with whom the Christian community has little or no contact. Consequently, the types of countercultural friendships which are the focus of this book frequently are not developed. The vast majority of friendships within most Christian communities are based on the principle that like attracts like. If an ethic of solicitude does exist, it tends to be property rather than agape-based. Yet, as Elliot Liebow quite correctly observes, "Whatever one's view of mental illness, it is probably true that the more one gets to know about a person, the easier it is to put oneself in that person's place or to understand his or her viewpoint, and the less reason one has for thinking of that person or treating that person as mentally ill."[1]

This is an important observation. Nicky Hayes, writing from the perspective of social psychology, points to the fact that in terms of friendship formation and development, people are inclined toward those with whom they can most closely identify.[2] However, his analysis of the research suggests that people tend to befriend those with whom they have regular contact. Even if they are quite different in many respects, there is a tendency to come to like people simply as a result of having regular personal contact with them.[3]

Theologically we might reflect on this phenomenon in the light of the apostle John's assertion that "perfect love casts out fear" (1 John 4:18). The fear of encountering those who are different can only be overcome through the act of encounter. Fear is disabled through encounter and through communal life with persons who may initially be perceived as radically different.

This being so, central to the process of friendship formation is the deceptively simple fact that *people need to meet one another before they can become friends.* The reality for many marginalized people is that they simply do not get the opportunity to meet people other than those with difficulties similar to their own, or those who are paid to deal with them. This has certainly been the case for people with mental health problems who in the past have been hidden from society in a physical way through the asylum system. However, it is also the case for many nonhospitalized people who often remain isolated and alone even when supposedly part of the "community." There is therefore very little opportunity for the development of the types of friendship which might lead to a valued identity and help break down many of the barriers of prejudice, fear, and ignorance that are so destructive to the mental health of people experiencing psychological distress. Because they rarely encounter "outsiders," many people, inside and outside of the church, have their perceptions shaped and governed by media representations and stereotyped images that do not necessarily bear any resemblance to the reality of the lives of the people to whom they refer. If the church is to be effective in its ministry of friendship, it will be necessary to bring the church and the marginalized together in such a way that both can encounter the humanity of the other and grow together toward mental-health-in-community. If the model of friendship described thus far is to find meaningful embodiment within the Christian community, the church will have to be *enabled* and *supported* as it struggles to overcome the "principle of likeness" and to live out the "principle of grace" within its community.

Developing a New Model of Care

In developing a model of care that will allow the Christian community to function in the ways that have been suggested, I want to begin by describing a system of care based on my personal experience as a community mental health chaplain. The model presented below was developed and implemented in the northeast of Scotland in my work with people living with mental health problems of various types. Through analysis of and reflection on the model of friendship development that was worked out within that context, it will be possible to indicate some of the ways in which the church can effectively care for people living with mental health problems and, in so doing, faithfully carry out its task of bringing freedom to the oppressed, and drawing the marginalized back within the boundaries of community.

Community Mental Health Chaplaincy

It will be helpful to clarify exactly what is meant by the term "community mental health chaplaincy." The word "chaplain"

> refers to a clergyperson or layperson who has been commissioned by a faith group or an organization to provide pastoral service in an institution, organization, or governmental entity. *Chaplaincy* refers to the general activity performed by a chaplain, which may include crisis ministry, counseling, sacraments, worship, education, help in ethical decision-making, staff support, clergy contact and community or church coordination.[4]

The chaplain is thus seen to be the representative of a particular faith community who is sent to work within a specific setting. A *community mental health* chaplain is someone whom the church has appointed as their representative within the dual contexts of a psychiatric hospital and the community, to authentically embody the faith community's desire to minister to those suffering from mental health problems, and to bridge the gap between hospital, community, and church.

Chaplaincy is a fluid and highly differentiated form of ministry that finds its shape and form according to the context within which it is carried out and the personality and vision of the individual chaplain. So the model of community mental health chaplaincy which will be presented within this chapter is not necessarily *typical* of community mental health chaplaincy in all places. The needs of persons vary from place to place, and the resources that are available are not the same in all places at all times. Also, chaplains meet with varying degrees of acceptance and cooperation from both church and mental health professionals, a fact that can profoundly affect the success of a model of care such as the one that will be presented. The model of mental health chaplaincy that will be outlined below is one I have developed and found to be effective in the facilitation of the types of friendships that have potential in the care of people with mental health problems. Nevertheless, with these reservations in mind, the ideas and practices that will be presented here are not parochial or wholly context dependent, and would be transferable, with appropriate modification, to other situations and to different contexts. I will begin by outlining the model of community mental health chaplaincy that will be the central focus of this chapter, before exploring some of the ways in which such a model can be used in the facilitation of health-bringing friendships within church communities.

Friendship in Action: The Basic Model

Within the particular model of chaplaincy that will be presented here, the basic task of the community mental health chaplain (referred to hereafter as the CMHC) was threefold. First, the intention was to set up a community mental health chaplaincy service that would participate constructively in the process of enabling persons with mental health problems who were either returning to the community from the hospital, or were already living within the community, to find an accepted and personally acceptable place within the life of a local church community.

Second, the chaplain's task was to facilitate the development of forms of education for local churches that would enable them to participate effectively and appropriately in the process of resettlement, and to begin to provide the type of community in which individuals suffering from mental health problems might find a valued place. This second task involved, among other things, dealing with issues of *advocacy* and *empowerment*. One of the tasks of the chaplain was to become an advocate for people with mental health problems and to facilitate the development of the role of advocate for others within the Christian community. For the reasons outlined previously, people with mental health problems are a particularly vulnerable group. It is easy for them to "lose their voices" within the public and private discourses that determine their life experiences. The chaplain, as the representative of the church—a sociopolitical, as well as a spiritual, institution that has a powerful public voice—was in a strong position to advocate on behalf of people with mental health problems and to speak out against exploitation and abuse at a personal and a social level. Likewise, an important task of the chaplain was to empower individuals to take control of their lives, to maintain enough confidence and self-esteem to be able to assert themselves constructively in social situations, and to develop positive forms of self-identity that would enable them to stand against the types of oppressive forces that have been highlighted.

Third, the task of the chaplain involved building up relationships with other agencies working in the community. This meant working in day centers, drop-in centers, and alongside organizations focusing on the rights of families and service users. In this way, relationships were developed and avenues opened which enabled people who might not normally have any contact with the Christian community (or any other religious community) to come into contact with it.

Chaplaincy and the Multidisciplinary Team

The CMHC functioned as part of a multidisciplinary rehabilitation team that consisted of various mental health professionals: a consultant psychiatrist, rehabilitation workers, community mental health nurses, social workers, occupational therapists, and ward nurses. Although this was a useful involvement, it was necessary to participate with caution. Though there were great benefits from being a part of such a team, the focus of the CMHC differed significantly from that of many other roles within the team. The chaplain's focus on spirituality, personal relationships, and the fact that his "professional boundaries" were often more fluid and less focused than those of many other professionals, meant that he often approached the care of people with mental health problems from a different perspective. This perspective prioritized the life experiences of people with mental health problems and focused on issues of *meaning* and *understanding* rather than *explanation* and *treatment*. While there was obvious potential for conflict and misunderstanding, the situation remained constructively balanced, as long as each member of the team was prepared to respect and listen to the perspective of the others.

From Care to Community

The chaplain's task was to act as a bridge between the hospital and the community. When a person was considered well enough to manage in the community, a person-centered care plan was developed, and the place and role of the chaplain within the overall care plan was negotiated.

The chaplain fulfilled his task with regard to the individual in two stages. To begin with, the CMHC developed a relationship with the individual while the person was still in the hospital, by spending time with him or her, working through difficulties and fears regarding the possible move, providing transportation to the hospital services, coming to understand him or her as a unique individual, and getting to know the ways in which the mental health problems affected the "patient" as a person. This stage was, at least ideally, marked by the development of a form of mutual acceptance that in itself was an important and therapeutic source of self-esteem for the individual.[5]

Once that relationship had been established, the task moved outside the boundaries of the hospital and into the community or, more specifically, the local church community. Over a period of time, the chaplain went with these individuals to a local church in the vicinity where they were to be resettled and gradually worked with them and the local congregation to enable each person to find a place within the Christian community. The church community was likewise helped to feel able to offer such a place. The main task at this stage was to enable each individual to find a congregation in which he or she felt comfortable, and to allow the church community to gain authentic understanding of the individual's needs by getting to know him or her in such a way that church members might be enabled to accept and understand any specific difficulties or peculiarities that such an individual might encounter. Within this context, the chaplain's long-term aim was to enable both congregation and sufferer to develop meaningful relationships, and in so doing, allow the chaplain to withdraw either completely or into a supervisory role.

The form the CMHC ministry took might best be described as an ongoing cycle of *introduction, education,* and *friendship enablement*—introduction of the individual to the church community (and vice versa) and education of both parties, which in turn facilitated integration and increased the possibilities for the development of acceptance and meaningful friendships. In this way, the CMHC developed a strong network of "bridges" between individuals who were leaving the hospital—individuals who were previously unknown to their local churches, but who were already in the community—along with the mental health professionals, the wider community, and, of course, the Christian community itself. The diagram below outlines the general network that the CMHC developed.

Within this model, the CMHC acted as a *key-worker* whose primary task was to enable the development of healthy interpersonal relationships between the individual suffering from mental health problems and the Christian community. At the center of this model is the CMHC, who might be described as a *friendship facilitator.*[6]

Once that network had been established, the CMHC began the process of introducing the individual to a particular church

The Basic Model

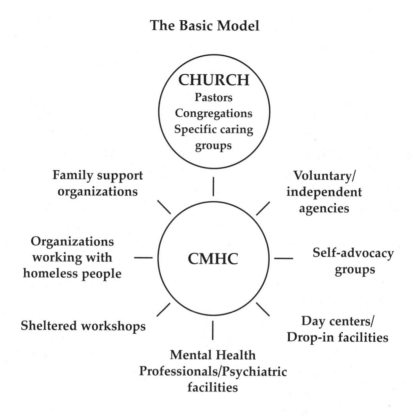

community that had been deemed appropriate for his or her needs. The decision as to which church was appropriate was made by the person who was moving out of the hospital, with the CMHC talking through the options with the individual in the light of the chaplain's own experience and knowledge of the local community churches. There was, therefore, a good deal of experimentation and moving from congregation to congregation, until a person eventually found a church community in which he or she felt comfortable and accepted. Gradually over a period of time, with the presence and support of the CMHC, the individual was introduced to the congregation, and the process of mutual "getting to know one another" began.

Enabling Friendship Formation

The need for friendships to be facilitated and enabled was absolutely crucial during the initial stages of the encounter between person and community. Within this context, the presence of the CMHC was very important. To draw an analogy from attachment theory, the CMHC provided a *secure base*[7] from which the individual was able to explore his new environment and discover the possibility of developing positive interpersonal relationships, and a subsequent new and more affirming self-identity.[8] This was often a difficult task. The inherent incomprehensibility of the person's illness experience, coupled with the inevitable difficulties of an institutionalized worldview—which often limits communicational ability due to its insularity and specialist-oriented regime—meant that often a person moving from hospital to community was severely lacking in appropriate communicational and relational skills. Therefore, it was vital that the CMHC provide a secure communicational and relational base from which the individual could explore the new landscape and to which the individual could return as he or she endeavored to learn the new skills of friendship-in-community.

Within this context, the CMHC also provided a similar "secure base" for the members of the congregation. One learns how to be friendly, and how to maintain one's friendships, in and through the process of experience and socialization. The need to learn friendship is even more pronounced when one is dealing with those who are, at times and in some ways, profoundly different. This is particularly so when that inherent difference is compounded by the socially constructed caricatured image of "the mental patient" and other frightening and highly negative media profiles. The church is a sociological as well as a spiritual entity and, as such, is very open to the adoption and assimilation of such negative societal attitudes. Congregations need to be educated, enabled, and supported if they are to overcome the "principle of likeness" and to embrace the "principle of grace."

From the perspective of the congregation, the presence of the CMHC with the person functioned on at least two levels. First, the CMHC's commitment to the individual seemed to make a strong statement to the congregation. In a very visible and tangible form, the relationship of the chaplain and these persons with the mental health problems physically manifested the church's response to the call to care for the "stranger." At first, the reaction was often along the lines of "I really admire you for being able to cope with 'these types of people,' but we could never do that ourselves." However, over a period of time, as the CMHC modeled the possibility of meaningful relationship, many people were able to move beyond their initially negative response and begin to embrace the possibility that friendship within the context of severe mental health problems was not impossible, nor primarily the task of the professional, but was potentially a powerful gift which that fellowship had to offer. The simple fact of the CMHC being with these persons and treating and communicating with them as full human beings, despite their sometimes bizarre speech and behavior, was a *crucial* step toward the breaking down of barriers and the overcoming of uncertainty in others. In showing solidarity with the person-as-person, the chaplain became "a tool of liberation" for both the congregation and the person with the mental health problem. The chaplain's relational bond of friendship very clearly imaged God's relationship with the person, and in so doing, helped to resurrect and sustain the humanity of the sufferers in the eyes of themselves and others. In showing solidarity-in-friendship with the person, the CMHC enabled others within the congregation to reframe their ideas. Instead of being someone for whom they must find ways of caring, or coping with, the person was reframed as someone who had human needs similar to their own, a real person, who desires to relate and who could be related to.

Second, as well as providing a secure base for both person and congregation, the presence of the chaplain with the individual also created a *safe* environment for both parties. This seemed to be particularly important from the perspective of the congregation. People suffering from the more incomprehensible manifestations of schizophrenia or bipolar disorder can be very different, bizarre, and occasionally, quite frightening. There was, therefore, a need to create what one might describe as an "experimental space" for the congregation, within which they could begin to develop an understanding of the persons, and find the confidence to relate to them, however tentative that initial encounter might be. At the same time, the creation of such a safe space enabled them to retain feelings of security, safe in the knowledge that there was someone there who cared for the person, but perhaps more important, someone who was, or at least was perceived as being, in *control*. One of the most common reactions when one experiences delusional talk and bizarre behavior is a deep inner sense of *chaos*. Stewart Govig conceptualizes this experience of chaos thus: "To me mental illness carries an ultimate: it hints at the yawning, formless void present at the beginning before God's wind swept over and brought light to original disorder (Genesis 1:1-3)."[9] The supporting presence of the CMHC provided at least the illusion of control and, in a sense, physically represented the peace and light of God in the midst of what appears to be dark chaos. In so doing, the CMHC enabled the possibility of developing understanding and tolerance by "protecting" both parties from the negative effects of their mutual confusion and uncertainty. In this way, the CMHC, as a secure base, was able to offer stability, safety, and the opportunity for the growth and interrelating of both parties. By offering encouragement and friendship to both parties, the CMHC was able to enable relationships between them, thus providing the relational context for the development of Christlike friendships and the overcoming of the "principle of likeness." Through regularly being with the individuals within the context of the church community, the CMHC provided a means of breaking down unnecessary barriers of miscommunication regarding the nature of persons who live with mental health problems, and allowed the congregation to come to know the persons behind the illness. In so doing, the chaplain became a catalyst which enabled the development of meaningful, liberating friendships.

Developing Trust, Encountering "Strangers"

In the earlier discussion on friendship formation, it was noted that people tend to befriend those with whom they have regular contact. Even if they are quite different in many respects, there is a tendency to come to like someone simply as a result of having regular personal contact. This was certainly the case within the experience of many congregations. While apprehensive prior to meeting an individual with a mental health problem, many people, but not all, began to discover that they were able to relate at a meaningful level simply by regularly coming into contact with someone living with the person with a mental health problem. What became clear, as this model was worked out within a number of congregations, was that it was not anything that the congregation *did* that enabled the development of friendship. It was more what it was prepared to *be* that was crucial—whether it was open, welcoming, tolerant, committed, and prepared to struggle with the difficult issues that occasionally arose. What was important was whether the community had absorbed the gospel *intrinsically* and sought to live that narrative out in its life and practice, or whether it understood the biblical narrative *extrinsically* and sought to live out its existence as a closed community that, while being safe from "intruders," was not necessarily faithful. In a sense, the person with the mental health problem could be understood as functioning as a form of "judgment" on the community, in that the presence of someone in this situation truly tested the authenticity and commitment of that community.[10]

David's Story: Learning to Care in Community

The following case study will help to illustrate some of the ways in which this model worked out in practice.

The CMHC first encountered David when he was an inpatient in a rehabilitation ward within the psychiatric hospital in which the CMHC was based. David was a twenty-two-year-old man who had had a serious mental health problem since he was twelve years old. Due to a disturbed family background, he had been in a children's home since he was eight years old. He had been diagnosed as having a severe mental health problem at the age of twelve, and had been in and out of psychiatric hospitals with varying degrees of regularity since that initial diagnosis. David's condition was cyclical, and there were long periods of lucidity during which he could lead a more or less normal life, although he was often impaired, to varying degrees, by the side effects of his medication. Primarily this manifested itself in tiredness, lethargy, a fine tremor of his hands, and reduced sexual libido. During the periods when he was not experiencing the acute symptoms of his condition, he was a very affable young man with a quick wit and a warm and often quite charming personality.

David had always had an interest in religion, and some of his delusional and hallucinatory experiences incorporated religious material. For example, he claimed he frequently saw Jesus, and occasionally heard the voice of God telling him to carry out particular tasks. He was, in his own words, "a very religious person." This being so, he was very interested in spending time with the chaplain, and over a period of some months, the two of them developed a good relationship. Despite the occasional distortions and exaggerations of his religious experience, it was obvious that David's faith was not simply a manifestation of psychopathology, but was in fact an important and meaningful part of his life.

On his first encounter with the chaplain, David was highly delusional and hallucinated almost constantly. In time, helped greatly by the use of atypical medication, David's symptoms were brought under control and the rehabilitation team deemed it appropriate for him to be discharged into the community. He was subsequently discharged into supervised private accommodation. Prior to discharge he had made a specific request for the chaplain to retain contact with him. While in the hospital, David had resisted any attempts to encourage him to develop contacts with a church outside the hospital, but on discharge he asked for assistance in finding a suitable church.

Initially the CMHC visited David in his new home on a regular basis in order to strengthen and reestablish the relationship outside the context of the hospital. With David's permission the CMHC, in confidence, contacted the minister of the local church, explained David's position, and talked through some of the specific needs he might have, such as unfamiliarity with "rules" of the church environment, difficulties with socialization, and poor concentration. The minister, although apprehensive and uncertain whether the church had the resources to deal with "these people," nevertheless was reasonably enthusiastic and prepared to help at whatever level was deemed necessary.

After three weeks of regular contact in David's new accommodation, the CMHC began to introduce him to the church community. The particular church that they attended was an open and relatively informal community that had a reasonably welcoming atmosphere. The initial encounters between the church and David were tentative on both sides. David, while keen and excited (sometimes inappropriately so) at being there, was at times strange, distant, and unpredictable. His contributions both on a personal and a public level were sometimes inappropriate, and his frankness concerning his sexual difficulties could be embarrassing and was undoubtedly off-putting for some within the congregation. David's concentration span was also somewhat limited, which meant that he tended to walk out of the service when he got bored and to re-enter at times that were often inappropriate, such as during times of silence and prayer. However, despite this, most of the congregation remained tolerant and keen for him to remain, although they needed reassurance and support from the CMHC.

David also attended a midweek Bible study, accompanied by the CMHC, in a small group setting that in many ways suited him better than the larger setting of the Sunday service. Within that context, people began to get to know David as a person. After a few weeks of settling in time within the small group he began to relate some of his life story. This was not always appropriate or beneficial to either David or the group. It was necessary at times for the CMHC to suggest to David that in the interest of his own confidentiality it might be best not to divulge certain information. Part of the difficulty that David encountered within this setting was the problem caused by institutionalization and poor boundary definition. In an institutional setting there are very often no, or very blurred, boundaries of acceptability in terms of what should or should not be said, or what is appropriate or inappropriate behavior in a specific situation. By gently restraining and correcting David's self-narratives, the CMHC was not acting in a paternalistic fashion, but was in fact helping him learn the art of friendship formation by enabling him to define and learn the importance of boundaries in the formation and maintenance of interpersonal relationships. The CMHC facilitated this process and in so doing opened the possibility for appropriate relationship and non-exploitative friendship.

In time, some members of the group began to respond very positively to David. They came to understand him as a person who, while at times almost completely obscured by a particularly unpleasant mental health problem, was at other times a person who not only needed to be cared for, but who cared for them and enjoyed their company. As David, within the safety of that group, for the first time began to develop friendships and encounter the acceptance of these relationships, so in a subtle way, his self-image began to alter. In his initial encounters he described himself as a "mental patient," partly because he was slightly mischievous and well aware of the kinds of reactions that such a statement could arouse, and partly because that is the particular social identity that had been bestowed upon him in his institutionalized life history up to that point.

In his initial encounters with the group, the primary focus of his conversation pertained to life within a psychiatric institution. Although his life chances had been potentially deepened and widened, they were still narrowed by his psychological attachment to the institution and his self-perception as a "mental patient." However, as he experienced the acceptance and comfort of the group, so his language began to change. Gradually he began to speak in the third person about "his illness" and how it had stopped him doing many of the things he had wanted to do in his life. He also began to speak about what was happening to him now and the hopes he had for the present and the future, rather than dwelling on what had happened in the past and the limitations caused by his mental health problem. In his self-perception and in the perception of the group members, the difference between person and illness slowly became a reality, with concomitant benefits and reframing of "illness to person" for both David and the group.

Neither David nor the group had an instant "Damascus road" type conversion in their understanding and perception. What happened was that through regular (initially guided) interaction, the two began to see each other and themselves differently and came to realize that they shared a common faith and a common humanity. As both parties' perceptions of the other and of themselves began to change, so also did their attitudes toward one another. Thus, by simply being with David in personal encounter the members of that group were enabled to work through their own prejudices and stigmatizing ideas, and begin to develop their relationships with him in a context of authentic personhood, rather than stereotypical illness images. In this way, as Gutiérrez has suggested, through gestures and ways of "being with" that some may regard as having little political effectiveness, liberation from oppressive self and social identity was achieved.[11]

Developing Friendships

In time, David developed solid friendships with certain members of the church community. Initially this involved offers to pick him up from his home and take him to church. However, as people grew more confident, so the scope of their friendships increased. One friend occasionally took David to soccer matches (David's poor concentration made this a difficult enterprize, which petered out after two partially unsuccessful attempts). Another met him regularly once every two weeks for coffee, and continued to do so for some six months before David left the church. This limited and bounded aspect of the friendship relationship, of course, marks it out from other relationships, in particular kinship relations. What was offered by the community was not constant companionship, but a relationship which, while demanding the commitment of both parties, had fixed boundaries and could be as intimate or as casual as either or both parties desired.

Breznitz, in his discussion on the therapeutic significance of hope, describes hope as a "protected area,"[12] a small area of experience that still maintains its positive features when everything else around it is threatening, "a small island of peace surrounded by storms and disasters."[13] This definition sums up the role of friendship within the context of caring for David. The church community in general (particularly in the small group setting) and those who made the effort to befriend David provided a protected area within which he could negotiate his new position. Even amidst the storms of his illness, the knowledge of that protected space held him and opened up hopeful possibilities for breaking the ongoing cycle of *withdrawal* and *return,* and the need for *forgiveness* and *acceptance* that marked his experience of mental health problems.

The key in this case was the inspiration of hope, both in David and in the congregation. Such inspiration of hope came from the development of understanding through personal encounter.[14]

Breakdown and Disconnection

Once David's relationships had begun to develop within the church community, gradually over a period of six months of regular contact, the CMHC was able to withdraw, although he remained a potential resource for both David and the church. Responsibility for David was then placed into the hands of the church community.

The course of David's encounter was not a smooth one. There were times when he was highly disturbed and had to leave church or group because of the disruption he was causing. This caused serious difficulties within the context of the main service, where a number of the congregation became quite hostile to his continuing presence. However, this was not the case in the smaller group, where people actually *knew* David and had begun to understand the true nature of his condition. Because this group of people within the congregation knew him, and through their encounter with him had come to know and respect him as a person, there was always a place for him when he returned to the church community after a period of disturbance. Importantly, as the CMHC's initial relationship had modeled the possibility of friendship and acceptance, so also those who had befriended David advocated on his behalf, and modeled the possibility of friendship to those who did not understand or were not prepared to tolerate David's speech or behavior. The small group's prophetic solidarity with David helped overcome the opposition to his presence that was expressed by some people within the congregation. Their own commitment and tenacity bore witness to the deeper meaning of fellowship that was missed by those who really did not understand the prophetic significance of what was going on.

After several months in this particular congregation, David decided that it was not the place for him, primarily because he had developed paranoid delusions that focused around the minister. Halfway through a service one Sunday evening he left, and never went back. At the time of writing, the CMHC is currently beginning the process of enabling David to find a place within the community of another church.

Reflection on the Model as it Worked out in Practice

This case study is helpful in that it illustrates both the joys and the difficulties of the ministry of friendship within the context of caring for people living with severe mental health problems. First, it clearly shows some of the ways in which the model of friendship can be implemented, and how in a relatively nonthreatening way the church community can be encouraged and enabled to liberate itself from its fears and false assumptions, and participate in the liberation of people with mental health problems. Negatively, it highlights some of the difficulties and pitfalls that are inherent in caring for persons with severe forms of mental health problems. Some in the church community will accept these persons, while others will reject them. There is a real possibility of friction and division, even if this form of ministry is carried out in a sensitive and considerate manner.

Second, because of the nature of the illness, there is always the possibility that the offer of friendship will be rejected. Church communities who are willing to offer such friendships must be prepared for disappointment, hurt, and rejection. The flipside of love and genuine caring is anxiety, pain, suffering, and the possibility of rejection. The concept of friendship based on the friendships of Jesus has certain messianic overtones that relate to issues of suffering and sacrifice. In striving to care for those with severe mental health problems, these themes can often be very much to the fore. These are inevitable, if at times upsetting, aspects of the practice of Christlike friendship. This is an important point to bear in mind. If the church is to engage in this type of relationship, then it must provide ways of supporting the befriender through the ups and downs of potentially difficult relationships of friendship.

The Significance of Hope

One of the main things that this system of care accomplishes is the inspiration of *hope*, both in the person suffering from a mental health problem and within the church community. In learning to understand David as a person, the church community was enabled to develop the hope and the expectation that it *could* in fact "deal" with "these people" and that, despite initial hesitations, it had something very special to offer in its gift of friendship and acceptance. Even though David ultimately rejected the friendship that the congregation offered to him (which, of course, was his prerogative), in the process of developing that friendship the congregation was liber-ated, empowered, and enabled to gain confidence, and to attain the hope of offering friendship to others in David's similar situations in the future. Equally important, David's encounter with the church community enabled him to discover hope in the midst of what was often a profoundly hopeless existence. It may well be that his relational history will consist of a string of broken friendships and itinerant connections with a number of Christian communities. However, his encounter with this particular community-of-friends opened up the possibility that *it does not have to be that way*, that perhaps he had more control over his life than he previously thought, and that he was in fact someone who was capable of relating and someone to whom someone else might wish to relate. Where there are friends there is hope. Where there is hope there are possibilities. If the wider church can implement strategies such as have been outlined here, and if it can find the forgiveness and acceptance necessary to welcome persons back even after they have rejected the community and offended or even despised individuals within it, then it should always be possible for someone like David to find a spiritual home and meaningful health-bringing friendships. Through the comforting presence of friends mental health problems can be reconceptualized, and the meanings ascribed to them radically redefined by both parties. Impossibility gives way to possibility, hopelessness is transformed into hope, and negative self-esteem is nurtured into a more positive self-perception. There may still be irreparable damage or loss, but that is not the end of the story. Through the gift of friendship, new and quite different chapters of a person's life can be written and the possibility of a hopeful future carved out and presented as a possible conclusion.

Chapter 10

Creating a Context for Care

Understanding and Overcoming
Congregational Resistance

At the heart of this form of ministry lies the struggle to create an atmosphere of acceptance, respect, and understanding within Christian communities. The successful implementation of a program such as the one being described here is wholly dependent on the cooperation of the church community and its willingness to offer time and resources. If, as has been suggested, "understanding is therapy," and if the church community is to be perceived as an open place of meeting, dialogue, and storytelling, then the development of such an environment is absolutely crucial. In my discussions with various agencies that deal with people with mental health problems, the consensus is that if friendship development is going to work in the ways in which this book suggests, an appropriate context must first be developed. The creation of an atmosphere of acceptance and respect is an absolute prerequisite for the development of meaningful, liberating friendships.

One aspect highlighted in the previous case study was the possibility of confusion, lack of understanding, and various forms of resistance from within a congregation. The very mention of the phrase "mental illness" can bring quite mixed responses from a congregation. The following vignette is not untypical of the attitude of many congregations to the presence of persons suffering from severe mental health problems in their midst.

The CMHC was contacted regarding some problems an inner-city church was having with what they described as: "ex-mental patients." The church was running lunch clubs and mid-day prayer meetings, and people with varying degrees of mental health problems were coming along and "disrupting" the prayer meeting. The church leaders felt that, as a congregation, they did not have the necessary expertise to deal with "these types of people," nor did they have the skills or resources to *do* anything for people "like them." In other words, they didn't feel equipped for this type of ministry. Their solution was that the CMHC should look at ways of arranging a "service of worship for the mentally ill," which "these people" could go to. This would enable the church to carry on their prayer and worship without any unnecessary disruption.

This was an unfortunate reaction to what is a not uncommon situation.[1] These "ex-mental patients," were indeed people with some history of mental health problems, but many of them had been living very happily in the community for up to ten years! Despite this, the church's attitude appears to have been, "once a mental patient, always a mental patient!" Rather than taking the time to get to know these people as people first, the congregation reacted according to certain preconceived stereotypes, which caused it to act on assumptions that were at best inaccurate, and at worst destructively ignorant.

It would appear that the stigmatizing attitudes and stereotyped assumptions that are so destructively prevalent within society are also present within the church. "Religious communities are subject to the same misunderstandings, fears, myths, and prejudices as the general public. The stigma attached to mental illness will prevail until people are educated otherwise."[2] The assumption was that this church had nothing to offer people with mental health problems. "These people" were automatically deemed to be the responsibility of the mental health professionals, and therefore the church assumed that it did not have any direct responsibility for them. This attitude spilled over into the realms of their understanding of how best to care for the spiritual needs of people with mental health problems. Once again the congregation presumed that these individuals had special needs that could be met only by the "specialist," this time in the form of the CMHC. The congregational resistance within this situation sprang from the fact that the congregation was fundamentally uninformed about mental health problems and the real, as opposed to the perceived, needs of people who live with them.

Creating and Sustaining Liberating Friendships: Education, Support, and Supervision

All of this would strongly suggest that *education* and genuine *encounter* are of fundamental importance in overcoming congregational resistance and facilitating meaningful friendships. In our previous discussions on the nature of friendship, it was argued that the type of friendships that resemble those of Jesus do not arise naturally from normal social encounters. Rather, forms of friendship that seek to move beyond natural attraction to embrace those who are often considered "strangers" need to be nurtured. Appropriate education is a central component to this process of friendship enablement. Education breaks down barriers for both sufferer and carer, and enables them to see the situation as it is, and not as they think it might be or should be, according to particular stereotyped ideas and understandings. However, precisely what is meant by the term "education" needs to be clarified.

Education and the Reframing of Illness Experience

At one level, such education pertains to the educating of people with mental health problems about the complexities of their conditions. Kirkpatrick and her coauthors in their research on schizophrenia found that "the importance of education for the client about the illness was not limited to symptoms and symptom control. Rather the schizophrenia was put in a framework for recovery, that is, letting people know that in spite of what is a fairly disabling mental illness, many people do go on to have fulfilling lives."[3] Thus, from the perspective of persons experiencing mental health problems, education with regard to coping with their problems and discovering the possibility of a hopeful future is central to the process of opening up new possibilities for the development of mental health. If one reflects upon David's experience of the church community, one can see the way in which the acceptance and friendship of people within the congregation enabled him to *begin* to alter his self-definition from *illness* to *person*. This was shown not to be a miracle cure, but rather the beginning of a process that may or may not find its final fulfillment. Yet, it is always worthwhile, for it enables a person to move toward mental health and the constructive realization of his or her personhood. A vital pastoral task will be to participate in the process of educating sufferers concerning the possibilities they still have for their lives, and the importance of developing respect for their personhood and relationships. Robert Coursey pertinently observes that persons with mental health problems "need help to gain perspective on it, education about the illness, familiarity with their symptoms and what makes them come and go and some ability to separate a sense of self from illness."[4] Education therefore demands the cooperation and participation of both the mental health professionals and those in the community who are willing to offer meaningful relationships that can constructively participate in the process of reframing the illness experiences of people with mental health problems.

Educating Congregations

At another level, education has to do with raising the consciousness of congregations to the situations of people with mental health problems and enabling an effective response. The previous vignette concerning the exclusive nature of some church communities showed clearly the need for congregations to be educated on matters of mental health and mental health care before they can effectively be friends.

How might a congregation best be educated in mental health issues in order that congregational resistance can be eased or even overcome? The most appropriate form of education within the Christian community is *interpersonal encounter*, and the most appropriate people to educate the community-of-friends on the experience of mental health problems are those who have mental health problems.[5] This was certainly the case in David's situation, where members of the congregation came to a very deep and intimate understanding of the nature of his mental health problem. They did this not by reading textbooks and recognizing symptoms, but by persevering with and learning to love a fellow human being who was struggling amidst the most unimaginable storms. The complex social, psychological, and spiritual reality of mental health problems means that only those who experience them can truly express what it means to live with them. It is therefore only through meeting people experiencing mental health problems and sharing with them in their experiences that people can truly become educated. Thus, education and friendship are seen to be inextricably intertwined. In order to be a friend it is necessary to be educated, but in order to be educated, it is necessary to take that first step toward friendship. Commitment to people with mental health problems, and a willingness to commune with them in critical solidarity is fundamentally an educational process within which there is a mutual and simultaneous exchange of information, experience, and friendship.

It would, however, be somewhat naive to suggest that in order for a person suffering from a mental health problem to be accepted and befriended, and a congregation successfully educated, all they have to do is to turn up at church! The ministry of education and enablement needs to be carried out sensitively and thoughtfully if it is to have any hope of taking root within a congregation. We might divide education into two models, both of which are different, but both of which are necessary for effective education.

Introducing the Person

The first model works on the premise that the most effective way of educating a congregation on the nature and experience of mental health problems is by inviting someone who has personal experience of such problems to come and tell his or her story. A person who is prepared to do this may well have to be supported, perhaps by a carer or a concerned other, as this can be a stressful situation for someone to be put into. Alternatively, a representative or representatives from local self-advocacy groups can be invited to talk about the experience of mental health problems, the ways in which they affect people's lives, and the types of responses that the church community might effectively offer. It is, of course, true that a large group situation may well be too threatening for some people. However, it is possible to structure such sessions so that the work can be done within small groups, which, as with David, are often more conducive to the development of a nonthreatening, accepting atmosphere. The important thing is that congregations be exposed to the lived experience of mental health problems, rather than a set of disembodied signs and symptoms that might be presented within a more formal academic setting. This personal approach to education has major advantages over a "classroom based approach." In terms of overcoming stereotyping and stigma, it allows the church community to experience firsthand the humanity of the sufferer. Instead of working according to ill-informed preconceived ideas, or vague, impersonal textbook definitions, the congregation is given the opportunity actually to share in the experiences of the other and, in so doing, to move toward the creation of an environment of acceptance and understanding. The individual is also given the chance to meet with a group of people who are genuinely interested in sharing his experience and learning more about his or her life experiences. In this way barriers can be broken down on both sides and a "clearing" can be hewn in which meaningful personal relationships might become a possibility. The important thing is that this form of education be both *personal* and *relational*, focusing on the person as person rather than the person as illness.[6]

Education as Empowerment

One great advantage of the form of education that is being discussed here is that it is a potential source of *empowerment* for a group of people who, as has been shown, often find themselves disempowered. The United Kingdom government document "Creating Community Care" makes the following statement:

> Most adults take for granted an expectation of respect and trust, a sense that their views will be listened to and their needs met with a sense of dignity. People with severe mental illness do not always share this experience and this results in enormous frustration. Whatever the nature of their illness, people with severe mental illness should be viewed first and foremost as individuals whose views should be taken seriously.[7]

Taking seriously the views of people with mental health problems may be the ideal, yet for the reasons discussed in this book, the reality is frequently quite different. As Pilgrim and Waldron point out, people with mental health problems lack *social credibili-*

ty.[8] In other words, the credibility of anything they say can very easily be destroyed by assumptions that it is nothing but the product of their illness experience. This form of discrediting is a significant part of people's daily lives, and it is also a significant part of their spiritual lives. Particularly for people who have delusionary or hallucinatory experiences, the discrediting and pathologizing of their faith and religious experiences is common. This is a point that will be addressed more fully later in this chapter. For now, it is enough to note that the lack of social credibility is a highly significant part of every aspect of the lives of people with mental health problems.

This being so, empowerment will have to do with enabling sufferers to find ways of gaining and maintaining enough self-confidence to enable them to retain a degree of control over their lives, also of enabling others to treat their opinions with respect and genuine concern. This has been done by mental health professionals by enabling people with mental health problems to participate in their own treatment programs and to be a part of the decisions that are made concerning their lives. Pilgrim and Waldron in their research into user involvement in mental health service provision carried out research where

> service users were encouraged to give opinions on service development and become active negotiators of change. To carry out the negotiations required the service users to become active and develop new skills. This included negotiating with professional managers by letter, phone and face to face. The group also had to develop co-operation among themselves. They needed to review their progress and decide on strategies and tactics. Questions of democracy and autonomy arose within the group itself. This led to the members of the user group being valued and respected by the researchers and by health and social services managers. They had become empowered, which along the way had also improved their self esteem and self worth.[9]

It is possible to transfer the general ethos of such an approach into the church setting and use it as part of the church's educational strategies. Empowerment has to do with the enabling of competencies that will allow individuals and communities to gain control over their lives.[10] While the model of friendship presented in this book is in itself an arena for empowerment—in that it provides a context for the development of positive selfûimages and relational competence—empowering relationship, the method of education we are exploring in this chapter, also has the potential to be a powerful source of consciousness raising and empowerment. The church, as a community of remembering and storytelling, can provide a public forum within which an individual or individuals can tell their stories in all their fullness. By listening to these stories of dangerous memories, the church community is thereby enabled to offer healing nurture to these broken individuals and, in so doing, connect with the heart of the church's own identity, which shapes its mission. In being enabled to tell their stories and in recognizing that they are listened to and respected, people with mental health problems can begin to explore the possibility that they are valued and that their stories are worthy of being listened to. When people with mental health problems are provided a platform from which they can share their experiences and enable others to come to an understanding that seeks not only to explain mental health problems but also to understand what it means to live with them, their views can be taken seriously and disempowerment considerably lessened.

Such an educational strategy also empowers the congregation. Ryles notes that "the true consequence of empowerment is . . . the development of competencies that allow people and communities to gain control over their lives. This can only be achieved by recognizing those forces that conspire to limit the scope of those lives . . . and then acting to effect change."[11]

Genuine empowerment can be enabled only when the consciousness of individuals and communities is raised to recognize the forces that conspire to disempower and limit the lives of significant sections of that community. When the congregation listens to the stories of people with mental health problems, collective consciousness can be raised and their memories jogged about the types of disempowering experiences that are being encountered on a daily basis by people with mental health problems. In listening, the community is empowered to stand with those who are being oppressed, and in so doing, to become the church in a faithful sense. In remembering, the community is called into relationships of critical solidarity that find their embodiment in committed friendship. In this way, through the process of education-through-encounter, consciousness is raised, individuals and communities can be empowered, and the eradication of ignorance and fear and of moving toward liberation is initiated.

Advocacy

Closely connected to issues of empowerment is advocacy, particularly the role of the chaplain, congregations, and friends as advocates for people with mental health problems. We have already explored some of the ways in which people with mental health problems are disempowered, oppressed, and discriminated against. Empowering people to take control of their own lives is a vital aspect of the model of care being presented here, yet there is also a need for others to take a stand against the things that depersonalize and damage the lives of people with mental health problems. Put simply, an advocate is one who pleads another's cause and who helps others by defending or comforting them. An advocate is someone who cares for others so deeply that he or she is willing to stand up for them in the face of oppressive forces that seek to harm those who, for whatever reason, are vulnerable.

Advocacy and Prophecy

It is interesting to compare the role of advocate with the role of the prophet.

> Prophets speak new truths to situations that are exhibiting injustice, or systems that have lost their way and are now functioning in a way that is a fundamental distortion of their original intention. The prophet recognises the weakest and most vulnerable within a community and takes a public stance against injustices that are perpetrated against them by unjust individuals and/or systems. Prophets recognise the personhood of the weak and adopt a powerful stance as advocate for the needy.[12]

The role of the advocate and the role of the prophet are deeply interconnected. Like the prophet, the advocate seeks to speak God's word into situations of injustice and oppression and, in so doing, move toward a form of transformation that reflects the will of God. Thus, in adopting a stance that seeks to defend those who have been made vulnerable by the attitudes and values of society and bring comfort to those whose hearts have been broken by the ravages of their life experiences, Christlike friends take on the role of advocate and prophet. Both roles are fundamental for a truly liberating church.

"Advocacy is about defining and fighting for citizens' rights, particularly those citizens who have had their rights devalued by a particular system. . . . Its aim is to ensure a better quality of life."[13] Advocates can be concerned citizens, mental health professionals, family members, friends, political organizations, individuals or groups of people with mental health problems, or any other interested parties who are not prepared to stand back and allow injustice to be perpetrated on vulnerable individuals or families. Advocates function on either an interpersonal or a political level and attempt to speak up on behalf of individuals or groups when others either cannot or will not intervene.

Defending the "Weak"

The dual role of the advocate to defend and to comfort is very important. For present purposes, it will be helpful to separate the two, although in reality they are inextricably intertwined. The Christian community as a liberating community of friends, is, by definition, called to a ministry of liberation that demands critical solidarity with those within society who may be vulnerable to the types of oppression that have been examined within this book. On a personal level this means entering into Christlike friendships with people who have mental health problems and working with them to bring about the Resurrection of people whose very personhood is called into question by the ways in which society is structured and the particular sets of values and expectations it chooses to prioritize. However, at a wider social and political level, if the problems that have been highlighted thus far are to be addressed at a macro-level, then the Christian community will have to think through the political implications of its critical solidarity with people who have mental health problems. The specific focus of this book precludes the possibility of exploring the dynamics of politically oriented pastoral care. It is nonetheless necessary to highlight the significance of such an approach for effective advocacy and liberating care. Conscientization without action is a contradiction in terms. Once people's consciousness has been raised through the types of educational strategies that have been outlined within this chapter, the revisioned community will have no option other than to become actively involved in critically addressing issues of poverty, oppression, and injustice wherever they are encountered. This action will have both an internal and an external dynamic. The internal dynamic will demand, for example, that congregations take a firm stand against stigmatization and offensive language as they emerge within the church community. The Christian community must learn "people first" language, such as referring to "a person with schizophrenia," not "a schizophrenic."[14] It must also create an atmosphere within which issues of mental health can be freely discussed, and people with mental health problems and their families can be at ease, even when things are difficult for all parties. This will involve educational programs such as those described here; and it will also require such things as positive preaching on issues of mental health, and Bible teaching that seeks seriously to address the reality of mental health problems.

The internal dynamic of advocacy will seek to work with others to create an atmosphere within which it is safe for people to tell their stories without guilt or fear of rejection. Such advocacy involves creating an atmosphere within which people with mental health problems can be incorporated into public worship, even if this means tolerating some degree of disruption at times. Thinking back to David's story, the small group acted as advocates for David in the face of discomfort and rejection from certain sections of the church. It was their advocacy that enabled David to remain a part of the wider worshiping community, and to participate with the whole church community in the worship of God. This type of advocacy within the Christian community will meet with resistance and may at times place the advocate at odds with the community as a whole. However, such rejection of those who stand in solidarity with the oppressed by religious authorities is not without good precedent! Both the prophets and Jesus himself paid a heavy price for their stance toward religious communities over issues that are not dissimilar to the ones under discussion here. To be an advocate within the church community is a dangerous business, but it reveals the heart of the coming kingdom of God.

The Politics of Advocacy

However, advocacy demands more than simply a change in the attitudes and structures of the Christian community. As well as an internal dynamic, the ministry of advocacy has a vital external dynamic that focuses on issues at the sociopolitical level. Despite the apparent decline in institutional religion, Christian commu-nities still retain a potentially powerful political voice. As such, they are in a position to take a solid stand against aspects of policy, practice, and public attitudes that may be causing harm to people with mental health problems and their families. The task of the Christian community is to use this voice effectively and appropriately. Adopting a stance of solidarity-in-advocacy will mean for example, taking a proactive stance against offensive media images that seek to stereotype and humiliate people with mental health problems. It will mean ensuring that congregations are effectively educated regarding mental health issues. But it will also mean pushing for similar educational strategies in significant educational establishments in the community. Local schools, colleges, and particularly seminaries and universities that are training the clergy, must be encouraged to emphasize issues of disability and mental health problems.

While the church does have a powerful public voice, it cannot advocate effectively on its own. It needs to learn to network with other organizations that have goals similar to its own. To advocate effectively with and on behalf of people with mental health problems, the church must involve itself with other organizations that are seeking after the rights of people with mental health problems and their families. Family-oriented organizations such as the National Alliance for the Mentally Ill in the United States or the National Schizophrenia Fellowship in Great Britain provide organizational networks that seek to further the rights of families, and work at both the interpersonal and the political levels to bring about changes in policy and attitudes that will improve the quality of life of people with mental health problems and their families. Similar networking can be developed with self-advocacy groups that have been formed by people with mental health problems with the specific purpose of working toward the eradication of the prejudice, discrimination, and injustice that mark the lives of so many people. Such groups work on a community and a political level, and seek to address issues of oppression and injustice in all of its fullness. Linking with such organizations allows church communities to experience and work alongside people with mental health problems and their families, toward a common purpose. All of this effort contributes to the process of liberatory education and the development of the role of advocate.

Comforting the Brokenhearted

As well as publicly defending those who are vulnerable, the advocate has another role. Think back to Jan's story that was presented earlier in the book, and remember the way in which she was excluded from the protection of the legal system. There was a dynamic within that situation that was not highlighted in the initial discussion. Throughout her ordeal, Jan was supported and cared for by a young woman who had befriended her during the weeks and months leading up to her altercation with the legal system. This young woman stood with Jan, helped her negotiate the complexities of the legal system, and sat with her in the midst of her brokenness as the whole thing fell apart. She became Jan's comforter, an advocate for her humanity when it appeared that the powers of the legal system were determined to strip that from her. Her faithful presence enabled Jan to find a degree of hope in what, for her, was a profoundly hopeless situation. The woman's critical solidarity with Jan was a powerful affirmation of Jan's self-worth and a powerful statement that she did not stand alone against the system.

To be an advocate has to do not only with actively standing against systems of injustice and oppressive social structures, it has to do also with coming alongside and comforting those who are injured by such systems. Friendship is by nature "advocating." The fact that it exists at all is a powerful statement to the world that people are of worth and that the way things are is not the way things have to be. To care and to offer comfort to another in their brokenness is to advocate on behalf of the humanity of the broken-hearted. To care in such ways is to image the one who "consoles us in all our affliction, so that we may be able to console those who are in any affliction with the consolation with which we ourselves are consoled by God" (2 Corinthians 1:4).

Advocacy as a Ministry of Reminding

A primary role of the advocate is to remind the Christian community and society at large that people with mental health problems exist, that they are worthy of being remembered, and that the church has something constructive to offer to their care. This ministry of remembrance can be brought into existence through the educational strategies that have been put forward in this chapter, and by engaging in the type of networking that was highlighted in the initial CMHC model. The task of the advocate is to gain a critical awareness of what is going on within the vicinity of the congregation, and to inform and urge the congregation into liberating forms of praxis.

Remembering People with Dementia

Let us take the example of people with dementia. We have already discussed some of the fundamental misunderstandings that exist surrounding dementia and the life experiences of people with this condition. Those who have worked within the area of dementia care will be familiar with the phenomenon of "dead people" being "resurrected" within a service of worship. Jimmy's story, presented previously, is a very good example of this form of resurrection. I have been struck by the way in which individuals who usually have little, if any, communication with others, and who do not respond to anything around them, are suddenly sparked into life by a hymn or the Lord's Prayer. If one takes seriously Kitwood's observations about the nature of the brain and the hidden possibilities that are contained within the "shells" of those who are "missing, presumed dead," then one cannot attribute such responses simply to residual memory. The act of worship is a deep and mysterious activity that reaches beyond our cognitive sensibilities and touches those regions of human experience where the "Spirit helps us in our weakness. . . [and] intercedes with sighs too deep for words" (Romans 8:26). The act of worship stands at the heart of what the church is and how it is called to function in the world. This being so, the church as a worshiping community has the potential to play a vital part in the spiritual resurrection of people with dementia through the gifts of praise, worship, and sacrificial friendship.

The task of the advocate is to remind congregations that people with dementia exist within their communities, in nursing homes, sheltered housing, with families, and that they exist as real and full persons who have very specific needs. The advocate reminds the Christian community that it is the task of the church to provide a context within which the Spirit can be allowed to work the ways of mystery and resurrection. This will mean reaching out in worship and friendship into those places within our communities where people with dementia live out their lives. It will mean offering resurrecting friendships to carers and cared for in order that new possibilities can be considered and fresh vistas of hope opened up. It will mean committing ourselves to regular services of worship, regular visiting, and a stance of critical and moral solidarity with those whom the world often forgets, and who often forget the world. In this way, the advocate, in raising the consciousness of Christian communities to the realities of what is going on around them, carries out a vital ministry. The advocate provides gentle avenues of hope and encouragement for people with dementia and their families, avenues through which the possibility of resurrection and hope can be made concrete and the challenge to be with the oppressed accepted in love.

Such a ministry is difficult and costly. To offer friendship to those who may not be able to reciprocate it, and who in fact may well forget who you are in the midst of your encounters, is a hard task. Yet, such freely given and costly commitment to vulnerable people is the stuff of the coming kingdom. To stand in solidarity with families whose loved ones have forgotten them, to befriend them and their loved ones, and together to work toward understanding and ways of maintaining the personhood of the sufferer, is to enter into the dynamic movement from chaos to resurrection that is contained in the promise and the presence of the resurrected Christ.[15] To behave in such ways is to reveal the reality of the kingdom of God and to recognize the possibilities for the future in the sufferings of the present.

Formal Education

The second model of education, which might run in conjunction with this *experiential-relational* education, is of a more formal type that seeks to explore other aspects of mental health problems. Organizations such as the Association for Pastoral Care in Mental Health[16] in the United Kingdom and the National Institute of Mental Health[17] in the United States provide extensive, but accessible, training courses to churches that are interested in dealing constructively with issues of mental health. Within the context of such a course, the congregation, as well as learning about mental health and ill health, is also introduced to other key workers within the area such as the hospital chaplain, the CMHC, social workers, community mental health workers, and other relevant mental health professions. A course such as this, run in conjunction with (and preferably with the participation of) the teaching that comes from people with mental health problems and their families, enables the church congregation to obtain an all-around picture of the nature and experience of people with mental health problems and the various services that are available to them and their families. Once again, it is important that people with mental health problems be involved with this aspect of education. The ways in which they experience mental health care as it is provided may be very different from the ways that professionals perceive things to be. By bringing service users and professionals into constructive dialogue within such an educational format, there is much possibility for all parties to share their hopes, fears, and expectations and develop forms of relating that together act toward the liberation of congregation and sufferer.

Finally, there is also a real need to develop modes of training and practice for pastors. For example, I would suggest that there should be a compulsory course in seminary training on mental health issues in the parish. For the parish minister, a system of pastoral consultation similar to the system proposed by Gerald Caplan in his model of preventative psychiatry might have an important part to play within the overall system of care and befriending.[18] Caplan envisaged a situation wherein psychiatrists provided a consultation service that could enable ministers, teachers, doctors, and informal carers to provide support for people encountering crisis and mental health problems. It would be possible to modify this system to provide a form of pastoral consultation whereby ministers within a particular area meet together regularly with mental health professionals to share their experiences and to work through any particular difficulties they had encountered within their parishes. Groups such as these might help prevent some of the difficulties that have been highlighted and enable churches to function more effectively in their ministry of friendship.

The important function that each of these forms of education performs is to allow the church community to define and confirm its self-image as a graceful community-of-friends called to minister to the marginalized. It also allows the Christian community to reframe its image of mental health problems and the persons who suffer from them, in such a way as to enable it to gain the confidence at least to begin to work toward the development of health-bringing, liberating friendships. Thus, the church, through its ministry of friendship development, can be enabled to participate authentically in the care of persons with mental health problems, in a way that respects the individuality and freedom of the person, while at the same time complementing the contribution of the other mental health professions, which also have a vital role to play in the recovery of people with mental health problems.

Religion, Spirituality, and Schizophrenia

A number of authors have examined the possibility that certain forms of mental health problems, such as delusions and hallucinations, are a form of mystical experience.[19] This is a potentially significant area for research and thinking, but the particular focus of this study makes it impossible to address this question here. Rather, the focus of this section will be on how one might go about discerning religious truth from delusion. One criticism that could be made against the idea of friendship as a model of pastoral care is that the religious community might in fact be unhelpful to a person suffering from religious delusions, since its belief structures might serve to reinforce unhealthy religious delusions. Under such circumstances close involvement with the church community may (this line of argument would suggest) be detrimental to the condition of the person. This criticism needs to be taken seriously. Due to the delusional nature of certain forms of mental health problems, there is indeed a real possibility that the person's experience of religion could become distorted and unhealthy. Within the context of the psychiatric hospital, I have encountered many people in highly disturbed states for whom religion has become a particular focus of their delusions. However, such delusional experiences of religion are not confined to patients! On one occasion two Christian befrienders (who were in fact nurses by profession) had to be excluded from an acute admission ward where I was working because they were convinced that a person's schizophrenia was in fact demon possession. They had carried out a service of exorcism in the hospital ward, with devastating consequences. The action of these well-meaning people compounded the delusions of the sufferer and in so doing exacerbated his condition to the point where he felt that the only course of action open to him was to attempt to bore a hole in his head through which the demons could escape! Thankfully this course of action was averted by the alertness of the ward staff. This incident is extreme both from the perspective of the reaction of the sufferer, and in the lack of insight shown by the befrienders; nevertheless, it provides a powerful lesson concerning the importance of friendship being *informed* in the ways that have been discussed in this chapter. It would be foolish to suggest that there are not difficulties and dangers in friendships that share a common element of religion. However, this does not annul the importance of religion for individuals or suggest that it is necessarily destructive of their mental health.

"Nothing But" Delusions?

With regard to spirituality and mental health problems, the risk of religion becoming distorted or incorporated into a person's delusional system does not in itself justify any implication that a person's religious beliefs are *nothing but* "a part of their condition." As Fuller Torrey comments, "like all human beings, persons with schizophrenia have a need to relate to a god or philosophical worldview which allows them to place themselves and their lives within a larger context."[20] A person's relationship with God and his or her ability to actualize that relationship is an important part of being human. Unless one wishes to argue that people suffering from mental health problems are somehow not human, or have desires that are radically different from those of the rest of humanity, then their religious aspirations *have* to be respected and appropriately nurtured. Certainly with regard to the impact of religion on delusional experience, there are very often difficulties in discerning "authentic" religious experience from the manifestations of psychopathology. As Frese points out:

> From the viewpoint of the person with the disorder . . . the phenomenon can be very much like a mystical experience. The young psychiatrist Carol North describes herself as being in a parallel reality or at a cosmic juncture . . . David Zelt describes himself as being "constantly in touch with the infinite and the eternal." The nature of the disorder is that it affects the brain's thought and belief systems, it affects a person's confidence in what is truthful. Therefore, to the person who is experiencing the disorder it very much can be a mystical journey where poetic relationships and metaphorical associations dictate truth. To the person who is experiencing the disorder, these subjective experiences are very real indeed. Therefore, while one should try to understand as much as possible about how the disorder is accompanied by biochemical irregularities, one should also understand that for the person who has the schizophrenia, it indeed can be a mystical or even a religious experience. Often these mystical experiences can be most seductive. One has the feeling that he is having special insights and even special powers. One is no longer restricted by the rigid control of rationality. One begins engaging in what experts have called paleologic or parataxic thinking. Many consumer/survivors prefer the term, "poetic" logic.[21]

Frese helpfully highlights some of the ways in which spirituality can indeed become distorted within the experience of a person suffering from a severe mental health problem. There is a need for critical discernment when dealing with spiritual matters.

Nevertheless, to suggest that religion may be incorporated into a person's delusional system is not to reject the potentially positive benefits of spirituality and the possible authenticity of religious faith and experience. Rather, a person who is entering into a relationship with someone suffering from a delusional condition should have access to a supervising person who can act as a sounding board against which this helper can work through any confusion that arises. Such a companion, whether a chaplain, mental health professional, or layperson with appropriate knowledge and experience, can work with the befriender to try and discern what is real and what is not, what is authentic religious experience and what is not, and how delusional material can best be dealt with. Acknowledgment of the possibility of distortion therefore forces the church, in its ministry of friendship, to ensure that befrienders have access to knowledge of both psychiatric symptomatology and the particular form of spirituality that the person with the mental health problem is striving to express.

Discerning the Cultural Reality of the Person's Religious Experience[22]

Psychiatrist Andrew Sims in "Psyche—Spirit as Well as Mind?" suggests that it is helpful to think in terms of *form* and *content* when attempting to discern the actual nature of religious experience in those suffering from mental health problems. If the religious belief manifests itself in the form of commonly acknowledged psychiatric symptomatology, and the belief holds no connection to the religious or social culture from which a person comes, then it may well be that the particular belief is in fact a part of the illness, in the sense that it does not connect with reality as it is perceived and interpreted within the experience of the person's own religious community.[23] This task of discernment is an important part of the process of understanding that has been shown to be so important in developing constructive friendships. With love, patience, and sensitivity to the fact that beliefs are *always* real to the individual, the informed friend can be enabled to stay with the person as he or she negotiates the reality of their spiritual journey. It is important to note that this process of staying with the person as a friend does not mean confronting the sufferer over the reality of his or her experience. It simply means being with the person, sharing in his or her experience, and allowing the person to share in one's own, in order that a mutual reality can be developed and negotiated over a period of time. To achieve this is no easy task. To be with a person in this situation is a skill that needs to be learned. It is not however a skill that *only* professionals can learn.[24]

Above all, what must be borne in mind is that the spiritual needs of people suffering from mental health problems are in essence no different from those of anyone else: to find a place of acceptance within which they can be allowed to be themselves, and where their illness experiences will be respected, understood, and tolerated in a spirit of love and care—a place where they can learn about and experience the embodied love of God and develop a meaningful relationship with God and with others within the community God has drawn together. Certainly there may be problems at a number of levels. However, this only means that they and the rest of the church must work toward developing ways and means of overcoming these problems in order that the person's religious experience can become authentic and meaningful.

Supervision

A final aspect of the developing model of care is the question of supervision. The development and maintenance of committed friendship within the context of severe mental health problems is never easy. It is therefore vital that this ministry be approached from a perspective of *perseverance* and *commitment*. Christlike friends must be prepared to accept the other as they are, and to be under no illusions that somehow they can change or cure the individual. In other words, the friendship that is offered must be *unconditional* friendship. It is possible that, in terms of the mental health problem, the presence of a friend will make no difference whatsoever to the progress of the condition. However, in terms of a person's humanity, a friend can make *all* the difference. Friendship does not cure mental health problems, but it does make a positive contribution to recovery and the enabling of the person to develop his or her true potential.

The case study about David demonstrated one of the major pitfalls in befriending people who live with schizophrenia—the possibility of *rejection*. It may be that a person or a congregation spends many hours working at a relationship with a person with a mental health problem, only to find themselves rejected, perhaps even despised due to paranoid delusions, and only to see the person moving on to another congregation or away from the church altogether. This can be devastating for the individual church member who had embarked upon the friendship relationship, and it can be deeply disheartening for the congregation involved. Although David's story embodied possibility as well as defeat, there are many situations where friendship simply will not function therapeutically, and where congregations and individuals simply cannot tolerate the disruption or cope with the difficulties. There is, therefore, a great need for *supervision* to enable individual and community to cope constructively with the pressures of maintaining friendships within the context of difficult situations. Part of the educational endeavors outlined above would include teaching people basic relational skills, such as the importance of listening, coping with frustration, boundaries, and empathy. These are skills that are vital for all relationships, so a basic knowledge of them will help a congregation at a number of levels. However, when people embark upon the practice of friendship and when they encounter the types of difficulties that have been highlighted in the previous chapters, there is a great need for support and supervision. Within this context, a key worker such as the CMHC would be responsible for the supervision. If a formal system of befriending is established, that supervisor would coordinate, support, and train those embarking upon this type of ministry. The key worker is thus available, in an unobtrusive way, to discuss, counsel, and work through any difficulties that either party within a particular relationship may be having. The aim of such supervision is to enable both parties to cope with the inevitable strains that arise within any relationship, but that tend to be amplified within the context of severe mental health problems.

For example, there may be difficulties with regard to *boundaries*. Because of the nature of the illness itself, plus the difficulties of having lived within a closed culture as is found within psychiatric hospitals, very often boundary definition and appropriate lengths of contact are difficult and have to be worked out clearly and carefully. The danger is that either party in the relationship may become overloaded by the demands of the other, and there may be a need for an intervening person to enable both parties to negotiate mutually acceptable boundaries. For instance, it may be worked out that the friends meet regularly for two hours every week. If the relationship is to remain strong on a long-term basis, and, if it is to be given the chance to grow appropriately with the minimal amount of stress for either party, it is very important that both stay within the boundaries of this arrangement. An important part of the supervisory process is to ensure that these boundaries remain safe and secure, and if they are to change, then it is with the agreement of both parties.

Such supervision is for the benefit of both parties, rather than for the protection of one. The supervisor exists as much for the sake of the person with the mental health problem as for the congregant. Both embark upon the relationship of friendship, and both are in need of support, encouragement and, if necessary, mending.

Confidentiality

It is absolutely necessary for the supervisor and the other parties to be very aware of questions of confidentiality. While it may be appropriate for a befriender to discuss general points and situations with the supervisor, such as how to deal with delusional material, understanding paranoia, and reacting to threats of suicide, it may be deemed wholly inappropriate to talk through issues that the sufferer has shared in confidence, or that are personal and not central to the relationship or to a difficulty being encountered at that time. The boundaries of confidentiality have to be worked through by all parties before difficulties arise in order that destructive miscommunication can be avoided. This is particularly so with, for example, suicidal ideation. Boundaries must be set up in such a way as to allow the befriender to have the freedom to report such situations to someone who is experienced in dealing with them. Therefore, boundaries, while flexible enough not to inhibit the development of meaningful relationships, must be set up in such a way that both parties are able to cope constructively in times of crisis.

The key worker is available to discuss particular difficulties and to minister in times of need, disappointment, frustration, and anger. The aim of such a system is that as the program of introduction, education, and facilitation develops and works itself out within the church community, so people will be enabled to find supervisors from their own congregations. In this way, over a period of time the key worker's role can move into the background and the congregation can become self-sufficient in both the practice and supervision of its ministry of friendship.

Reframing Recovery

We need to think through the implications of how the term "recovery" might be understood within the developing model of care. It has been suggested that many forms of mental health problems, while not necessarily degenerative in a Kraeplanian sense, are interminable; that is, they will be with the person for the rest of his or her life. This being so, it will be helpful to ask the question, *How exactly should one understand the concept of "recovery" when there is little possibility that the mental health problem will ever be cured?*

It has been argued that there is often a profound difference in perception over the ways in which people interpret, and attribute meaning to, the experience of mental health problems. This has been illustrated in the various vignettes that have been presented in the previous chapters. There it was noted that one important difference in definition often occurs between professional expectations and the expectations that a sufferer or relative may have. For many mental health professionals the concept of recovery is primarily perceived as having to do with the cessation or control of symptoms and the ability to live a "normal" life (although the definition of precisely what "normal" is can be quite variable). Such a cure-oriented definition of recovery denies any real possibility of recovery to the person suffering from long-term mental health problems who does not remain asymptomatic. In this view "the most obvious sign of recovery is the cessation of symptoms to the point of permitting one to have the ability to find and keep steady employment. More broadly, it might include living independently, forming meaningful relationships, being financially self-support-ing, and not having to be rehospitalized for psychiatric reasons."[25]

However, this is not the only way the situation of the person can be defined or the notion of recovery conceptualized. The American self-help support organization "Schizophrenics Anonymous" offers a useful understanding of the concept of recovery as it applies within the context of schizophrenia. They argue that recov-ery from serious mental health problems is much more than being free from symptoms, or being able to meet social norms, or fulfill-ing particular cultural expectations. Rather they believe that

> . . . some level of recovery is achieved if the person is function-ing at that person's highest possible level. As victims of one of life's most disruptive illnesses, S.A's cardinal goal is for each member to get well and to stay well. But recovery—as in the severity of the illness—is always an individual matter. Chronically ill persons may achieve their full potential by living in a group home environment, adhering to their rules and work-ing part-time in a sheltered workshop. Other individuals may be living independently, working full-time, maintaining personal relationships, and perhaps attending school. Still others are doing their best by residing on a locked ward at a state-run hospital, taking medication, eating and behaving the best they can. To be "recovering" is to function to the maximum extent of individual capacity, within the limitations imposed by the severity of the ill-ness, personal abilities and talents, and the environment.[26]

According to this definition, recovery has to do with the ability to live one's life to the full within the constraints of the particular mental health problem. Recovery has to do with enabling persons to move along the mental health continuum, and in so doing, find the strength to be human and to remain human even in the midst of the vicissitudes of his or her condition. In this way, persons can be enabled to develop their God-given potential to the maximum degree possible, even in the midst of apparent chaos and hopeless-ness. Understood in this way, it becomes clear how important friendship can be within the overall process of recovery. By enabling persons to develop their relational potential and to work with them in the process of the redefinition of their personhood, the presence of a faithful friend acts as a powerful catalyst in the movement toward recovery, defined in these terms.

The Art of Being

Perhaps the most confusing thing about the therapeutic value of friendship for the modern mind is the simple fact that friends do not actually have to do anything. To ask "what is it that friends actually do in the process of recovery?" is to miss the point. Friends bring about healing and growth simply by being there. As Erickson and his colleages conclude in their research into the needs of people with chronic mental health problems:

> Lay persons, sometimes with tacit encouragement from professionals, believe that nothing of lasting value can occur unless the patient is expressing deep emotion or exploring painful memories, usually in the context of formal and private one-to-one conversations. Such vanities are harmless enough except when they discourage efforts at maintaining normal social intercourse and giving practical help. Alternatively, a confused church person in search of a rationale for giving help may tacitly steer the conversation toward religious material (assuming evangelism provides the missing focus or justification), or steer clear of the religion, mindful of social caricatures of the practice. In point of fact, the "doing of therapy" is often unwelcome or inappropriate, and the judicious sharing of one's faith is not always inappropriate. What is most needed is the consistent offering of a friendly relationship. . . . Skills associated with such relationships are characterised more by their common sense and good natured persistence than by special or secret knowledge. In short, *helpers need to be taught to disenthrall themselves and to relate to patients with a chronic mental illness as persons without constant second guessing.*[27]

In a world that struggles to understand what is going on within the sufferings of the person with mental health problems, the Christlike friend accepts and acknowledges the fundamental relational personhood of the individual (even when it is not yet an existential reality). A patient and tenacious friend enables the person to experience the types of relationships that image Christ and bring health and wholeness. When professionals, family, and friends struggle to hold on to the personhood of the individual, the messianic friend acknowledges that there is a unique and incommunicable element to the other that is not destroyed by the illness. This friend strives in weakness and in sacrifice to enable the actualization and maintenance of a positive social identity, a "true self," even in the midst of fragmentation and dislocation.

Now we have completed model of friendship development presented in diagrammatic form.

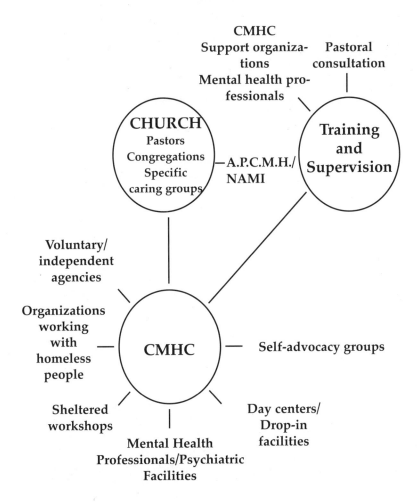

Chapter 11

Caring for the Carers

Creating a
Hopeful Future

A final but important portion of the model of friendship needs to be addressed: *In what ways can the model of friendship and friendship development minister to and partake in the development and maintenance of the mental health of those who care for people with long-term mental health problems?*

The earlier discussion on the impact of expressed emotion on relapse in schizophrenia, and Warner's cross-cultural observations on the impact of family structures on recovery,[1] emphasized the importance of the family in caring for people with mental health problems. Research studies have indicated that "40-65 percent of adults with severe and persistent mental illness either reside with their families or receive primary care-management from their families. The ability of family members to provide a benign, understanding, and predictable environment for their ill relative is a key factor in the capacity of the ill family member to stabilise and remain in the community."[2] One major difference between the type of friendship that has been the subject of the previous discussion and the type of relationship that occurs within families is that the contact that friends have with people who have mental health problems is limited and, while committed, can be terminated by either party at any time. Families do not normally have the option of withdrawing from a situation when it gets too tough. They have to live with the situation all the time. This being so, the stress placed on families can often be immense. David's story illustrated the pattern of wellness-illness-wellness, as well as the movement between acceptance of relationship and rejection that is typical of certain forms of mental health problems. Some of the ways in which the friends might be enabled to cope with this were mentioned in the preceding discussion on education, support, supervision, and enablement. However, within the context of the family, the pressure of such fluctuation and disappointment is greatly exacerbated.

In my discussions with mental health professionals and representatives from organizations who focus specifically on the needs of people with mental health problems and their families, the consensus was that what is *not* required is for the church to provide a specific befriending service for relatives and carers. On the whole, partly because of the stigmatizing nature of mental health problems, and partly because of the need to be with others who are sharing the same experience, what carers tend to want is the friendship and support of other carers. This being so, a formal system of befriending may prove to be inappropriate. It would be more appropriate for the church to be aware of particular services and groups within an area and to be in a position to link people into existing support groups, rather than try to set up a service on their own. This would be an important outcome of the networking that was previously shown to be of great importance.

This does not mean that the model of friendship and friendship development that has been presented is irrelevant for the mental health care of families and carers. Quite the opposite. If the church is to take seriously its ministry of friendship and implement strategies similar to those outlined above, this effort will inevitably be beneficial for families struggling to cope with particular situations that can easily become isolating and claustrophobic. Entering into committed friendship with a sufferer not only eases the burden on the family in a physical and emotional way,[3] it also helps them deal with their own "referred stigma" (that is, the social impact of the illness on the family). Through the process of befriending, the friend confirms that in fact their loved one *is* valued and acceptable, despite personal and social pressures that might suggest otherwise. The act of setting up a befriending scheme and working through the issues of introduction, education, supervision, and so forth, raises the profile of mental health issues within a church community. In so doing, the development of an atmosphere of care and acceptance is facilitated, within which stigma and isolation can be broken down, problems can be discussed, and health-bringing friendships developed.

From the perspective of families, this is perhaps the most important contribution that the framework for friendship development can offer them, in terms of long-term pastoral care. Due to the stigma and alienation that is referred onto the family because of the negative public persona of mental health problems, there is a real danger that families can become isolated and turned inward. As psychiatrist David Enoch observes in his work with people with schizophrenia:

> The lack of sympathy and understanding from the members of the family, neighbours and members of the church only accentuates the difficulties and isolates them further. Just as friends of the schizophrenic himself tend to desert him, often at the instigation of their families, the carers and relatives of the schizophrenic also feel that they are looked at as contaminated. Hence further isolation occurs between them and their friends.[4]

As has been illustrated, the situation is often no different within the context of the church community. Enoch notes that "several parents told me that when their son or daughter developed schizophrenia, members of the church gave no support; in fact they often became hostile and discontinued past friendship. . . . It is a terrible indictment of Christians that when families are suddenly told that they have a schizophrenic son or daughter, they are more frightened of informing their Christian friends than others."[5]

As Cannon correctly observes, "Most families do not want or need therapy. More than anything else, they need to feel accepted, understood, and cared about by the spiritual community and God."[6] Stewart Govig's research into the needs of families caring for people showed that the families' priorities were:

- Counsel on family stability and marital tensions;
- Preaching that includes words like "paranoid" and "schizophrenia";
- Help in dealing with guilt, shame, and embarrassment;
- Promoting adult religious education about chronic mental illness;
- Noncondemning acceptance of family anger and frustration;
- Information about treatment options as Community Mental Health Centers;

- Encouragement to "tell our stories";
- Clergy calling at the hospital during acute stages;
- Congregations should encourage persons with mental illness to attend public worship.[7]

This suggests that what families require from society in general and from the church in particular is the provision of an accepting, sympathetic, and well-informed community. Within this community, their situation can be understood, and empathized with and they can be given the opportunity to express their feelings and share their experiences in a meaningful, nonthreatening manner without fear of rejection or condemnation. This would seem to confirm within the context of the family the important proposition previously stated in connection with caring for people with mental health problems: *understanding is the therapy.*

By implementing some of the strategies presented previously and by advocating for families, the church can be enabled to move toward creating a community of friends that incarnates and actualizes such a desire for acceptance and understanding. Within such a context there are opportunities for families of sufferers to develop the types of friendships and structures of social support that are so important for the development and maintenance of their own mental health, particularly in times of stress and crisis. The framework of friendship development that has been presented holds out real possibilities of contributing to the reconnection of families who have been dislocated from the community because of the particular difficulties that they encounter in caring for someone with mental health problems, and of enabling them to develop and maintain their own mental health. In this way it is possible to open lines of healing communication and in so doing to take seriously the apostle Paul's plea to "bear one another's burdens" and thus to open up and share sadness, loss, grief, and joy within a context of hopeful possibility and shared responsibility.

The Significance of Loss

Providing families who are struggling with the effects of mental health problems a space within which they can express the reality of their pain and hopelessness in an atmosphere that is under-standing and noncondemning is of great importance. Perhaps it is in the creation of such a space that the Christian community can find its primary task. The person with a mental health problem, while possibly altered, is certainly not lost to the illness. The act of the community's entering into a relationship of friendship with people with mental health problems declares that they remain val-ued and acceptable despite the difficulties and changes imposed upon them by their condition. This is a crucial point that must not be forgotten or downplayed. Yet, for many families whose loved ones experience mental health problems, there remains a profound sense of loss—loss of vital aspects of the person they knew and loved, loss of hopes for their future, and often, due to their com-mitment to care for the individual, loss of freedom to do many of the things that they were previously able to do. That loss is real.

As was indicated by the adaptation of Lipowski's ideas into a model of meaning attribution, illness can be interpreted in a vari-ety of ways and viewed from a number of different perspectives. For many families the primary interpretation that is put on the con-dition of their loved one is that of irreparable loss. Stewart Govig illustrates the way in which many parents experience the "loss" of their loved one to mental health problems:

> It was like trying to put the pieces of a shattered vase together only to find the glue never quite stuck. It dawns on you that the vase actually comprises the pieces in your hand. You welcome a new son, daughter, or sibling into the family circle—what your loved one has become today.[8]

Annie Borthwick likewise argues that loss is central to the experi-ence of families, primarily the loss of the person they once knew.

> What is the nature of the loss or losses that are experienced? It is rather simplistic to assert solely that illness has changed the per-son. Those doctors who see a person in the sequence of psychosis after psychosis have never seen that person as he or she was once known to the family. They have not seen him before, and there-fore it is not surprising that the enormity of the loss may be diffi-cult for them to comprehend. It is not surprising that denial of

197

this loss may be continued for some time. After all, the person is still there physically. And yet the "personhood" of the loved one is radically altered. Where once there may have been a feeling of expansion, of unlimited potential, particularly where a bright young son or daughter is concerned, this is now replaced by a sense of limitation and dependence. There is a strange illusory quality, too, that this cannot be true, because so often, the patient will seem to be all right. And yet, when he or she tries to do [a] thing which previously would have been easy, anxiety, distress, or psychotic symptoms are the result.[9]

Borthwick here usefully highlights the clash of understanding and interpretation that frequently occurs between the perceptions of "outsiders" such as health professionals, and the perceptions of families who actually experience a sense of loss. Within this situation there is the potential for a great deal of strife, confusion, and miscommunication.

Sveinbjarnardottir and Casterle in their research into the emotional experiences of families who had a member suffering from severe mental illness make several observations: First they point to the impact of *hope* on the ability of families to cope.

Hope was an important element in helping relatives to come to terms with the mental illness. Experience had taught them to keep their expectations within realistic limits. . . . The expression of realistic hope for the future of the mentally ill family member seemed to be an integral part of acceptance of the illness. Expectations centered around the mentally ill person being able to live a decent life within his or her limited capacity.[10]

It has already been shown how important hope is for people with mental health problems. These researchers highlight the importance of hope, from the carers' perspective. Continuing, they note that

family members expressed the need for emotional support to be able to handle the various problems associated with serious mental illness. The need to talk about private or difficult information to a confidant, usually a close relative or a friend, was notable, as was the need to be listened to by a person showing an interest in and understanding of the issues. Family members viewed emotional support as being able to express uncomfortable feelings to someone they trusted: "It is always difficult to watch my mother getting sick. I never imagined it could be so serious. My husband supports me in dealing with my feelings—at least he listens to me."[11]

They conclude that

the possibility of a positive emotional experience with the patient seemed to increase when the family members had succeeded in making sense out of their situation. . . . Important factors contributing to family members' process of accepting the illness seemed to be increased understanding and manageability of the situation, putting sense into a sometimes harrowing situation, and using cognitive restructuring to make the situation more positive.[12]

Central to the coping ability of the families in these researchers' survey was their ability to find some degree of hope, some confidant whom they could trust with the pains of their situations, and some mechanism through which they could perceive their situation in a more positive manner.

Other researchers have made similar observations. For example, Antonovsky points toward the fact that people's ability to adapt constructively to stressful situations depends on how comprehensible, manageable, and meaningful they understand their situation to be.[13] Hill and Mullen, commenting on the importance of the work of Antonovsky for the developing field of psychoneuroimmunology, draw out some of the implications of this aspect of his work for pastoral care.

Antonovsky . . . advocates a salutogenic model which addresses how the mind can contribute to health. Based on his research Antonovsky contends that what he calls a sense of coherence (SOC), defined as an orientation that views life as comprehensible, manageable, and meaningful, helps sustain good health. The qualities essential to SOC are foundational to the ministry of pastoral care. The pastoral caregiver seeks to enable persons to find meaning in their struggle to understand stressful life events and to mobilize coping resources to manage the stress they encounter.[14]

From these observations it can be seen that the inspiration of hope, meaning, and understanding (which are central to the pastoral task) can, in and of itself, (quite apart from strategies implemented within the counseling relationship) bring health.[15]

The Disabled Christ:
Faith, Hope, and Survival

Within this overall context, a person's religious beliefs can be of great importance. However, the significance of religion does not lie in its ability to lift one out of one's circumstances. Such triumphalism bears little relevance to the day to day lives of people wrestling with the complexities of mental health problems. David Karp in his research into the nature of depression notes that the type of religion that best enables coping is a religion that understands the place of human suffering and seeks to incorporate it into everyday life in a way that enables people to make some kind of sense of it.[16] Thus, a healthy religious response will enable a person to make sense of his or her suffering, rather than escaping from it. *But what is a healthy religious response?*

A healthy religious response provides a spiritual framework within which people can express the reality of their situations and find meaning and hope, even in the midst of their pain. It is a way of viewing the world and of understanding God within it that holds in critical tension the reality of human pain and suffering, and the possibility that there is more to life than that which is experienced in the present.

Stewart Govig suggests that the spirituality of individuals and families is fundamental to the process of coping with mental health problems in a family member. Defining spirituality is a notoriously difficult task. However, the following definition offers a helpful if somewhat broad definition of spirituality.

> A person's spirituality is the overarching framework within which a person interprets and makes sense of their reality. It is a set of beliefs and understandings about reality that acts as a lens, through which people view their experiences and attribute understandings, meaning and purpose. As such it has the potential to be a powerful force in the defining and redefining of the illness

experience. . . . What a person's spirituality does then, is to anchor them to the world in a very particular manner, enabling them to understand and interpret their illness in terms which may well be very different from the ways in which the professional understands and sees the illness.[17]

This being so, the particular ways in which a family interprets their experience will be profoundly influenced by the particular spirituality that undergirds their lives.

Govig reflects on the miracle story in Matthew 8:14-16, in which Jesus healed Peter's mother-in-law. He notes Matthew's statement that this "was to fulfill what had been spoken through the prophet Isaiah, 'He took our infirmities and bore our diseases' " (8:17). Govig wrestles with the question of what Matthew actually meant in his use of Isaiah's suffering servant imagery. "Here . . . stands the very One chosen by God—the disabled Christ?—who has taken our infirmities [handicapping conditions] and shouldered our diseases . . . [mental health problems]. The book of Hebrews reminds believers of a Jesus who 'in every respect has been tested' as the rest of us are, yet is without sin (4:15). Our fellow sufferer also humbled and 'emptied himself' (Philippians 2:6-11). Who among us, I ask, can experience more testing and humiliation than persons like Jay [Govig's son] who must contest with those tormenting voices of auditory hallucinations? The disabled Christ, I answer, who stands side by side with them."[18]

Once again, we encounter the motifs of cross, resurrection, and critical solidarity with those who are oppressed that have previously been shown to be so significant. By entering fully into the pain of people with mental health problems, Jesus takes on their infirmities, and in so doing, himself becomes disabled. It is not that he simply empathizes or passively sits alongside those who are going through the experiences of mental health problems. Just as on the cross he entered fully into the pain of humanity, and suffered with and for them, so also he actually enters fully into and shares the pain of those who are oppressed by mental health problems and the families who struggle to cope with those so oppressed. In this way he breaks down the barriers of alienation and isolation and injects hopeful possibilities into situations that often appear to be profoundly hopeless.

By presenting this concept of the "disabled Christ," Govig's intention is to reframe what might be considered the normative emphasis on the triumphant risen Christ toward an image of Christ that accepts and incorporates the reality of pain and suffering into human existence, yet still offers the possibility of hope and meaning in the midst of it. From this perspective religion ceases to be a utopian escape, but instead is incorporated into the earthiness of painful worldly existence. Christ comes to suffer with the family in passion and commitment, sharing in their experience, bearing the same scars they bear, yet transforming the pain of those scars by offering commitment, solidarity, hope, and healing. Such a theology gives no explanation for suffering. The "disabled Christ" does not offer a solution as to why suffering exists. What this image does do however, is to reveal clearly that God exists in solidarity with the world's suffering. The cross is God's protest against suffering, and Jesus' words from the cross are God's lament for the brokenhearted. His cry of desolation "Eli, Eli, lema sabachthani?" which means, "My God, my God, why have you forsaken me?" (Matthew 27:46) provides a shared *lament* that expresses confusion and pain and is the frequent cry of both carer and cared for.

Lamentation

Lamentation is important and frequently forgotten in contemporary theology, but is of great pastoral significance for people with mental health problems and their families. While the psalms are used extensively within the worship and devotion of the church, they tend to be used selectively, with the psalms of lament posing difficulties to our triumphalistic longings. As Glen Weaver correctly points out:

> By far the most frequent type of psalm in the Scriptures is the individual lament. It is probably fair to suggest that this type is also the most neglected by Christians today. The individual laments carry us from our baseline sense of security downwards to the nadir of a person's anguish and misery. And this descent is ordinarily no mere device to set in motion a more triumphant divine ascent. The psalms of lament can take up residence in the depths and, by turning over the many sides of suffering in a poet-

ic parallelism, encourage us to think and feel our way into the potential ruin of our own condition. Engaging in that kind of lament seems wrong to our Christian sensibilities. It runs over into harsh complaining and lack of charity toward our enemies.[19]

And yet, engaging in such a process of lamentation is a reaffirmation of one's humanity in the midst of apparent dehumanization. To engage in the process of lament is to enter into a process of protest within which one screams against the injustice of the way things are. It is a human act that points to the possibility that we are not trapped in a providential trap within which we have no control and no voice with which to grasp hold of our futures. The lament is a way of asserting that the way the world is cannot be legitimated by blind triumphalism and that the pain of God's creation needs also to be embraced alongside the joy.

Mary Elizabeth Moore notes that lament is a neglected form of protest in many cultural traditions.

> Lament is also a common expression of the prophetic ministry of women in the Hebrew Bible. . . . Lament arose when the people of Israel experienced "their strength choked off and their ability to resist falter." In Judges, for example, the lament is more than a request for help from God; "it is also a public expression of the people's pain." This echoes stories of Exodus in which God hears the groans and cries of the people (3:7-10; 2:23-24).[20]

Lament arises from the recognition that humanity is bound in covenant with God and one another, a covenant within which God stands with and for the oppressed. Lamentation reminds us that "people are now faced with what it means to meet in covenant when the gift of covenant is broken, when response to covenant is called forth, but is instead denied or destroyed."[21] Thus, lament is a public protest against the way things are, in the light of how they should be if creation retained its fidelity to its covenant with God. For families, the process of lament enables them to express their anger and disappointment with God and the ways things are. Yet they do so in the context of the crucified and risen Christ, kno that God has promised not only to answer their lament, but journey with them until the promise reaches its ultimat ment. Thus, lamentation is a powerful process of catharsis, affirmation, and empowerment. As Walter Brueggemann puts it:

> In the public utterance of such pain, both parties emerge with freshness. Obedience turns out to be not blind *submissiveness* required by common theology. It is rather a bold *protest* against a legitimacy that has grown illegitimate because it does not seriously take into account the suffering reality of the partner. Where the reality of suffering is not dealt with, legitimate structure is made illegitimate when the voice of pain assumes enough authority to be heard.[22]

On the cross, Jesus' lament, "Eli, Eli, lema sabachthani?" legitimates and gives meaning to the laments of those families who suffer in covenant brokenness. The disabled Christ descends into the depths with the whole of humanity and struggles in protesting solidarity against the way things are in the light of the way that things will be. Lament gives a voice to suffering and in so doing brings comfort, peace, and healing. Govig continues:

> Besides reframing my normative emphasis on the risen Christ and Lord, life within limits has become a vital reality and slowed down my pursuit of religious and psychological crutches. Anger recedes and the strangest reframing of all has taken place: rebirth within the boundaries of God's salvation. Lament has given voice to suffering and becomes a means to approach the One who can take it away. It spurs a movement toward God.[23]

Thus, rather than being an expression of doubt or rejection of God, lamentation in fact is an avenue to God through which one can pass as one encounters the pain and suffering of human existence as it is, in the light of the way it will be.

Caring and Curing

As well as revealing the potential that theology and spirituality have for reframing the illness experiences of both carer and cared for, these theological reflections also point toward another important theme that has run throughout this book. Theologian and philosopher Thomas Moore speaks of the difference between "care" and "cure."

> A major difference between care and cure is that cure implies the end of trouble. . . . But care has a sense of ongoing attention. There is no end. Conflicts may never be fully resolved. Your character will never change radically, although it may go through some interesting transformations. Awareness can change, of course, but problems persist and never go away. . . . Care of the soul . . . appreciates the mystery of human suffering and does not offer the illusion of a problem free life.[24]

It has been argued that Christian friendship gains its identity and finds its form in reflecting the life of Christ. At the heart of this form of friendship lie the central tenets of care—passion, commitment, solidarity, the desire to be *with* and *for* the other—all aspects that were manifested within the earthly life of Jesus and that typify the nature of Govig's "disabled Christ." The reclamation of the significance of lamentation and the reconceptualization of Christ's stance as one of solidarity with people with disabilities provide ways in which individuals and families can begin to understand their situation theologically and to conceptualize their situation differently. Reflection on these images enables people to incorporate their religious spirituality into the pain, suffering, and disappointment of everyday life in such a way that hope is sustained and loneliness is eased, as they experience the soothing presence of the passionate love of God, who actively shares in the tragedy of human existence.

If it is true that a person's spirituality provides the primary lens through which they see and interpret the world, such a realignment of emphasis will inevitably have beneficial practical consequences. However, such theologizing only makes sense when it is incarnated within the lives of those who claim to follow that same Christ. Lamentation needs to be heard not only by God, but by the whole community. The disabled Christ is not merely an image of God, but provides a template for Christian living. The Christian community of friends is called to enter fully into the pain, suffering, and ch of those who struggle to cope with the confusion of mental h problems. It is called to embody the disablement of individu' their families, and to live lives that display empathy, understanding, and critical solidarity. It is called to become a community that listens to the laments of its people, and in the power of the Spirit reaches out and seeks to address the pain at both a personal and political level. The task of the Christian community is to incarnate the "disabled Christ" in its attitudes, behavior, commitment, and actions. This embodiment of Christ is fundamental to the healing and growing process that will enable the strength to be human and to remain human, irrespective of circumstances.

Churches are not immune to the alienating and stigmatizing attitudes that are present within society. The literature and the author's personal experience reveal very clearly the sense of alienation and "differentness" often felt by families who have a member suffering from mental health problems. The Christlike friend, by entering into the family's difficult situation in commitment and solidarity, reveals something of the nature of the God whom they represent, and also offers them a connection with the church community. Whereas previously they may have been awkward or embarrassed about their situation, now through the graceful presence of the community of friends, the family can begin to feel accepted. It can be enabled to redefine its situation in the light of the biblical narrative, the "disabled Christ," and the warmth of the community of friends. The community of friends, by living, preaching, and teaching the kingdom, provides a context for change—a witness to the world that speaks of the possibility of acceptance and love to those whom the world rejects and chooses to stigmatize. By stretching beyond the boundaries of accepted normality, the church can become a vital catalyst in the movement toward changed practice and restored relationships. In providing a safe space or sanctuary where people living with mental health problems can find a valued place and a vital stepping stone back into society, the church will fulfill its true goal, which is to image Christ and reveal the nature of the God. In educating itself and reaching out to educate the world, the church will find a focus for its mission which will give it a vital role and strong identity in a culture in which it is struggling to hold onto both.

Conclusion

From "Mental Patient"
to
Person-in-Relation

This book has presented a critical practical theological perspective on the life experiences of people with mental health problems that will both guide and enable the effective praxis of the church as it struggles to participate faithfully in God's continuing mission of liberation to the poor. It has become clear that people with mental health problems rank among the poor and the oppressed within contemporary Western societies. In a multitude of different ways, their personhood is undermined, their life expectations limited, and their possibilities for meaningful, health-bringing relationships severely restricted. Within such a context, the church is called into a pastoral ministry of liberation and radical befriending focused on enabling the overcoming of such injustices and allowing people with mental health problems to be resurrected from being nonpersons into full personhood.

Perhaps the strangest thing about this process of liberation is its ordinariness. It calls upon the whole church community to become advocates and prophets, yet it asks them to image the gentleness and sensitivity that was a primary mark of the ministry of Jesus. Certainly, all of us should be angry and outraged at the injustices perpetrated against people with mental health problems. Righteous indignation in the face of injustice and oppression is a sign of living humanly. Nevertheless, the outworkings of liberatory pastoral care must focus as much on love as on justice. Liberating pastoral care is the product of meaningful personal encounters between fellow human beings who fully recognize one another's humanity. The liberation of people with mental health problems will involve times of righteous anger and a proactive and publicly advocated preference for the poor. Yet such liberation, while being revolutionary in the sense that it signals the revolutionary new worldview of the coming kingdom, focuses less on aggressive or violent confrontation and more on patience, kindness, humility, trust, hope, and perseverance. People with mental health problems find liberation when the consciousness of others is raised to the possibility that those who might otherwise be considered "other" and unworthy of attention are human beings, worthy of respect and meaningful relationship. Such liberation is brought about through apparently minor and insignificant changes in everyday assumptions, understandings, and language. It comes about when people commit themselves in loving solidarity to those whom society casts aside. Such love will refuse to accept any form of injustice that is perpetrated upon the weak and the vulnerable and will be prepared to stand up and confront it wherever it is encountered. Liberating love embraces the "mental patient," and loves him or her into a new identity as a "person-in-relationship," made in the image of a God who *is* love, a person loved by God beyond all measure.

Friendship is the embodiment of such liberating love. The types of friendship that have been outlined in this book point toward a particular way of being human that embodies the love of Christ for the outsider. As such, they provide a powerful reminder to the church as to its true nature and the primary purpose of its mission—to show critical solidarity with those whom society oppresses, marginalizes, and alienates. When the consciousness of the community of friends is raised to the issues presented within this book, and when that raised consciousness is embodied in the types of countercultural friendships revealed in the friendships of Jesus, new possibilities for rehumanization and liberation are opened up, and the church is given the opportunity to be the church in a deep and meaningful way.

Community Care

By shifting the focus of mental health care away from an emphasis on *cure* toward an emphasis on *relationships, critical solidarity, liberation,* and *care,* this book has developed a model of mental health care that respects and fully acknowledges the important contributions that the whole church community has to make in the continuing process of mental health development and care. While society struggles to see beyond a person's illness, the Christian community is called to stand in critical moral solidarity alongside people with mental health problems. In and through the relationship of friendship, the community of friends is called to work toward discovering new and innovative ways of enabling persons positively to reconstruct their personhood and identity, and live lives that are appropriate to their status as full human beings. While acknowledging the importance of specialist modes of caring, such as psychiatry, psychology, counseling, and psychotherapy, the model presented within this book opens up the field of mental heath care to nonspecialists, and points toward the ultimate value that such contributions can make to the process of mental health care.

Caring with Passion

This book has called the church back to its fundamental identity as a community of people who *love* and *care* with the sacrificial *passion* of God. The form of love that the church is called to live out, however fragmentarily within its earthly structures, is precisely the shape of the love that is revealed in the life of Jesus.[1] In a world that flees from pain and stigmatizes suffering, this book calls for the church to retrieve its fundamental identity as a community that cares with the passion of God and reveals that care in and through its precious gift of friendship. This is not to say that the quest for a "cure" is unimportant. McGlashan, in comments inspired by the last paragraph Silvano Arieti wrote in his 1974 edition of *Interpretation of Schizophrenia*, reflectively observes that ". . . the warmth of the human embrace can sometimes burn off the fog of grey that permeates the schizophrenic patient's mind. Sometimes it can't, but the warmth and the embrace must still be extended to shelter those who suffer, until the day when the storm of schizophrenia can be lifted and blown out to sea by the high pressure front of research."[2]

However, until that day, it is the quest to care that forms the foundational motivation for the whole of the church's ministry as it struggles to actualize God's ideal of mental health under the shadow of the cross and in the hope of the Resurrection.

Notes

Introduction

1. For a fuller discussion of this model, see John Swinton, *From Bedlam to Shalom: Towards a Practical Theology of Human Nature, Interpersonal Relationships and Mental Health Care*. New York: Peter Lang (In Press).
2. G. D. J. Dingemans, "Practical Theology in the Academy: A Contemporary Overview," *The Journal of Religion*, vol. 76, no. 1, January 1996, p. 83.
3. Duncan B. Forrester, *Theology & Practice*. Epworth Press, London. 1990. p. 5.
4. Rebecca Chopp, *The Praxis of Suffering: An Interpretation of Liberation and Political Theologies* (Maryknoll, New York: Orbis, 1986); James H. Cone, *God of the Oppressed* (New York: Seabury, 1975); James H. Cone. *For My People: Black Theology and the Black Church* (Maryknoll, N.Y.: Orbis, 1984); Nancy Eiesland, *The Disabled God: Toward a Liberatory Theology of God* (Nashville: Abingdon Press, 1994).
5. Gustavo Gutiérrez, *A Theology of Liberation* (London: SCM Press, 1988), p. 6.
6. Ibid., p. 5.
7. Such reflection is done for example, within Ecclesial Base Communities—100-150 people who meet regularly to pray, worship, and plan community action in the light of experience.
8. Gutiérrez, *A Theology of Liberation*, p. 12.
9. See, for example, Psalm 82:3-4: "Defend the cause of the weak and fatherless; maintain the rights of the poor and oppressed. Rescue the weak and needy; deliver them from the hand of the wicked." Psalm 89:14: "Righteousness and justice are the foundation of your throne; love and faithfulness go before you."
10. Richard Bauckham, *The Bible in Politics* (London: SPCK, 1985) p. 110.
11. Gutiérrez discusses more fully this understanding of promise revealed in the present in *A Theology of Liberation* (London: SCM Press, 1988), pp. 91-97 and 121-40. Pastoral theologians who have used the liberationist perspective include Rebecca S. Chopp and Duane F. Parker, "Liberation Theology and Pastoral Theology," *Journal of Pastoral Care*, Monograph, Journal of Pastoral Care Publications (North Myrtle Beach, SC); Stephen Pattison, *Pastoral Care and Liberation Theology* (London: Cambridge University Press, 1994); Nancy L. Eiesland, *The Disabled God*.
12. Leonardo Boff, *Ecclesiogenesis: The Base Communities Reinvent the Church* (Maryknoll, New York: Orbis Books, 1986).
13. I am grateful to Stephen Pattison for his advice and helpful suggestions regarding the appropriate form of liberating stance that can be taken by those who do not have immediate experience of particular forms of oppression.
14. Pattison, *Pastoral Care and Liberation Theology*, p. 227.
15. Gutiérrez, *A Theology of Liberation*, p. 15.
16. Bryan P. Stone, *Compassionate Ministry: Theological Foundations* (Maryknoll, N.Y.: Orbis Books, 1996), p. 102.

17. Ibid.
18. Robert McAfee Brown in Gustavo Gutiérrez' *Liberation Theology*, p. vii.
19. For a fuller discussion on the implications of this movement from the perspective of caregivers, see Stewart D. Govig, *In the Shadow of Our Steeples: Pastoral Presence for Families Coping with Mental Illness* (Binghamton, N.Y.: Haworth Press, 1998).
20. Pattison, *Pastoral Care and Liberation Theology*, p. 84.
21. Marion Young, *Justice and the Politics of Difference* (Princeton, N.J.: Princeton University Press, 1990), p. 148.
22. Tom Kitwood, *Dementia Reconsidered: The Person Comes First* (Orlando, Florida: Open University Press, 1997), p. 12.
23. Rebecca S. Chopp, *The Power to Speak* (New York: Crossroads, 1989), p. 7.
24. Gutiérrez, *A Theology of Liberation*, p. xxx
25. John Wilkinson, *Health and Healing* (Edinburgh: The Handsell Press, 1980), p. 5.
26. Sinclair B. Fergusson and David Wright (Eds.) *New Dictionary of Theology* (Downer's Grove, Ill.: InterVarsity Press, 1978), p. 777.
27. Gutiérrez, *A Theology of Liberation*, p. xxx
28. Pattison, in *Pastoral Care and Liberation Theology*, very helpfully uses the perspective of liberation theology to show how "the mentally ill" as a group fall into this category within contemporary British society, as do women. Similarly, Susan Sontag masterfully shows the social impact of AIDS and its potential for disenfranchising individuals of positive social identity. Susan Sontag, *Illness as Metaphor: AIDS and Its Metaphors* (London: Penguin Books, 1991).
29. "The Spirit of the Lord is upon me, because he has anointed me to bring good news to the poor. He has sent me to proclaim release to the captives and recovery of sight to the blind, to let the oppressed go free, to proclaim the year of the Lord's favor (Luke 4:18-19)."
30. Gustavo Gutiérrez, *The Power of the Poor in History* (Maryknoll, N.Y.: Orbis Books, 1983), p. 140.
31. John MacMurray, *Persons in Relation* (Atlantic Highlands, N.J.: Humanities Press International, 1991).

1. Community and Friendship

1. Thomas Szasz, *The Myth of Mental Illness* (London: Penguin Books, 1973).
2. R. D. Laing, *The Divided Self* (London: Penguin Books, 1990).
3. John Swinton, *Building a Church for Strangers*, Contact Pastoral Monographs, No. 9, 1999, pp. 16-17.
4. John S. Strauss, "The Person—Key to Understanding Mental Illness: Toward a New Dynamic Psychiatry, III," *British Journal of Psychiatry*, Vol. 161 (Supplement 18) 1992, pp. 19-26, 109.
5. Ibid., p. 104.
6. Nancy L. Eiesland, personal correspondence. Used with Dr. Eiesland's permission.
7. Stanley Hauerwas, *Resident Aliens* (Nashville: Abingdon Press, 1989).

8. Avery S. J. Dulles, *Models of the Church* (London: Gill and Macmillan, 1976).

9. Henri Lubac in Dulles's *Models of the Church*, p. 59.

10. Jürgen Moltmann, *The Church in the Power of the Spirit* (London: SCM Press, 1992).

11. Stanley Hauerwas, *The Peaceable Kingdom: A Primer in Christian Ethics* (Notre Dame, Ind.: University of Notre Dame Press, 1983).

12. Brian Easter, "Sacraments and MH People," in *Liturgy*, Vol. 9, No. 5, June/July, 1985, p. 193. He is discussing John Calvin's definition of sacraments.

13. Dulles, *Models of Church*, p. 61.

14. Ibid.

15. Ibid., p. 6.

16. The use of the term "institution" is not meant to limit conceptualizations of the church to the institutional church. The term "institution" indicates the whole church in all its variegated forms as it works out its historical existence.

17. John Patton, *Pastoral Care in Context: An Introduction to Pastoral Care* (Louisville: Westminster/John Knox Press, 1993), p. 25. Quoting Peter Hodgson, *Revisioning the Church: Ecclesial Freedom in the New Paradigm* (Philadelphia: Fortress, 1988), p. 52.

18. Ibid.

19. Moltmann, *Church in the Power of the Spirit*, p. 196.

20. Hodgson, *Revisioning the Church*, pp. 58-63. (Quoted in Pattison).

21. Dulles, *Models of Church*, p. 66.

22. J.C. Hoekendijk, *The Church Inside Out* (London: SCM Press, 1967), pp. 71-72.

23. Ibid., p. 71.

24. Ibid., p. 105.

25. Ibid.

26. Ibid., p. 93.

27. Ibid.

28. Sallie McFague, *Models of God: Theology for an Ecological, Nuclear Age* (London: SCM Press, 1988), p. 161.

29. John Swinton, *From Bedlam to Shalom* (In press).

30. Jürgen Moltmann, *The Open Church—Invitation to a Messianic Lifestyle* (London: SCM Press, 1978), p. 56.

31. Swinton, *From Bedlam to Shalom* (In press).

32. Moltmann, *The Open Church*, p. 60.

33. Stephen G. Post, *The Moral Challenge of Alzheimer Disease* (Baltimore: Johns Hopkins University Press, 1995), p. 37.

34. A. Soble, *The Structure of Love* (Newhaven: Yale University Press, 1990), pp. 5, 6.

35. Stephen G. Post, *The Moral Challenge of Alzheimer Disease*, p. 38.

36. In Stanley Hauerwas, *Sanctify Them in the Truth: Holiness Exemplified* (Edinburgh: T&T Clark, 1998), p. 111.

37. Aristotle, *The Nichomachean Ethics* , David Ross, tr. and intro. (New York: Oxford World's Classics Set, Oxford University Press, 1998).

38. Andrew Mackie and John Swinton, "Community and Culture: The Place of the Virtues in Psychiatric Nursing," *Journal of Psychiatric and Mental Health Nursing,* January, 2000, p. 36.

39. Stanley Hauerwas, *A Community of Character* (Notre Dame, Ind.: University of Notre Dame Press, 1981), p. 116.

40. Stanley Hauerwas, *Sanctify Them in the Truth,* p. 111.

41. For a development of this point, see Alasdair Macintyre, *After Virtue: A Study in Moral Theory* (Lubbock, Texas: Duckworth, 1996).

2. Setting the Context

1. Trevor R. Hadley, Matt Muijen, Howard Goldman, and Geoff Shepherd, "Mental Health Policy Reform and Its Problems in the UK: Déjà Vu," *Current Opinions in Psychiatry,* Vol. 9, 1996, pp. 105-8.

2. E. Fuller Torrey, *Surviving Schizophrenia: A Manual for Families, Consumers, and Providers* (New York: Harper Collins, 1995), p. 24.

3. J. W. Browning, "Caring for People: Community Care in the Next Decade and Beyond," Chaplaincy Modes in Mental Health (Unpublished paper), p. 1.

4. E. Fuller Torrey, *Surviving Schizophrenia,* p. 24.

5. Stewart Govig, *In the Shadow of Our Steeples: Pastoral Presence for Families Coping with Mental Illness* (New York: Haworth Press, 1999), p. 1.

6. Stephen Pattison and Paul Armitage, "An Ethical Analysis of the Policies of British Community and Hospital Care for the Mentally Ill," *Journal of Medical Ethics,* Vol. 12, p. 137.

7. Ken Kesey, *One Flew Over the Cuckoo's Nest* (New York, NAL-Dutton, 1963; London: Calder & Boyars, 1972).

8. Andrew McKie, "Changing Attitudes to Mental Illness," *Third Way,* March, 1991.

9. Urban expansion has meant that many are now situated in the midst of communities. In this sense community care is not an option. Psychiatric hospitals are part of our communities whether we desire them or not. However, despite this physical closeness, there remains a symbolic segregation within the perception of the general public.

10. J. W. Browning, *Caring for People,* p. 4.

11. Pattison and Armitage, "An Ethical Analysis of the Policies of British Community and Hospital Care for the Mentally Ill," p. 137.

12. Erving Goffman, *Asylums* (London: Penguin Books, 1991).

13. Goodman et al. note that there is an emerging body of research on the physical and sexual abuse of seriously mentally ill women that documents a high incidence and prevalence of victimization within this population. Lisa A. Goodman, Stanley D. Rosenberg, Kim T. Mueser, and Robert E. Drake, "Physical and Sexual Assault History in Women with Serious Mental Illness: Prevalence, Correlates, Treatment, and Future Research Directions," *Schizophrenia Bulletin,* Vol. 23, No. 4, 1997, pp. 685-96.

14. Pattison and Armitage, "An Ethical Analysis of the Policies of British Community and Hospital Care for the Mentally Ill," p. 154.

15. Peter Barham, *Schizophrenia and Human Value* (London: Free Association Books, 1993), p. 178.
16. Pattison, *Pastoral Care and Liberation Theology,* p. 155.

3. What Is Schizophrenia?

1. This diagram was developed from the thinking of Z. J. Lipowski in the paper "Physical Illness, the Individual and the Coping Process," *Psychiatry in Medicine,* Vol. 1, 1979, pp. 91-102.
2. Jay E. Adams, *Competent to Counsel,* pp. 31-32.
3. The Enlightenment was a period of Western cultural history marked, among other things, by a movement away from the primacy of religion and God to the primacy of reason and human beings. Among the central ideas that have arisen from this period are such things as *the belief in progress* (where humanity is assumed to be master of its own fate and should approach the future with confidence in its ability to transform the world through the technological power of science and the effective use of reason), the assumption that *all problems are in principle solvable through the use of reason and technology,* and the belief that *people are emancipated, autonomous individuals.* Within such a cultural milieu, medicine and the medical model have come to provide the dominant discourse and epistemological framework within which we strive to develop our understandings, not only of what is healthy and what is unhealthy, but also of what forms of physical and psychological states and behaviors are accepted as normal.
4. David L. Rosenhan and Martin E. P. Seligman. *Abnormal Psychology* (New York: W. W. Norton, 1984) p. 365.
5. Ibid., p. 368.
6. Barbara A. Turner, "First Person Account: The Children of Madness," *Schizophrenia Bulletin,* Vol. 19, No. 3, 1993, p. 649.
7. *Wild Haemorrhages of the Imagination: A Personal Experience of Schizophrenia* (Edinburgh: National Schizophrenia Fellowship, 1986) p. 7. Whereas religion in the past has featured highly in the delusinal thinking of persons diagnosed as having schizophrenia, nowadays the content of delusions is as likely to contain elements of science fiction, cinematic characters, and other contemporary cultural themes. This suggests strongly that the content of delusions is not free floating, but culturally bound.
8. *Mental Illness and Schizophrenia* (Edinburgh:National Schizophrenia Society, 1993) p. 8.
9. *Wild Haemorrhages of the Imagination,* p. 10.
10. In other words, the people cannot separate themselves from the world.
11. *Diagnostic and Statistical Manual of Mental Disorders, Third Edition, Revised* (American Psychiatric Association: 1987)
12. Charles V. Gerkin, *Living Human Document: Revisioning Pastoral Counseling in a Hermeneutical Mode* (Nashville: Abingdon, 1984).

13. This is, of course, a context dependent observation in the sense that it is, for example, socially appropriate for people to cry at particularly happy events, such as weddings, births, christenings, and so forth.

14. David M. D. Shore (Ed.), *Schizophrenia: Questions and Answers* (Rockville: The National Institute of Mental Health, 1995), p. 3.

15. Ibid., p. 4. Shore suggests that in his experience and research, around 20 percent of patients have only one episode and had no impairment of function or personality; 35 percent go on to have several episodes with no impairment between; about 10 percent have multiple episodes of schizophrenia with a static level of functional and personality impairment between; and 35 percent have multiple episodes with increasing levels of impairment. In a study that looked at the 35-year outcome of schizophrenia, 20 percent of those with a first episode in the 1940s were incapacitated by their illness; 67 percent had never married, and 58 percent had never worked since their first episode.

16. Ibid., p. 7.

17. Glenn R. Marland, "Atypical Neuroleptics: Autonomy and Compliance?" *Journal of Advanced Nursing*, 1999, Vol. 29, No. 3, pp. 615-22.

18. D. E. Casey, "The Relationship of Pharmacology to Side Effects," *Journal of Clinical Psychiatry*, 1997, Vol. 58, Suppl. 10, pp. 55-62. For more on Casey's perspective see B. B. Sheitman, H. Lee, R. Strauss, and J. A. Lieberman, "The Evaluation and Treatment of First-episode Psychosis," *Schizophrenia Bulletin*, Vol. 23, No. 4, 1977, pp. 653-61.

19. Peter Barham and Robert Hayward, *Relocating Madness: From the Mental Patient to the Person* (New York: NYU Press, 1995) p. 60.

20. David Karp, *Speaking of Sadness: Depression, Disconnection, and the Meanings of Illness* (New York: Oxford University Press, 1996), p. 102.

21. Ibid., p. 88.

22. Even when we appear to be talking about hard, scientific issues of biology and pharmacological interventions, we find ourselves having to address fundamental issues of power, personhood, and interpersonal relationships. Even at this early stage in our investigation it is becoming clear that it is not possible to understand the total experience of schizophrenia if we confine ourselves to the biomedical model of understanding. Medications are certainly useful, but on their own, they are not enough. Unless we strive to understand the psychological and hermeneutical dimensions that underlie the taking of medication, and strive to take very seriously the wider social dynamics of the experience of mental health problems, we risk missing aspects of the total picture that are fundamental to the person-as-person.

23. Barham and Hayward, *Relocating Madness*, p. 61.

4. Beyond the Medical Model

1. Alastair G. Cardno and Peter McGuffin, "Aetiological Theories of Schizophrenia," *Current Opinions in Psychiatry*, Vol. 9, 1996, pp. 45-49.

2. Ibid., p. 48.

3. Ibid., p. 45.

4. Ibid., p. 48.

5. Agencies such as The National Alliance for the Mentally Ill, The National Mental Health Association, Yale University Psychiatric Research Unit in America, the National Schizophrenia Fellowship and the Schizophrenia Fellowship of Great Britain, to name but a few, all place great emphasis on the need to educate the public regarding the neurobiological nature of schizophrenia.

6. E. Fuller Torrey. Excerpts from "Surviving Schizophrenia," Bristol-Myers Squibb Pharmaceutical Group, Montreal, Quebec, Canada. 1985. p. 2.

7. G. Bateson, D.D. Jackson, J. Hayley, and J. Weakland, "Towards a Theory of Schizophrenia," *Behavioural Science*, Vol. 1, 1956, p. 251.

8. Sue Walrond-Skinner, *Family Matters: The Pastoral Care of Personal Relationships* (London: SPCK, 1988) p. 15.

9. Agnes Miles, *The Mentally Ill in Contemporary Society*, Oxford, 1981, Martin Robertson, p. 11.

10. The National Alliance for the Mentally Ill in America, and the National Schizophrenia Fellowship of Great Britain both point to the counterproductive effects of such an understanding of schizophrenia.

11. J. Leff and C. Vaughn, Expressed Emotion and Families New York: Guilford Press, 1985. T. Bradshaw "Does Family Intervention Reduce Relapse in Schizophrenia?" *Psychiatric Care* (4) 1997 pp. 30-3. Families can be stressful places at the best of times, and this can undoubtedly *exacerbate* the experience of schizophrenia. Several studies have shown that persons with schizophrenia are more likely to relapse if family members living in the same household adopt a critical attitude, are hostile, or are over involved with the individual. "In families where at least one member showed high expressed emotion, the relapse rate over a period of a year proved to be three to six times higher than in families where expressed emotion was low. Patients who did not take antipsychotic drugs were most vulnerable to this effect. One study also found that if the level of expressed emotion in a family fell, the rate of relapse also fell. It is less clear whether any particular type of treatment or counseling can reduce expressed emotion, but the possibility has excited interest among professionals who work with schizophrenic patients." *The Harvard Medical School Mental Health Letter* "Expressed Emotion and the Schizophrenic Patient." Published by the Harvard Medical School via the internet, July 1997.

12. John Swinton, *Building a Church for Strangers*, p. 20.

13. It is true that within an institutional situation people with severe mental health problems like schizophrenia often develop strong bonds of friendship with other patients. Likewise, strong bonds of friendship can be formed within the community setting, in drop-in centers, day hospitals, self-advocacy groups and so forth. Elliott Liebow presents a fascinating insight into some of these relationships as they developed among homeless women in his *Tell Them Who*

I Am: The Lives of Homeless Women (Penguin Books, 1995) (cf. especially ch. 5). However, the sad fact is that many people with mental health problems who have been released into the community have tremendous difficulties initiating and developing relationships of any type. Often their only real contact with other people is via visits from comiciliary mental health professionals, or visits to mental health clinics for checkups, medication, and so forth.

14. The Mental Health Foundation, "Creating Community Care: Report of the Mental Health Foundation Inquiry into Community Care for People with Mental Illnesses," 1994, p. 27.

15. John S. Strauss, "The Person—Key to Understanding Mental Illness: Towards a New Dynamic Psychiatry, III," *British Journal of Psychiatry*, Vol. 161 (Supplement 18), 1992, p. 20.

16. George M. Furniss, *The Social Context of Pastoral Care: Defining the Life Situation* (Louisville: Westminster/John Knox Press, 1994), p. 20.

17. Rosenhan and Seligman, *Abnormal Psychology*, p. 366.

18. Courtney M. Harding, Joseph Zubin, and John S. Strauss, "Chronicity in Schizophrenia Revisited," *British Journal of Psychiatry*, Vol. 161 (Supplement 18) 1992, p. 27. These authors suggest that for Kraeplin, "prognosis confirmed diagnosis." However, Wing observes that he also recognized that onset could occur later in life, and that recovery was possible. K. Wing, *Schizophrenia: Toward a New Synthesis* (London: Academic Press; New York, Grune & Stratton, 1978), p. 2.

19. The input from psychiatry to the caring process is highly significant. While always wary of the misuse of power by groups of professionals, it is not my intention to advocate forms of care that seek to exclude psychiatry from the overall process of caring. My point is that standard psychiatric definitions and understandings can only offer a part of the picture. In order to fully understand schizophrenia it is necessary to look beyond the psychiatric paradigm and begin to explore the wider social dimensions of schizophrenia. This will mean developing collaborative strategies that include, but are not defined by, the perspective of psychiatry.

20. Peter Barham, *Schizophrenia and Human Value*, p. viii.

21 R. Warner, *Recovery from Schizophrenia* (London: Routledge, 1985), pp. 135, 188-89.

22. Horacio Fabrega, "The Self and Schizophrenia: A Cultural Perspective," *Schizophrenia Bulletin*, Vol. 15, No. 2, 1989.

23. Carr, for example, shows some of the ways in which sufferers can use particular techniques ranging from behavioral change, socialization, and cognitive control to cope with their illness, that is, to retain their sense of agency and control over their lives. Vaughan Carr, "Patients' Techniques for Coping with Schizophrenia: An Exploratory Study," *British Journal of Medical Psychology*, Vol. 61, 1988.

24. Helen Kirkpatrick, Janet Landeen, Carolyne Byrne, Harriet Woodside, Julie Pawlick, and Anna Bernardo, "Hope and Schizophrenia: Clinicians Identify Hope-Instilling Strategies," *Journal of Psychosocial Nursing and Mental Health Service*, Vol. 33, No. 6, January, 1995, pp. 15-19.

25. Jerome Kroll, "Religion and Psychiatry," *Current Opinion in Psychiatry*, Vol. 8, 1995, pp. 335-39.

26. Fabrega writing from the perspective of social anthropology notes that while disturbances such as schizophrenia are universal to human groups, there is a wide variety in the appearance and significance of the disturbance, which differs markedly from culture to culture. He points to the danger within contemporary Western psychiatry of cultural bias and a consequent ignoring of the importance of a person's social history (although his usage of this expression is implicit rather than explicit) and its impact on the experience of schizophrenia. Horacio Fabrega, "On the Significance of An Anthropological Approach to Schizophrenia," *Psychiatry*, Vol. 52, February, 1989.

27. Arthur Kleinman, *The Illness Narratives: Suffering, Healing, and the Human Condition* (New York: Basic Books, 1988), p. 3.

5. Creating Nonpersons

1. Rex Ambler, "What Is a Person?" in Stephen Pattison (Ed.), *Mental Handicap, Theology and Pastoral Care: Proceedings from the Pastoral Studies Spring Conference*, University of Birmingham, England, 1986.

2. Tom Kitwood, *Dementia Reconsidered: The Person Comes First* (Buckingham: Open University Press, 1998), p. 12.

3. Roy Porter, *The Social History of Madness* (London: Weidenfeld and Nicholson, 1987) p. 3.

4. Ibid., p. 3. Quoted by Barham and Hayward, *Relocating Madness*, p. 2.

5. Roy Porter, "Bedlam and Parnauss: Mad People's Writing in Georgian England" in G. Levine (ed.) *One Culture*, Wisconsin: University of Wisconsin Press, 1987. Quoted by Barham and Hayward, *Relocating Madness*, p. 2.

6. Ibid.

7. Sue E. Estroff, "Self, Identity, and Subjective Experiences of Schizophrenia: In Search of the Subject." *Schizophrenia Bulletin*, Vol. 15, No. 2, 1989, p. 189.

8. W. T. Carpenter, "Approaches to Knowledge and Understanding of Schizophrenia," *Schizophrenia Bulletin*, Vol. 13(1), 1987, p. 3.

9. All of this deeply affects people's material existence. If a person cannot find and hold down employment, he or she is unlikely to be able to afford good living conditions on social security benefits.

10. *The Fundamental Facts*, London: The Mental Health Foundation, 1993, p. 23.

11. Swinton, *Building a Church for Strangers*, p. 28.

12. David A. Pailin, A *Gentle Touch—From a Theology of Handicap to a Theology of Human Being*. London, 1992, APCK, p. 120.

13. For a further development of this argument, see Swinton, *From Bedlam to Shalom* (In Press).

14. Pailin, *A Gentle Touch*, p. 118.

15. R.J. Van Den Bosch. "Schizophrenia: Inner and Outer Worlds." *Communication and Cognition* 28. 1995, p. 327.

16. Allan V. Horwitz, The Social Control of Mental Illness (New York: 1982), Academic Press, p. 16.
17. Ibid., 16.
18. Horwitz highlights the research of Yarrow et al., who showed that, far from using the psychiatric services as a form of social control, wives resist labeling their husbands' behavior as symptomatic of mental illness for a number of years, but instead use various techniques to normalize behavior. Horwitz, The Social Control of Mental Illness, p. 32. As a consequence most people are in acute stages of disorder when brought to the attention of the authorities. The thesis that close relations tend to deny and normalize mental illness contradicts the belief that any persons enter mental hospitals because they have been rejected by their families or other intimate relations. Persons enter psychiatric institutions because their behavior has become so disturbed and incomprehensible that families can simply no longer cope with the situation.
19. Hurding, Roots and Shoots, p. 34. Empathy is concerned with recognizing and understanding the feelings of another as if they were being experienced by oneself, whereas sympathy involves being emotionally affected by the feelings of another.
20. Torrey acknowledges that "friendship is needed by persons with schizophrenia, just as it is by everyone." However, Torrey suggests, the physical and emotional symptoms of schizophrenia can be a barrier to friendship. E. Fuller Torrey, Surviving Schizophrenia, p. 235.
21. In other words, although schizophrenia may well a a "physical" disease in the sense that it has some kind of biological etiology, this does not mean that this somatic origin dictates the relational life-course of the individual.
22. David Karp, Speaking of Sadness, pp. 191-92. What we need to recognize is that mental health problems, like all forms of human disorder, are always shaped and constructed by the particular contexts within which they are experienced. Psychological disease and illness are not "things" that are simply out there waiting to be discovered. Rather they derive their meanings, what they are as social objects, through a process of human interpretation. This is not to question the reality of disease or illness states but rather to emphasize that these states and experiences are understood and interpreted within certain social contexts. It is important to realize that the way a thing is defined and the particular meanings that are ascribed to it will profoundly affect the ways in which we react toward it and the particular forms of intervention we deem appropriate to use when dealing with it.
23. Agnes Miles, The Mentally Ill in Contemporary Society (Oxford, Martin Robertson, 1981), p. 60.
24. Ibid., p. 62. Miles notes "In a study carried out by Elinson et al., three-quarters of a New York sample agreed with this statement: "unlike physical illness, which makes most people sympathetic, mental illness tends to repel most people" (p. 63).
25. MIND is an organization that works within the United Kingdom to provide a

better life for people diagnosed as mentally ill. It does this through campaigning, community development training, publishing, and a comprehensive information service.

26. MIND Information: "Dangerousness" (London: MIND, 1994).
27. Greg Philo. Media and Mental Distress. London and New York: Longman, 1996, p. 96.
28. Otto F. Wahl, *Media Madness: Public Images of Mental Illness.* New Brunswick, Rutgers University Press, 1995, p. 98.
29. Ibid., p. 99.
30. Kirkpatrick et al., *Hope and Schizophrenia*, p. 18.
31. Erving Goffman, *Stigma* (London: Penguin Books, 1990), p. 9.
32. Ibid., p. 13.
33. Ibid., p. 12.
34. Ibid., p. 15.
35. Miles, *The Mentally Ill in Contemporary Society*, p. 63.
36. Goffman, *Stigma*, p. 18.
37. Ibid., p. 19.
38. Ibid., p. 20.

6. Stories from Dark Places

1. Rosenhan and Seligman, *Abnormal Psychology,* pp. 348-55.
2. Robert M. Young, "The Moral and the Molecular," paper presented to Conference on the Bi-centenary of the Founding of the York Retreat, The Retreat, York, 4 October 1996.
3. Ibid.
4. One of the interesting things about public reactions to bipolar disorder is that this particular disorder has a history of being accepted as a biological disorder. Nevertheless, this does not protect individuals from the powerful processes of dehumanization that are central to the life experiences of many people with this disorder.
5. There is evidence to suggest that the physical and sexual abuse of women with mental health problems is quite widespread, and understandably, markedly underreported. Goodman *et al.,* note that there is an emerging body of research on the physical and sexual abuse of seriously mentally ill women that documents a high incidence and prevalence of victimization within this population. Lisa A. Goodman, Stanley D. Rosenberg, Kim T. Mueser, and Robert E. Drake, "Physical and Sexual Assault History in Women with Serious Mental Illness: Prevalence, Correlates, Treatment, and Future Research Directions," Schizophrenia Bulletin 23 (4):685-96, 1997.
6. Oliver Sacks, *The Man Who Mistook His Wife for a Hat* (London: Picador, 1985), p. 36.
7. Tom Kitwood "Toward the Reconstruction of an Organic Mental Disorder," in Alan Radley, *Worlds of Illness: Biographical and Cultural Perspectives on Health*

and Disease, (London: Routledge, 1995). See also Tom Kitwood, "Personhood, Dementia, and Dementia Care" in *Dementia: Challenges and New Directions, Research Highlights in Social Work,* 31. Susan Hunter (ed.) (London: Jessica Kingsley Publishers, 1997).

8. Kitwood, in *Worlds of Illness,* p. 153.

9. Ibid., p. 151.

10. Kitwood, *Dementia Reconsidered,* p. 151.

11. Ibid., p. 152.

12. Ibid.

13. Ibid., p. 55.

14. Ibid., p. 62.

15. Stephen G. Post, *The Moral Challenge of Alzheimer Disease* (London: Johns Hopkins Press, 1995), p. 3, drawing on the research of E.T. Lucas, *Elder Abuse and Its Recognition Among Health Service Professionals* (New York: Garland, 1991).

16. Ibid., p. 9.

17. Stanley Hauerwas, *Suffering Presence* (Edinburgh: T & T Clark, 1986), p. 162. Quoted in Stephen G. Post, *The Moral Challenge of Alzheimer Disease,* p. 9.

18. Ibid., p. 176. Quoted in Stephen G. Post, *The Moral Challenge of Alzheimer Disease,* p. 9.

19. Ibid., p. 178. Quoted in Post, Ibid., p. 9.

20. Ibid.

21. This section of the chapter is drawn from a paper originally presented by John Swinton at the Annual Wheaton College Theology Conference, April, 1999.

22. Margaret G. Hutchison, "Unity and Diversity in Spiritual Care." Paper originally presented at the Sydney University Nursing Society First Annual Conference for Undergraduate Nursing Students in NSW, September, 1997.

23. Andrew Oldnall, "A Critical Analysis of Nursing: Meeting the Spiritual Needs of Patients." *Journal of Advanced Nursing,* Vol. 23, 1996, pp. 138-44.

24. For further development of the theological significance of memory in the context of Alzheimer's Disease, see David Keck, *Forgetting Whose We Are: Alzheimer's Disease and the Love of God* (Nashville: Abingdon, 1996).

25. Swinton, *Building a Church for Strangers,* pp. 18-21.

26. David Karp, *Speaking of Sadness: Depression, Disconnection, and the Meaning of Illness* (New York: Oxford University Press, 1996).

27. For further reading on this topic see Susan Sontag, *Illness as Metaphor* and *AIDS and Its Metaphors* (London: Penguin Books, 1991).

28. Judith Lorber, *Gender and the Social Construction of Illness* (London: Sage Publications, 1997).

29. Although profoundly affected by their biology, people are not determined by it. People are considerably more than simply a mass of genes and chro-

mosomes, and the impact of mental illnesses such as schizophrenia are considerably more complex than is implied by the idea of malfunctioning biological processes alone.

7. Memory, Resurrection, and Hope

1. Patton, *Pastoral Care in Context*, p. 15.
2. Psalms 63:6-7; 74:2; 119:49-50.
3. In Patton, *Pastoral Care in Context*, p. 28.
4. Ibid., p. 29.
5. Johann Baptist Metz, Glaude in Geschichte und Gesellschaft. Studien zu einer praktischen Fundamental Theologie, Mainz: Grünewald 1984.
6. Russell A. Butkus (1987) "Dangerous Memory and Social Justice Education." *Religious Education* Vol. 82, No. 3: 426-46. p. 445.
7. Patton, *Pastoral Care in Context*, p. 28.
8. Gustavo Gutiérrez, "Solidarity: The Victory of Life." A homily of Gustavo Gutiérrez. This article can be obtained via the Internet at the Epica Library, Challenge Articles: 1989-1997. http://www.ipc.org/epica/solid.htm
9. Richard Bauckham, *The Theology of Jürgen Moltmann*, Edinburgh: 1996, T & T Clark, p. 36.
10. Marcella Althaus-Reid, "Doing a Theology of Memory: Counting Crosses and Resurrections," From an article which first appeared in *Life Out of Death: The Feminine Spirit in El Salvador*, published by CIIR. This article can be attained via the internet at: The Epica Library, Challenge Articles: 1989–1997. http://www.igc.apc.org/epica/doinga.htm
11. Ibid.

8. Resurrecting the Person: Friendship, Hope, and Personhood

1. This is not, of course, the case for all sufferers. Some persons suffering from enduring mental health problems manifest the negative symptoms of the illness for the majority of their lives. Even so, Harding, Zubin, and Strauss argue that even this type of chronicity is not a necessary accompaniment to schizophrenia, but a product of the types of social processes which are being outlined within this chapter. "Derived simply from the Greek word *chronos*, meaning time, the label "chronic" denotes an illness of long duration or one of frequent recurrence. However, when chronic is paired with schizophrenia, as in "this person is a chronic schizophrenic," the connotation becomes an expectation of deterioration, defect, or deficit states . . . These perceptions have also stripped hopes of recovery from patients and their families." Harding, Zubin, and Strauss, *Chronicity in Schizophrenia: Revisited*, p. 27. Thus, lowered expectations *can* become self-fulfilling prophecies thus contributing to chronicity and alienation.

Important on this point is the work of Wing and Brown who found that the negative symptoms of schizophrenia were exacerbated by an under-stimulating social environment, was closely related to three aspects of the patients condition: *social withdrawal, blunting of affect, and poverty of speech*. Similarly, an over-stimulating social environment which was noted as precipitating the more acute symptoms of schizophrenia and led to relapse. Although many hospital environments try very hard to provide appropriate levels of positive stimulation, lowered staffing levels, lack of resources, and poor morale due to such things as job insecurity and changing management structures, mean that for many within the hospital system the possibility of stagnation and institutionalization remain a reality. Thus psychiatric hospitals have the potential both to enhance and to restrict a person's life possibilities.

A good example of the effects of institutionalization can be found in the changing nature of one particular form of schizophrenia, *catatonic schizophrenia*. In catatonic schizophrenia a person may exhibit stuporous or frozen behavior, during which they will sit fixed in the same position for many hours. If someone moves them they will "freeze" into the new position. Rosenhan and Seligman note that a kind of statuesque "waxy flexibility" is charactistic of catatonic schizophrenia (Rosenhan and Seligman, *Abnormal Psychology*, p. 371.) However, with improved hospital services that emphasize the importance of an appropriate level of stimulation for persons suffering from schizophrenia, this condition has been reduced to the point where very few people will actually experience it outside of textbook descriptions. It would appear that it was in fact a manifestation of the neglect and under-stimulation which typified many of the old psychiatris "back wards," rather than something which is inherent in the illness itself.

2. Rosenberg. *A Symbolic Interactionist View of Psychosis*. page 291.

3. Harding et al note that "Zubin & Spring considered the patient to be a person with a persistent underlying vulnerability—an essentially well person with intermittent episodes of good health." Courtney M. Harding, Joseph Zubin and John S. Strauss. 'Chronicity in Schizophrenia: Revisited.' *British Journal of Psychiatry* 161 (Supplement) 18 1992: pp. 27-37, page 32). In the light of the evidence which seems to suggest that schizophrenia has a strong biological component, it might be debatable whether one would wish to take such an absolutist stance. Nevertheless, this understanding would make sense in the light of the following discussion on the processual nature of mental health and the dangers of understanding health in terms of a fixed static entity. The importance of this reconceptualization of schizophrenia will become apparent as the argument progresses.

4. Keith Tudor, *Mental Health Promotion: Paradigms and Practice* (London: Routledge, 1997), p. 22.

5. Ibid.

6. Ibid., p. 23.

7. Carl R. Rogers, *On Becoming a Person*, Boston: Houghton Mifflin, 1961.

8. Vicktor E. Frank., *Man's Search for Meaning: From Death Camp to Existentialixm*, (Boston: Beacon Press, 1962).

9. Kirkpatrick et al., *Hope and Schizophrenia*, pp. 15-19.

10. Emmanuel Y. Lartey, I*n Living Colour: An Intercultural Approach to Pastoral Care and Counseling* (London: Cassell, 1997).

11. Moltmann, Jürgen, *God in Creation: An Ecological Doctrine of Creation* (London: SCM Press, 1985).

12. Karl Barth, *Church Dogmatics III/4* (Edinburgh: T & T Clark, 1961).

13. John Swinton "Reclaiming the Soul: A Spiritual Perspective on Forensic Nursing," in David Robinson and Alison Kettles, *Forensic Nursing and Multidisciplinary Care of the Mentally Disordered Offender* (London: Jessica Kingsley, 1999), p. 123.

14. John DeGruchy in Trevor Hart and Daniel Thimmel (Eds.) *Christ in Our Place.* (London: The Paternoster Press, 1989). See also Motlmann Jürgen, *God in Creation: An Ecological Doctrine of Creation* (London: SCMN Press, 1985); Barth, Church Dogmatics III/4.

15. If one understands a mental health problem as something that is experienced at particular times by a person, but which remains in a sense separate from that person, one opens up the possibility that, given appropriate support and motivation, the person as an active agent, can interact with the disorder in ways which will influence the course of that disorder. It is not possible to take this line of thought further within this book. For another development of this approach see Marius Romme, and Sandra Escher, *Accepting Voices* (London: MIND, 1993); Vaughan Carr, *Patients' Techniques for Coping with Schizophrenia;* A. Breier and J. S. Strauss, "Self-Control in Psychotic Disorders," *Archive of General Psychiatry,* p. 40; and V. Carr and M. Katskitis, "Illness Behaviours and Schizophrenia." *Psychiatric Medicine,* 5, pp. 163-70 1987. These authors develop this area quite comprehensively, exploring various ways in which sufferers can interact with and develop some degree of control over their symptoms.

16. John S. Strauss. "Subjective Experiences of Schizophrenia: Toward a New Dynamic Psychiatry—II." *Schizophrenia Bulletin* Vol. 15. No. 2. 1989, p. 182.

17. At first sight, this distinction may appear to be merely playing with semantics. However, underpinning all of the arguments in this book is the proposition that the ways in which one conceptualizes human beings, and the ways in which they conceptualize themselves, can have a major impact on the forms of practice which one seeks to use in one's attempts to care for them.

18. Ibid., Strauss, "Subjective Experiences of Schizophrenia," p. 184.

19. The research of psychiatrists Romme and Escher in *Accepting Voices,* adds support to this suggestion and develops it further.

20. Ibid., Strauss, "Subjective Experiences of Schizophrenia," p. 184.

21. Ibid.

22. Kirkpatrick et al., *Hope and Schizophrenia*, p. 15.

23. Ibid.

24. Ibid., See also Harding, Zubin and Strauss, *Chronicity in Schizophrenia: Revisited,* for further development of this point.

25. J.F. Miller, *Coping with Chronic Illness: Overcoming Powerlessness.* (2nd Ed) Philadelphia: F. A. Davis, 1992, p. 414.

26. Kirkpatrick et al, *Hope and Schizophrenia*, p. 16.
27. Carolyne Byrne, Helen Kirkpatrick, Harriet Woodside, Janet Landeen, Anna Bernardo and Julie Pawlick, "The Importance of Relationships in Fostering Hope," *Journal of Psychosocial Nursing and Mental Health Service*, Vol. 32, No. 9, September 1994: p. 31.
28. Ibid.
29. Kirkpatrick et al, *Hope and Schizophrenia*, p. 33.
30. Byrna, et al. "The Importance of Relationships," p. 33.
31. Thomas H. McGlashan, "What Has Become of the Psychotherapy of Schizophrenia?" *Acta Psychiatr Scand 90* (Supplement, 384) 1994, pp. 147-52.
32. Ibid., p. 150.
33. Harris Brown and Robinson in their research into the role of friendship in depression found that "what is beneficial about befriending is the knowledge that someone cares enough to visit without being paid and that "the sense of equality afforded by the mutual self-disclosure of friendship may contribute to their sense of self-worth and security" (p. 219) Results showed a significant effect of befriending upon remission, with 65% of those allocated befriending compared to 39% in the control group experiencing remission when other variables were controlled for." T. Harris, G.W. Brown, and R. Robinson (1999) "Befriending as an intervention for chronic depression among women in an inner city: Randomised control trial, *British Journal of Psychiatry*, Vol. 174, 219-24.
34. In the same way as a catalyst changes something not because of what it *does*, but because of what *is*, so also friends enable mental health not by doing something for the person, but by *being* something for them.

9. Enabling Friendship-in-Community
A Ministry of Introduction, Education, and Enablement

1. Liebow, *Tell Them Who I Am*, p. XIV.
2. Nicky Hayes, *Principles of Social Psychology* (Hove, United Kingdom: Lawrence Erlbaum Associates, 1993), p. 78.
3. Ibid.
4. Smith, in Rodney J. Hunter, *Dictionary of Pastoral Care and Counseling* (Nashville: Abingdon Press, 1990), p. 136.
5. Weissman and Appleton's research is helpful on understanding the therapeutic implications of acceptance. They sought to determine how six inpatients (ages 13 to 18 years) at a psychiatric hospital described how they experienced acceptance from psychiatric mental health nurses. The following themes emerged: (1) The nurse who shows acceptance is seen as a friend; (2) acceptance generates a sense of well-being; and (3) acceptance produces feelings of comfort with the nurse. Thus, through the nurse's acceptance, adolescents

experience nurses as unique individuals who provide comfort and nurturing. This relationship connection helps adolescent clients use their inner strength to gain a sense of well-being. As will be shown, acceptance is central to the model of care which is being worked out within this book. Jodi Weissman, Cathy Appleton, "The Therapeutic aspects of acceptance," *Perspectives in Psychiatric Care,* 1995 Jan.-Mar. Vol. 31(1); pp. 9-23.

6. The CMHC has of course many other roles such as counselor, advocate, support worker for staff and carers, but for the purposes of this part of the investigation it is the important role of the chaplain in facilitating friendship that will be the primary focus of interest.

7. John Bowlby, *The Making and Breaking of Affectional Bonds* Routledge, (London and New York: 1994).

8. This is particularly so for individuals who are "emerging" from the hospital, but it is also the case for people who are already living within the community but who, for the reasons outlined previously, have difficulties socializing.

9. Stewart D. Govig, *Souls Are Made of Endurance: Surviving Mental Illness in the Family* (Louisville, Kentucky: Westminister/John Knox Press, 1994).

10. It is important to note that there were many people, some with quite severe mental health problems, who simply fitted straight into a congregational situation with no need for the presence of the CMHC other than at the initial stage of introduction. However, there were a number of people who had real struggles. The focus of this chapter will be on those people for whom acceptance and a genuine place in the community can be very difficult for both church and person.

11. Gutierrez, *A Theology of Liberation,* p. XXX.

12. Shlomo Breznitz, "The Effect of Hope in Coping with Stress," in Appley, Mortimer, and Trumbull (Eds.) *Dynamics of Stress: Physiological, Psychological, and Social Perspectives* (New York and London: Plenum Press, 1986), p. 297.

13. Ibid.

14. In times of crisis and amid the acute manifestations of the illness, when David was unable to be a part of the worshiping community, it was the *symbolic* knowledge that the friendship relationship was always there which was as important as the actual practice of it. Certainly that symbolic aspect of the friendship relationship was "made flesh" through the continuing ministry of the CMHC who continued to visit David in times of crisis or hospitalization, but it was the *symbolic connection* with the wider church community that moved beyond his illness and helped sustain his sense of connection with others.

10. Creating a Context for Care: Understanding and Overcoming Congregational Resistance

1. This highlights some important areas of challenge and difficulty and raises some important issues for the church community. It is easy to forget that many people with severe mental health problems come to the church "uninvited."

Although there is currently a great public emphasis on deinstitutionalization and care in the community, the truth of the matter is that the majority of people suffering from mental health problems already live in the community. The CMHC model points toward some of the ways in which the church can reach out to those who live with mental health problems. However, in reality many people will, for various reasons, be drawn to the church. Sadly, the church community is very often unprepared for the appearance of "strangers" in its midst.

2. John M. Cannon, "Pastoral Care for Families of the Mentally Ill," *Journal of Pastoral Care*, Vol. XLIV, No. 3 (fall 1990), pp. 213-21.

3. Kirkpatrick et al *Hope and Schizophrenia*, p. 18.

4. Coursey in T. H. McGlashan, "What Has Become of the Psychotherapy of Schizophrenia"? Acta Psychiatr Scand 1994 (Suppl. 384) p. 150. Although the intention of Coursey and McGlashan is to present an argument for supportive psychotherapy, the tasks they highlight as important to the therapeutic process—support, reality testing, assistance in the development of positive self images, and so forth—would in practice be a central part of the practical application of the model of friendship which has been worked out within this book.

5. There is a strong precedent for this approach within contemporary mental health practice. "Service user involvement" is now a part of both nursing and medical curricula within the United Kingdom. There is also a very strong "users movement" which seeks to empower people suffering from mental illness and to educate the public in a personal manner as to the nature and experiences of mental illness and the expectations that people suffering from them have for their lives. A very useful overview of the literature on user involvement and user involvement groups is to be found in M. J. Rudman, "User Involvement in Mental Health Nursing Practice: Rhetoric to Reality," *Journal of Psychiatric and Mental Health Nursing*, Vol. 3 (1996), pp. 385-90.

6. It would be beneficial for congregations to gain similar access to the experience of families. As part of the overall educational process, family members should also get the opportunity to speak with congregations and to share their experiences with them. However, the experience of family members is often very different from the experience of people with personal experience of mental health problems. If we think back to Lipowski's model of illness attribution, the ways in which families interpret their member's illness may be quite different from the ways in which the sufferer interprets it, and not just because of the distortions of illness. This being so, while the perspective of the family remains vital, it is just as important the the voice of a person with mental health problems be heard, listened to, and given respect.

7. *Creating Community Care: Report of The Mental Health Foundation Inquiry into Community Care for People with Severe Mental Illness* The Mental Health Foundation (London: 1994), p. 19.

8. D. Pilgrim and L. Waldron (1998) "User Involvement in Mental Health Service Development: How far can it go?" *Journal of Mental Health*, Vol. 7, No. 1, pp. 95-104.

9. Discussed in Simon Fitsall, "Evidence Based Practice in Mental Health Nursing." *Nurse* 2 1999. http://wkweb5,cableinet.co.uk/garyblatch/contents.html

10. Paulo Freire, The Pedagogy of the Oppressed Penguin Books, (Longon: 1980).

11. Shaun M. Ryles, "A Concept Analysis of Empowerment and its Relationship to Mental Health Nursing," *Journal of Advanced Nursing* 29 (3) 1999, pp. 600-607.

12. John Swinton, "Reclaiming the Soul," p. 123.

13. Simon Fitsall, "Evidence Based Practice in Mental Health Nursing,"

14. Rosaline Carter, "Advocating for the Mentally Ill, Mental Illness: A Spiritual, Emotional, and Physical Perspective Online Conference, A. Christopher Hammon and Vicki L. Hollon (Louisville: Wayne E. Oates Institute, 4 October, 1999). http://www.oates.org/conference_center/fall99/conf_hall/presentations/r_carter.html

15. Glen Weaver, "Senile Dementia and a Resurrection Theology," *Theology Today,* Vol. XLII (April 1985–June 1986), pp. 444-56.

16. The APCMH (formally the Association for the Pastoral Care of the Mentally Ill has been active since 1986, working with churches of all denominations to raise awareness of the needs of people with mental helath problems, and to encourage and develop good pastoral practice within this field. Local branches provide a range of services including drop-in centers, help-lines, befriending schemes, and carer groups.

17. The National Institute of Mental Health produces excellent literature on mental health problems that can easily be incorporated into a course such as this.

18. G. Caplan, *Principles of Preventative Psychiatry* (New York: Basic Books, 1964).

19. For example, Anton Boisen, *The Exploration of the Inner World: A Study of Mental Disorder and Relisioug Experience,* New York: Harper and Brothers, 1962; Anton T. Boisen, "Religious Experience and Psychological Conflict," *Journal of Pastoral Care,* Vol. XIII, 1959, pp. 160-63; Peter Breggin, *Toxic Psychiatry* (London: Harper Collins, 1991); David Lukoff, "The Diagnosis of Mystical Experience With Psychotic Features," *Journal of Transpersonal Psychology,* Vol. 17, 155-81, 1985; Raymond Prince, "Religious Experience and Psychosis," *Journal of Altered States of Consciousness,* pp. 5167-181, 1979; Michael A. Siglag, "Schizophrenic and Mystical Experiences: Similarities and Differences." Presented at the 95th Annual Convention of the American Psychological Association, New York, August 30, 1987.

20. Fuller Torrey, *Surviving Schizophrenia,* p. 309.

21. Frederick J. Frese, "Twelve Aspects of Coping with Schizophrenia," *Innovations & Research,* Vol. 2, No. 3, 1993, pp. 39-46. Used by permission.

22. The expression "cultural reality" is used to differentiate between the reality that the individual is experiencing and the religious "reality" as it is defined within a particular cultural context. What one might describe as "delusional reality" is no less real to the individual. It is the cultural verifiability which makes it "acceptable" or "unacceptable" within a particular religious and social context. This cultural reality is, or course, not a fixed reality and differs

from context to context. For example, in some cultures the manifestation of hallucinatory activity, the hearing of voices, and the possession of obscure knowledge may be deemed as the mark of a true holy man.

23. Andrew Sims, "Psyche—Spirit as Well as Mind?" *British Journal of Psychiatry* 165, 1994. Sims's definitional criteria are helpful as a loose framework for determining the nature of the person's religious experience. However, there is a good deal of room for argument and debate as to how conclusive such criteria might actually be in practice.

24. One particularly useful text which offers strategies for understanding and dealing constructively with delusional experiences is Rebecca Woolis, *When Someone You Love Has a Mental Illness: A Handbook for Family, Friends and Caregivers* (New York: G.P. Putnam's Sons, 1992).

25. *Schizophrenics Anonymous: Self-Help Support Group*, Mental Health Association in Michigan, 1994, p. 12.

26. Ibid.

27. Richard C. Erickson, David Culture, Victoria Brandon Cowl, and George E. Nobler, "Serving the Needs of Persons With Chronic Mentall Illness: A Neglected Ministry," *The Journal of Pastoral Care*, Vol. XIV, No. 2 (Summer 1990), pp. 153-62. Emphasis added.

11. Caring for the Carers:
Creating a Hopeful Future

1. Richard Warner, *Recovery from Schizophrenia: Psychiatry and Political Economy* (London: Routledge, 1985), pp. 1-10.

2. Journey of Hope Family Education "Ten Principles of Support." California Alliance for the Mentally Ill, 1996.

3. If, for example, a person commits herself to meeting with a schizophrenia sufferer for say, two hours a week, then this will inevitably be beneficial to the mental health of the carer(s).

4. Mary Moate and David Enoch, *Schizophrenia: Voices in the Dark* (Sussex, Great Britain: Kingsway Publications, 1992), p. 28.

5. Ibid., p. 28.

6. John M. Cannon, *Pastoral Care for Families of the Mentally Ill*, p. 213.

7. Stewart D. Govig, "Mental Illness and the Family: Contexts for Pastoral Care." *The Journal of Pastoral Care*, Vol. 47, No. 4, Winter, 1993, pp. 105-9.

8. Ibid., p. 107.

9. Annie Borthwick, *Invisible Pain: The Experience of Being a Relative of a Person with Schizophrenia*. N.S.F. Scotland. (no date) p. 5.

10. Eydis Sveinbjarnardottir and Bernadette Dierckx de Casterle, "Mental Illness in the Family: An Emotional Experience," *Issues in Mental Health Nursing*, Vol. 18, 1997, p. 51.

11. Ibid., p. 53.

12. Ibid.

13. Anton Antonovsky, *Health, Stress and Coping* (San Francisco: Jossey-Bass, 1987).

14. Wayne E. Hill and Paul M. Mullen, "An Overview of Psychoneuroimmunology: Implications for Pastoral Care." *The Journal of Pastoral Care*, Vol. 50, No. 3, (Fall 1996), pp. 239-47.

15. Although the implications of this observation cannot be drawn out here, it is important to note that if that sense of coherence could be embodied within and meaningfully manifested through positive interpersonal relationships, there would appear to be great potential for holistic healing. Hill and Mullen draw out some of the implications of this observation as it might apply within a pastoral context from the perspective of current developments in psychoneuroimmunology. Hill and Mullen, "An overview of Psychoneuroimmunology: Implications for Pastoral Care," p. 243.

16. Karp, *Speaking of Sadness*, p. 96.

17. J. Swinton and A. M. Kettles, "Resurrecting the Person: Redefining Mental Illness—A Spiritual Perspective" *Psychiatric Care*, Vol. 4(3), 1997, p. 1.

18. Govig, *Souls Are Made of Endurance*, p. 84.

19. Glen Weaver, "Senile Dementia and a Resurrection Theology," p. 445.

20. Mary Elizabeth Moore, *Ministering with the Earth* (Missouri 1998: Chalice Press), p. 61.

21. Ibid., p. 64

22. Walter Brueggemann, *Old Testament Theology: Essays on Structure, Theme, and Text*, pp. 18-19, 21.

23. Govig, *Souls Are Made for Endurance*, p. 84.

24. Thomas Moore, *Care of the Soul* (New York: Harper Collins, 1992), pp. 18-19.

Conclusion

1. W. H. Vanstone, *The Stature of Waiting, (Loneon: 1982) Darton, Longman &* Todd, p. 95

2. McGlashan, *What Has Become of the Psychotherapy of Schizophrenia*, p. 151.

Index